# Fashion India
## Spectacular Capitalism
### Edited by Tereza Kuldova

akademika" publishing

© Akademika Publishing, 2013

ISBN 978-82-321-0319-5

This publication may not be reproduced, stored in a retrieval system or transmitted in any form or by any means; electronic, electrostatic, magnetic tape, mechanical, photocopying, recording or otherwise, without permission.

Layout: Johnny Kreutz, Museum of Cultural History
Cover Layout: Johnny Kreutz, Museum of Cultural History
Printed and binded by: InPrint Ltd., Latvia
Paper: MultiArt Matt 130g

Photos by Kirsten Jensen Helgeland, Museum of Cultural History:
p. 4, 10, 30, 49, 50, 71, 94, 119, 120, 166, 193, 196, 223
Photos by Adnan Icagic, Museum of Cultural History: p. 224, 228, 229, 230, 231, 232 and inside cover
Cover photo by Raghubir Sing

This book has been published with funding from and in cooperation with Museum of Cultural History, University of Oslo

We only use environmentally certified printing houses.

Akademika Publishing
Oslo/Trondheim
www.akademikaforlag.no

# Contents

*Introduction* .................................................................................................. 5
Tereza Kuldova

*The World Fashion Fair: India on Display* ................................................ 11
Nilanjana Mukherjee

*When the Local is in Fashion. How to spend a few hours waiting for a delayed flight in the middle of the night at the Delhi airport and receive an ethnographic enlightenment* ....................................... 31
Paolo Favero

*'The Maharaja Style': Royal Chic and Double Vision* ............................... 51
Tereza Kuldova

*Fashion Zeitgeist in Northeast India* ........................................................ 73
Marion Wettstein

*Seamingly Known: A Photoessay* .............................................................. 89
Meher Varma

*Dressing India Anew: Fashion Designers Betwixt and Between* ............. 95
Janne Meier

*Memories of Luxury, Aspirations Towards Glamour, and Cultivations of Morality: How south Indian Muslim women craft their style* .......... 121
Caroline Osella

*The Quality of a Copy* ............................................................................. 143
Constantine V. Nakassis

*Laughing at Luxury: Mocking Fashion Designers* .................................. 167
Tereza Kuldova

*Walking with Kolhapuri Artisans: On the Art of Designing and Wearing Shoes* ....................................... 195
Catherine Willems and Kristiaan D'Août

*Hindi Cinema and Masculinities: From Salman Khan to John Abraham* .......... 211
Némésis Srour

*Epilogue* ................................................................................................... 225
Thomas Hylland Eriksen

*Author Biographies* ................................................................................. 233

# Introduction
## Tereza Kuldova

> *I want this funeral to be spectacular! Manish darling, you have to design some fabulous embroidered dresses for us and change the interior, we need controlled opulence, luxury and modesty in one, lots of white! It is all about business, you know that darling!*

Anjali's uncle was still fighting against cancer in the hospital when she began planning his spectacular funeral together with one of India's leading fashion designers. Wealthy businessmen, politicians and celebrities were invited the day before her uncle's death. The carefully designed funeral 'festivities' spanning over a week were planned to manifest the power, status and wealth of the family. Business deals worth millions were sealed.

The designer dress that Anjali wore was handmade in Lucknow and took six girls more than five months to embroider. It cost more than a 5-year salary of one of the embroiderers working on the dress. Anjali wore the dress only once.

India is often imaged as consisting of two parallel worlds: the world of the poor and that of the rich or middle class. In reality, however, these two worlds are profoundly dependent on each another; one cannot exist without the other. The rich reproduce poverty in multiple ways, knowingly and unknowingly, in order to satisfy their needs, while the poor have to find ways of surviving, depending on scraps from the rich's table. Nowhere is this more visible than in the emerging Indian fashion industry, where the beautiful dresses, like the lotus flower, grow out of the mud.

Indian fashion, as a social, aesthetic and economic phenomenon, has, until very recently, been a *terra incognita* for anthropologists and scholars. This volume is in fact the first one on the market that attempts to rectify this lack in scholarship by bringing anthropologists together to think through fashion seriously and to prevent further stigmatisation of fashion studies as 'feminine', unserious and worthless. The essays in this volume clearly show that fashion is, like other pleasures, predicated upon privileges as much as on exploitation and oppression, which is precisely why it should be taken seriously and interrogated (Smith 1996). Taking the Indian fashion market, in its multiple manifestations, as a point of departure for an investigation of politics of identity and authenticity, of commodification of past, heritage, culture and tradition and of questions pertaining to cultural property rights, this volume offers a unique perspective on the dynamic overlaps between market, aesthetics and culture in contemporary India. The ambition of this book is to throw light on contemporary India from a vantage point never taken before, arguing the potential of trying to make sense of a society by focusing on its aesthetic production that is in current economy necessarily bound to the global marketplace.

Contemporary Indian fashion and interior design thrives in re-enactments of India's royal pasts and the heritage luxury industry is booming. This trend may be read as a materialisation of the current politics of tradition and identity symptomatic of the dominant discourse of the rise of India as a new global economic power. This new India is, according to its ideologues, economists and business elites, no longer imitating the West but instead presents itself to the world as true to itself and as confident, proud and powerful because of its Indianness. This proud Indianness is visually constructed through an aesthetics modelled upon the re-imaginations of the lifestyles of the pre-colonial Indian royalty, be it the Rajputs or Mughals. We must not forget that this trend also relates to the global (or rather diversely localised) processes of heritisation of aristocratic pasts (and presents) and to attempts at distinguishing local 'capitalisms' through inflected nationalistic identity politics.

This volume was written at the occasion of the exhibition 'Fashion India: Spectacular Capitalism' that opened at the *Museum of Cultural History* in Oslo on 13th of September 2013, an exhibition grounded primarily in my research in India, while also interweaving all of the present essays. The book itself, exploring this confusing landscape between economy, aesthetics and politics, was motivated by my doctoral research, conducted in New Delhi and Lucknow (2010-11), which pointed towards the necessity of taking aesthetics, materiality and visual representations seriously in anthropological study of the contemporary world. I have brought together scholars working on India from around the world to address this relationship together with me; the result is a visually striking and exciting volume, where each essay presents a unique point of view on this shared field.

During my research in New Delhi, the members of the Indian business elites often spoke to me about retaining tradition, about distinctly Indian capitalism and about succeeding as Indians and precisely *because* of their Indianness, something that involved invocations of largely invented traditions (Hobsbawm and Ranger 2003), celebration of national heritage and cultural aesthetics of commodified and packaged 'authenticity'. This shift towards a powerful aesthetics of the new proud and confident India, where categories like tradition and modernity have to be continually reinterpreted and negotiated (Janne Meier, p. 95-118), is visible anywhere from the fashion ramp (Tereza Kuldova, p. 51-70), via the bodies of the muscular Bollywood actors (Nemesis Srour, p. 211-222), to the lounges at the international airport in New Delhi (Paolo Favero, p. 31-48). All these representations comprise part of the creation of the mythologies of contemporary neoliberal India, with its spectacular capitalism. These mythologies of spectacular capitalism incorporate ideas such as that anybody can make it if they work hard enough, or that, over time, capitalism will eradicate inequalities. The realities on the ground more often than not resist these myths (Tereza Kuldova, p. 167-192).

This volume not only traces the logic of the spectacle and capitalism back in time, analysing the current modes of representation, such as fashion shows, in terms of a continuation and reinterpretation of former modes of representation within the capitalist market (Mukherjee, p. 11-29), but also focuses on the complex relationship between lived culture and commercialised culture and the lives of the lower classes who are producing the material symbols of powerful Indianness and serve as ideological objects of the nation *par excellence* but whose material bodies are rejected from the portrayals of this 'new' and 'booming' India. The volume clearly shows that the aesthetic cannot, and should not, be separated from the political and the economic.

Aesthetic beauty cannot be conceived of without its juxtaposition, without the mud from which the lotus flower grows. The arguments spanning these pages, driven by a series of juxtapositions, resemble the white lotus as they take us on a journey from the impoverished conditions of the embroiderers, hidden 'under the water' from the gaze of elite luxury shopaholics to the lavish, material and sensual montages of distinctly Indian and post-2008 *confident* prestige placed within the global economic playground, montages that themselves (re)produce, depend on and feed off their opposite – the poor, polluted and dirty mud that, paradoxically, when sanitised and heightened by means of abstraction, becomes the purest of 'soul material' with which the elite self can fashion itself. The fashion business in India depends on the aesthetics of India's crafts and thus on the direct linkages to the craftspeople in order to satisfy the elite's cravings for national belonging and royal-like heritage luxury (Khaire 2011). In this respect, the fashion and garment industry in India is a sphere par excellence where the *vernacular economies* (Jain 2007) meet and interweave with capitalism and neoliberal logic, where the informal blends with the formal, where notions such as 'heritage' and 'tradition' intermingle with challenges posed by late modernity. It is a sphere where aesthetics and class merge, where nostalgia for grand imagined past redefines tastes and styles as well as meanings of the present directed at the future; it is a sphere that caters to the 'new modern maharajas' (Brosius 2009) at the same time as it is a sphere that employs hundreds of thousands of those labelled as poor. Today, the idea of Indian heritage, wrapped up in exotic images of the flamboyance of royal courts as much as the colourful and stylish native of the Indian village has become a proven and effective sales strategy, one that has moved from the realm of the state-run craft emporiums and governmental schemes to the high-end designer boutiques and the luxury segment. Indeed, heritage and even more so heritage luxury is big business (Rowlands 2002).

The obsession with excess, lavishness and distinction merges the neo-liberal valorisation of 'culture of excess' (Mani 2008:44) with the Indian elite's need to show off hierarchical distinction, cultural belonging and regained confidence in India, one that, as one of the elite fashion designers pointed out to me, 'compared to the West, has real history'. Indeed as David Harvey points out, capitalists increasingly 'trade on values of authenticity, locality, history, culture, collective memories and tradition' (Harvey 2001:109) and the fashion designers are no different in this respect. However, what is interesting is how this trend, which can be observed on a global scale, is played out in the particular settings and acquires radically different meanings for different people.

The emphasis on reclaiming confidence in Indianness and the prestige of India was often connected to a parallel critique of copying and imitating of the West, which was, according to my elite interlocutors, best left to the 'frustrated middle classes'. Several essays in this volume point to the ways in which the non-elites navigate the terrain of fashion and craft their own aesthetics, while displaying an everyday creativity in their re-appropriations and redefinitions of style, glamour and fashion (see Nakassis and Osella p. 121-165). The worlds of high-end fashion and vernacular style engage in mutual borrowings, which have to be accounted for and investigated in more depth. In this unclear terrain, issues of copyright, claims to creativity and originality, accusations of imitation and counterfeit emerge both as pressing empirical topics and stimulating analytical questions.

In order to address these larger issues, the authors of this volume pose concrete questions, such as what have the contemporary Indian spectacular fashion shows in common with the Western nineteenth-century department store fantasy palaces, the royal *durbars*, the elaborate museum displays of the colonial era and the lives of erstwhile Indian royals? What can the Delhi International Airport reveal about the current obsession of Indians with Indianness, the 'local' and the refashioning of India for the global audience? How does the 'royal chic' – the current trend in luxury Indian haute couture that recreates the splendour of the aristocratic lifestyles of the bygone era – depend on poverty for its visual and material existence? Why does the Indian government invest in the Northeast Indian fashion scene and in the production of ethnic glamour and tribal chic? How do the glamour seeking Kerala Muslim women appropriate the sexy Bollywood fashions while still retaining their codes of modesty? How do the world of Delhi and its fashion designers look from the perspective of the village craftswomen that work for them, while mocking and laughing at them and their hectic life? What is the science and artisanship behind the production of traditional Kolhapuri sandals, turned into luxury items for the international consumer? Finally, how do Bollywood cinema and the changing male fashion and body ideals reflect the transforming India?

Without further ado, I wish you pleasant reading and convey my gratitude and thanks to all the dedicated authors and everyone involved in this book project!

# References

Brosius, C. 2009. 'The Gated Romance of 'India shining': Visualizing Urban Lifestyle in Advertisement of Residential Housing Development.' In K. M. Gokulsing & W. Dissanayake (Eds.) *Popular Culture in Globalized India*. London: Routledge.

Harvey, D. 2001. *Spaces of Capital: Towards a Critical Geography*. London: Routledge.

Hobsbawm, E. J. & Ranger, T. O. 2003. *The Invention of tradition*. Cambridge: Cambridge University Press.

Jain, K. 2007. *Gods in the Bazaar: The Economies of Indian Calender Art*. Durham: Duke University Press.

Khaire, M. 2011. 'The Indian Fashion Industry and Traditional Indian Crafts.' *Business History Review*, 85:2, 345-66.

Mani, L. 2008. 'The Phantom of Globality and the Delirium of Excess.' *Economic and Political Weekly*, 43:39, 41-47.

Rowlands, M. 2002. 'Heritage and Cultural Property.' In V. Buchli (Ed.) *The Material Culture Reader*: 105-15. Oxford: Berg.

Smith, M. D. 1996. 'The Empire Filters Back: Consumption, Production and the Politics of Starbucks Coffee.' *Urban Geography*, 17:6, 502-24.

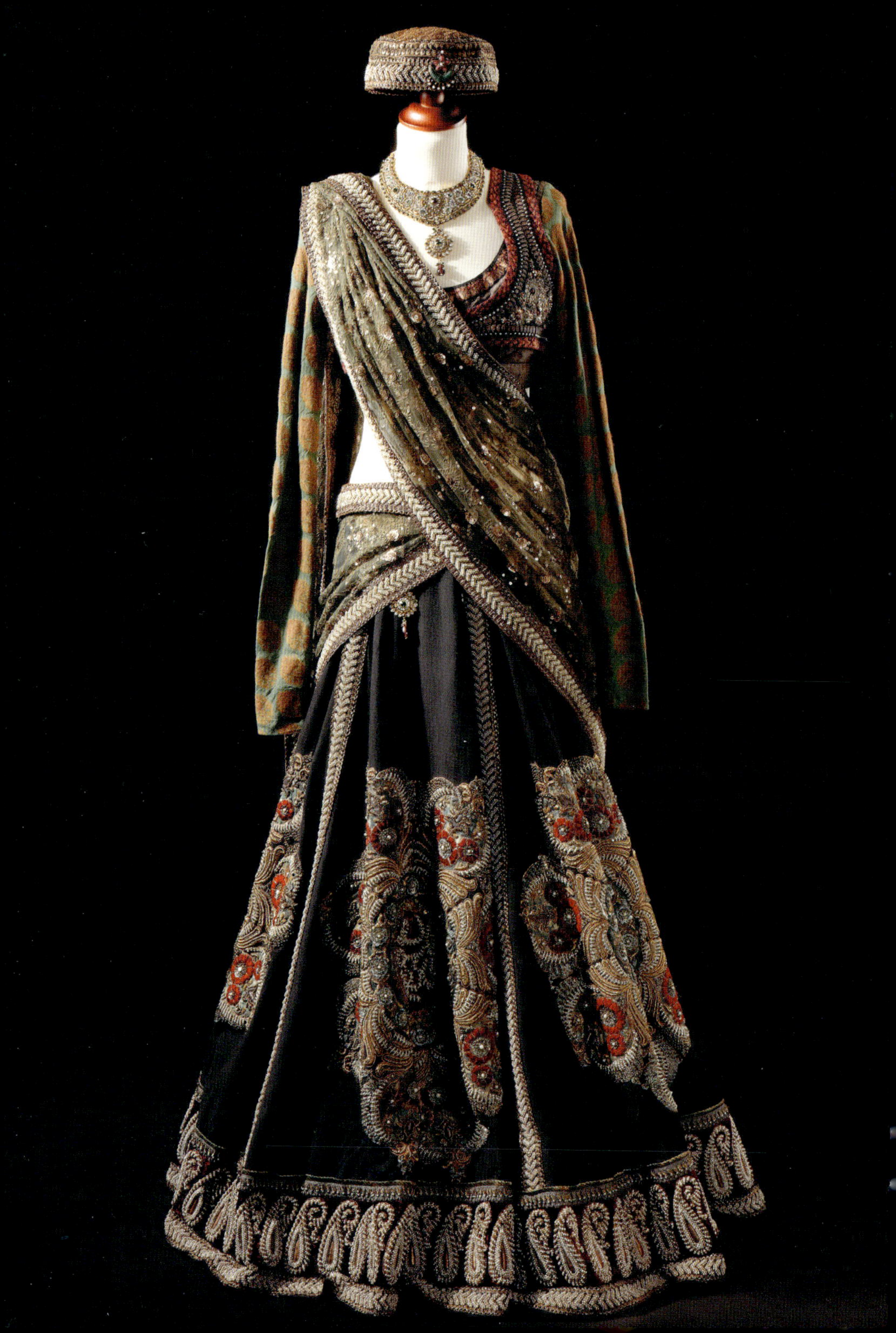

# The World Fashion Fair
## India on Display
Nilanjana Mukherjee

Fashion is obviously an economic issue as much as it is a socio-cultural one. As the historian Fernand Braudel points out, 'costume is linked to the possibilities of the material situation [...] The history of costume [...] touches on every issue – raw materials, production processes, manufacturing costs, cultural stability, fashion and social hierarchy'. (Braudel: 1981, Steele: 1985, 18) Although technically temporality of fashion deliberately drives older forms into obsolescence, what is often noticeable is a recurrence of the past within an inevitable cycle. This means that we need to trace continuities of the past into the present. Therefore, my main objective here is to study and trace the image-making; working; and the historicity of the spectacle of fashion show. This essay is divided mainly into two parts: the first section talks of the fashion-related theatrical formations developed in the backdrop of the emerging modern city in the late nineteenth century West, and its appropriation of the 'traditional other' in a rapidly advancing capitalist economy surviving on spectacle-making; the second section extends the lineage of cultural representations in such as the fashion pageant, dating back to postcolonial India in order to trace the continuation and engagement with visual cultures manufactured typically in the imperial West. I argue that the fashion industry in India thrives in a strange crucible, which amalgamates what is imagined as tradition and that which expresses modernity. An investigation into the contemporary Indian fashion industry thus necessarily leads us into post-Independence debates and to, earlier still, the British rule and colonial era. In my paper, I shall recall the tussle between ideas of tradition and modernity in the initial years after Independence, whereby the new nation drew her symbols from pre-colonial tribal and ethnic culture: with the rural landscape, with its autochthonous arts and crafts, emerging as the site of recovery of pristine and essential India in visual culture such as art and cinema.

## Temporality, Fashion and the Public Spectacle
The catwalk show is a public event, a marketing exercise, where each show guards and maintains its own aura of the ephemeral, fugitive, the contingent and the exclusive. Such exclusivity is part of its marketability, where the audience becomes part of the spectacle and the product portrays an image that is reflected only in its semblance; as the final consumer in such fashion shows and pageants is often absent. Howev-

er, with the progressive advancement of technology and media culture, such shows are able to reach a global audience. In this process, the audience becomes a market rather than a public. In the present consumerist society, sales promotion of fashion, including garments, cosmetics and sundry consumer items, which resort to advertisement, also reflect the same networking. It is said that fashion is all about change. For centuries, people perceived the changing form of fashion as essentially inexplicable. Throughout time immemorial, fashion has been personified as a deity, which periodically issued yet another capricious decree, signifying the temporality of fashion. Similarly, the everyday practice of getting dressed also involves a conscious awareness of time and so the temporal constraints of fashion cannot be avoided. The experience of fashion imposes an external sense of time. Time is socially constructed by the fashion system through the circle of collections, shows and seasons, which serve to halt the flow of 'now' by means of projections into future (Entwistle: 2000, 32). The fashion system, and that which is within it, particularly fashion journalism, constantly freezes the flow of everyday practices of dress and orders them into distinct entities of past, present and future. For example, 'this winter brown is the new black' or 'forget last year's lime-green, cool beige is the colour to wear this summer'. These artificial indictments only attempt to perpetuate the production process. Adorno and Horkheimer argue that the role of such a cultural industry is that of generating and creating false needs through 'mass deception' (Adorno and Horkheimer: 2002). The modern catwalk, ramps and fashion shows celebrate this temporality through its intensified pace, where the fluidity of ceaseless images of models walking one after another construct a constant series of 'nows'. Considering the situation in which an activity such as the pageant takes place, such techniques of the body become not only a part of the interaction order, but also serve to reproduce it.

Earlier, in the 1940s and '50s, for example, only a very small number of people could experience the old-fashioned intimacy of such shows, seated close enough to the models to see the fine detailing of the clothes. However, since the 1990s. the number of people familiar with fashion collections has been rapidly increasing, as these designs began to be conveyed to a mass audience through the new visual media, such as magazines, books, videos, the television and the internet. More remarkable, in this respect, are the International Beauty Contests such as the Miss World or Miss Universe Contests, which are able to reach and influence a global audience. The enterprise here is to woo the audience, entice and seduce them through simulation and illusory visions of excess. I would argue that the spectacle from the 1990s onwards has mutated into one of pure image. This evokes Susan Sontag's claim that 'a society becomes 'modern' when one of its chief activities is producing and consuming images" (Sontag: 1978, 153; White: 2000, 164). Therefore, it is essential to study the nature and process of constructing these images to see how a post-colonial society striving to become part of the global economy is nurtured and nourished by them. Here, I shall mainly concentrate on the representation of national costumes in international beauty pageants, trying to trace the lineage of the spectacle through time. The conglomeration of the exotic and the erotic through a mechanics of spectacle-making is my central focus.

## The Spatial Trope in Staging Fashion

I argue that the creation of late-twentieth century spectacle, exemplified by beauty contests and fashion shows, for example, does not depart entirely from past traditions. In fact, many scholars have tried to understand analogies and similarities of such fashion shows in terms of the emergence of capitalism and therefore of the 'modern city'. With the city becoming the site of modernity and late capitalist ideals, the countryside and the village became constantly 'other'-ised and exoticised in order to be consumed. In the West, the nineteenth century theatrical formations often extended beyond the countryside and generously embraced the colonised geographies, revelling in representations of cultural differences, essentialisations and stereotypes. The world of entertainment came to be marked by ingredients and tropos from the non-West. For example, colonial locations were also seen as suitable sites for maximising sexual opportunities and therefore even served as locale for nineteenth century pornographies. As the European societies revelled in the representations of cultural differentials and essentialisms, the non-West was embraced and incorporated into the realm of urban spectacles. Colonial topographies became the location for many theatrical performances, as did the cultural markers for example, and clothes and rituals played a crucial role in such performances. As David Cannadine points out, the colonial other, the 'Orient' was copiously appropriated through motifs and decorations, a process he calls 'Ornamentalism' (Cannadine: 2001). Spaces meant for amusement, such as the supper boxes in Vauxhall, were designed to capture this growing interest in the colonial picturesque. Cultural motifs and ethnic designs metonymised the colonies, which existed only to be consumed as spectacles in the metropolis.

From the beginning of the nineteenth century, department stores in Paris, with their radical new technique of retail and display, rapidly turned into theatres of consumption. Shop windows became astound-

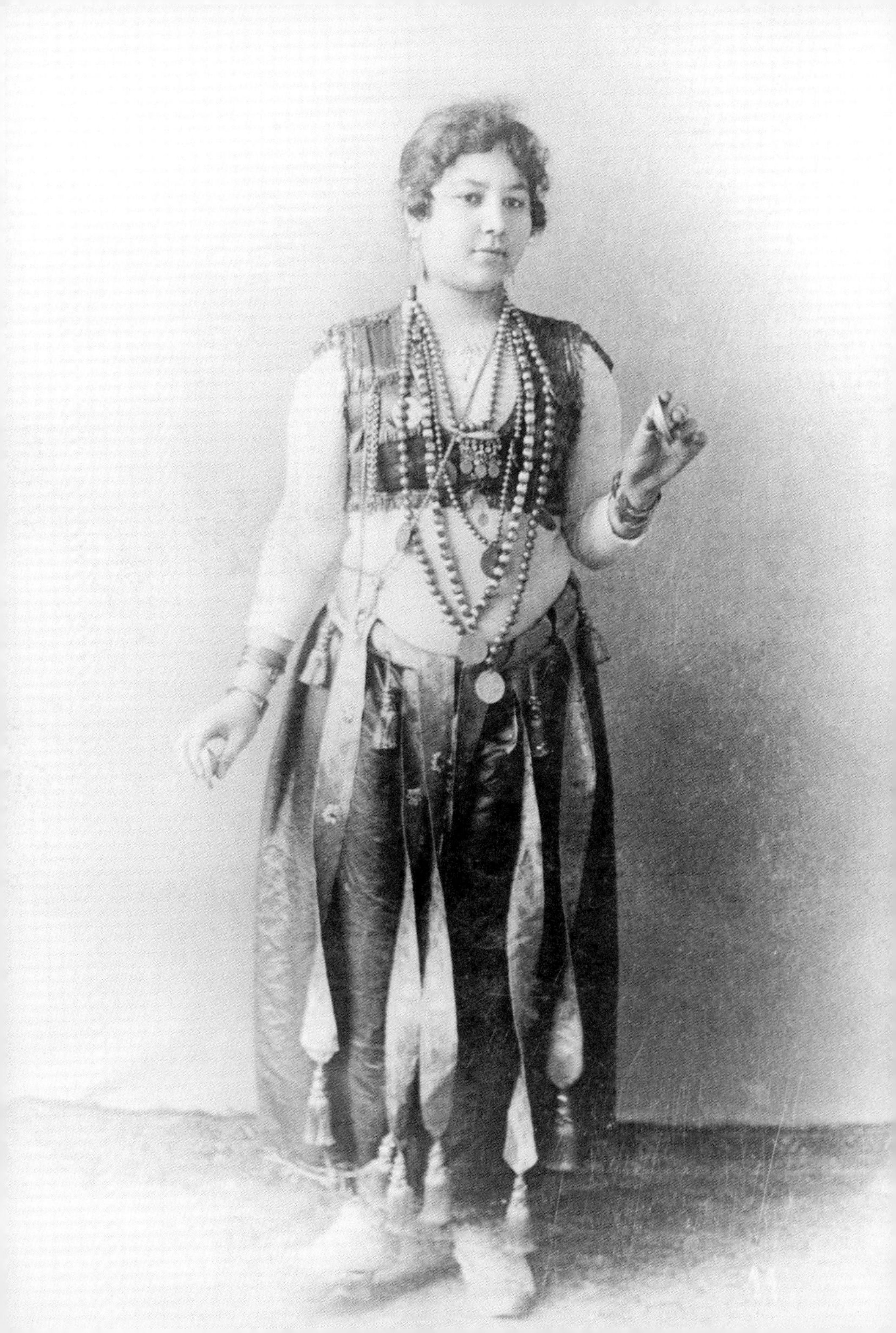

ing sources of display, as did the goods inside the store, where everyday objects were rearranged together with decorative sculptural forms of flowers, caged live birds and, later on in the century, splashing electric fountains. All kinds of the latest technical innovations were utilised. Flashy electric lightning further galvanised some of these displays into fairy-tale scenes. In addition, and most importantly, department stores often drew on the convention of theatre and exhibitions to produce orientalist scenes, including living tableaux of Turkish harems, Cairo markets or Hindu temples, with live dancers, music and oriental products. In such departmental stores, and occasional world fairs and exhibitions, the real commercial nature of the transaction was disguised by the creation of the seductive 'dream worlds' in which the consumer lost him or herself in fantasy and reverie. In the nineteenth century, female consumption was nurtured, trained and encouraged through spectacles and dreamy scenarios staged in the department stores. Simultaneously, the great exhibitions that granted a vision of luxury consumption to mass audience strengthened the connection between consumerism, material culture and the exotic.

Today's spectacular runway shows and beauty pageants that incorporate enticement and advertisement are highly innovative and could be perceived as advancing the tradition of linkage between spectacle and commodity culture, which was established in the nineteenth century city, with its departmental store fantasy palaces. The modern fashion shows fulfill a somewhat similar role, with the only difference being that the audience remains seated while the spectacle unfolds before them like a mobile panorama. Perhaps the show itself, in which the stationary spectator is dazzled by lights, effects and rapid-fire presentation, has more in common with the fantasy journey of the world fairs. In the spectacles of the exhibition of 1900, colours, cultures and sounds were fused in a way very similar to today's Miss World or Miss Universe contest. Here the 'Cairo belly dancers' and 'Andalusian gypsies' of the world fair are not dissimilar to the performing models representing different nationalities and cultures. Such international pageants employ techniques of historical pastiche and cultural collage to fuse disparate cultures and places, much as the World Tour did in the 1900 Paris Universal Exhibition by abutting a Hindu temple, a Chinese pagoda and a Muslim mosque enlivened by live jugglers and geishas. The effect, of both the 1900 Exhibition as much as that of the present day internation-

---

Left:
Egyptian dancing girl, World's Columbian Exposition, Chicago, Illinois, 1893
Photographer: Unknown | Source: Library of Congress (Public Domain)

al pageants, is to normalise, contain and manage non-European cultures by recreating them in the form of a spectacle. The 'people and cultures on display' paradigm in these performances intertwines exotic and the erotic, by the same logic it also mixes ethnicity, gender and geography. The organisation of the beauty pageants at various picturesque locales of the world caters to a taste for a burgeoning touristic desire to see the most touted sites, albeit only in representation.

This fantasy carnival of human figures, colours and confetti takes the form of an endless celebration of crowning the Queen. A feeling of 'presentness' pervades the aesthetics of world exhibitions as much as that of today's global contests, which, as Georg Simmel points out: 'increases our time consciousness, and our simultaneous pleasure in newness and oldness give us a strong sense of presentness' (White: 2000, 153). It is this sense of 'presentness' in a late twentieth century fashion show with its brevity and drama that is created precisely to make us conscious of the new juxtaposed the old, creating not only a cultural but a historical pastiche. Fashion sociologist, Elizabeth Wilson has focused exclusively on the nexus between women, modernity, fashion and the city, arguing that fashion and modernity share a duality because they are both formed in the same crucible: that of the early capitalist city (Wilson: 1985, 9). Both Georg Simmel and Walter Benjamin have pointed out how the urban landscape has undergone considerable aesthetisation and enchantment through its architecture, billboards, shop displays, advertisements, packages, street-signs and through the adorned bodies who move through these spaces, that is, those individuals who conduct their movements and walk in particular stylised ways. (Benjamin: 1999) The enchantment and stylisation were replayed in the make-believe, hyper-real space of the late twentieth century catwalk.

## Romantic Fantasy and the Bourgeois experience

This brings us to the unique quality that combines an elusive, mysteriously exciting and illusory attractiveness called glamour. (Gundle: 2009) This is the much-publicised quality which stirs the imagination and appeals to a taste for the unconventional, the unexpected, the colourful or the exotic. Walter Scott is said to be the author who first introduced glamour into literary language. As the inventor of the historical novel and a great promoter of Romanticism, Scott specialised in creating illusion and visual deception hence transporting one to a different time and space. By blending real historical setting with fiction, he offered a romanticised vision of a medieval past that thrilled nineteenth century readers and fired their imagination. For the newly-empowered middle-class readers, the stories of violent passion, terrible feuds, great loves, chivalrous acts and deadly battles which took place in faraway alien natural settings of lakes, mountains, forests or amidst gothic architecture of castles and towers, became vehicles for their dreams and desires. This fantasy aspect born out of a feeling of nostalgia for a lost aristocratic order is significantly linked to the development of modern consumerism. Even advertisements today tap the sentiment and use narratives predominantly of romance and exoticism to allure customers. The insatiable desire, often expressed in day-dreaming or fantasy, became a crucial part of the bourgeois experience and modern consumerism.

Bourgeois consciousness in the beginnings of capitalism facilitated the emergence and articulation of ideas, images and figure that were alluring and enticing, often borrowing from attributes and characteristics of the currently overthrown aristocracy. The late aristocracy continued to define luxurious living, the most significant component in the valorisation of any product meant for sale. This historical juncture, on the one hand, nurtured growth of the new cities and market places, while, on the other, the newly formed bourgeoisie increasingly adopted and manifested aristocratic attributes including style, taste and beauty. However, this new visual language of display was not entirely different from past traditions. The royal courts often became the model for imitation. As the established elite lost its monopoly of splendour, the resources widened and provided access to the rising social class. Another major role was played by the opening up of high-society to the exponents of arts, show-business and the worlds of money and an increased role of appearances in social relations. Up to the eighteenth and nineteenth centuries, the social bearer of glamour was the aristocracy, but increasingly this class was losing its political and economic power. Aristocracy:

> .... offered only a paradigm. More important was the semblances or reproduction of distinction, stylishness, wealth and breeding that could be manufactured by commercial culture or through the media. This artificial aura, detached from the class that had created it and turned into a manufactured property, was the essence of glamour. (Buckley and Gundle in Bruzzi eds: 2000, 335)

The new visible elite and role models were those who were photographed, painted and talked about in the press. The foremost prerequisite for this would be photographic beauty, style, excitement and an artifice acquired through consumption of various luxury items and fashion. Visibility or appearance and artifice thereby became more important. Yet, as the visual horizons of the public were being widened, magazines and shop windows also functioned as distancing mechanisms. By virtue of serving to prevent immediate access, along with seduction,

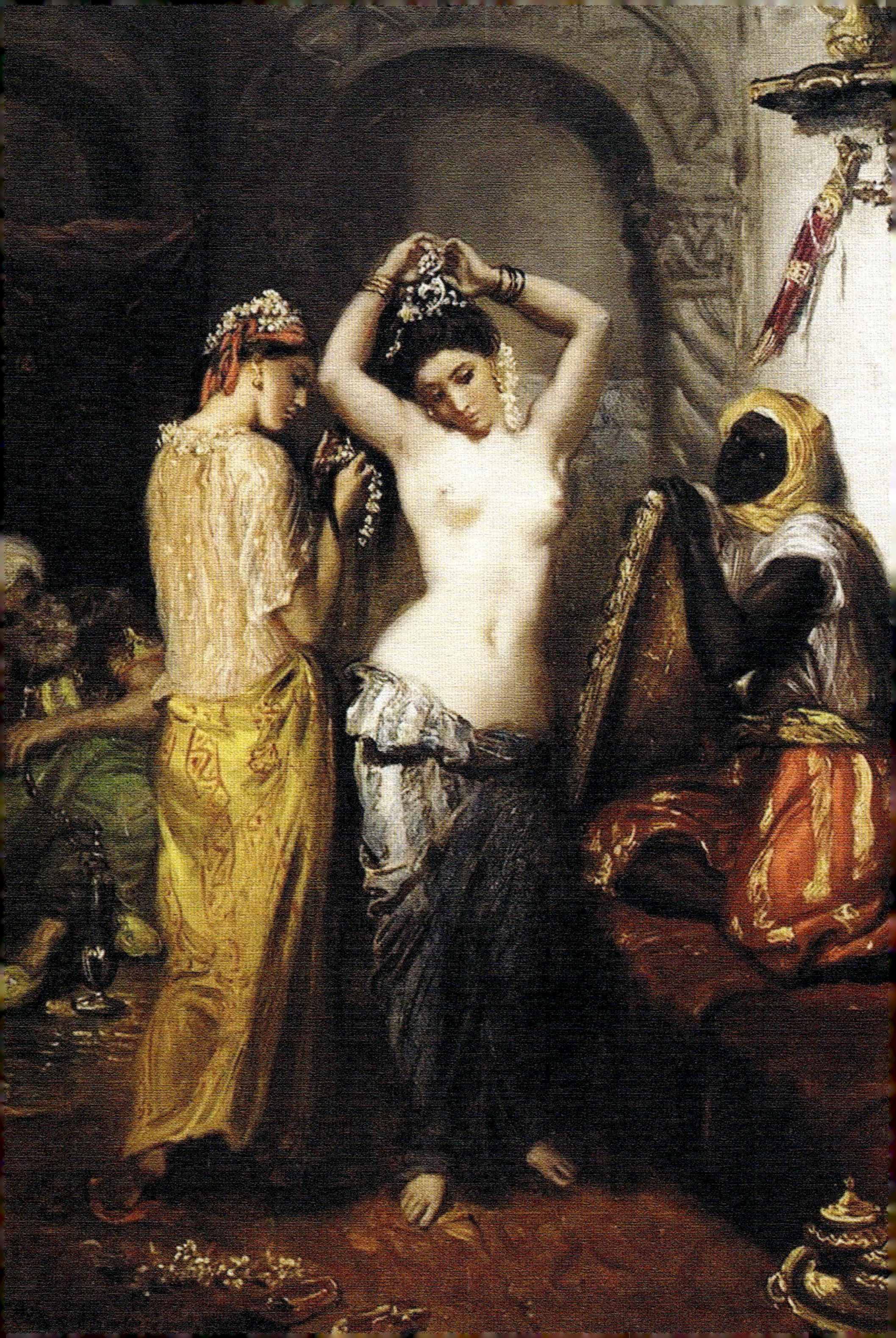

they fuelled envy and desire - the crucial weapons through which consumerism and conspicuous consumption thrive.

## Sex and Seduction

What is this seduction? In its dictionary definition, it refers to the act of causing a person to 'err in conduct or belief', to the 'leading astray' or enticement of another, particularly with regard to sexual matters. It refers to getting another to carry out one's will, not by force or coercion, but by an exercise of the other's own (albeit often mistaken or misguided) free will. Seduction is the idea that the other cannot be forced to follow, that in any such forging, there is always an ambiguity, a possible resistance by the other. According to Baudrillard, seduction refers to the idea that we cannot have a relationship without it being possible to determine whether it is we who lead the other or the other who leads us. (Baudrillard:1990) Today's beauty contests with their opulence, glitz, glamour and splendour principally deploy this tool of seduction, where consumption of certain brands becomes a prerequisite for a happy living and attainment of apparent aristocracy through 'mock-queendom'. This can work in times like ours: in an age when people no longer want things for what they are, or for what they can be used for, but only because somebody else wants them. Moreover, the bourgeois longing and nostalgia for an eroded aristocracy results in the embracement of a pseudo-aristocracy which mimics the appearance and lifestyle of the lost monarchy. Indeed, what could engender this seduction more than a sexual body, that is, the body of a woman, or better still, the body of the prostitute?

Going back to the nineteenth century city, the low cultural forms that provided inputs into the dynamic image of the city alongside aristocratic refinement were popular theatre, cafe and the world of commercial sex. Sex and the theatrical mixed openly. Within the brothels, sexual practices became more elaborate and increasingly staged. Spectacles and tableau vivants [living pictures] were enacted on gigantic revolving turn-tables; simple peepholes were replaced by draperies, mirrors, binoculars and acoustic horns hidden in the wall. Prostitutes were required to perform a greater range of activities. That which had previously been perceived as aristocratic taste was now turned into a lower and middle-class spectacle. Interestingly, contemporary descriptions of brothels reveal fantasy settings not dissimilar to those of department

---

Left:
Harem
Painting by Théodore Chassériau (1819 – 1856) | Source: Wikimedia (Public Domain)

stores. Many brothels also renovated their establishments in the form of opera settings, oriental scenes, Louis XV salons or electric fairylands.

The everyday act thus becomes glamorous and mystified through artificial rendering, sensational and exciting when it is turned into a spectacle. In contemporary advertising and publicity stunts, spectacle seems to have greater force in public conscience than ever before: as popular arts, music and film tend to invest greater confidence in sensibility, intuition and emotion. Therefore, every such image contains an overt or covert theme of fairy-tale romance and melodrama combined with neat detailing – not unlike that of children's picture books. This may have eventuated as a reaction to centuries of an emphasis on reason and scientific technology, which is thought to have brought little else than misery for the substantial majority of the world's population, as well as depletion and destruction of ecological resources and international strife. Spectacle and public entertainment of this kind deliberately takes recourse to sentiment, fantasy and romance, eschewing overtly modern technology.

Fashion is about extorting the maximum media coverage, and, the more spectacular the presentation the better. The spectacle is the theatre through which capitalism and consumer culture works. Such a spectacle invariably uses heightened, hyperbolic images instead of the actual and real. In his essay, The Work of Art in the Age of Mechanical Reproduction, Benjamin argued that in this age there was born 'a desire to bring things closer spatially and humanly'. Benjamin says:

> Everyday the urge grows stronger to get hold of an object at very close range by way of its likeness, its reproduction unmistakably, reproduction as offered by picture magazines and newsreels differs from the image seen by the unarmed eye. Uniqueness and permanence are as closely linked in the latter as are transitoriness and reproducibility in the former (Benjamin: 1973, 225; Buckley and Gundle: 2000, 334).

These images do not exist in some distant realm of art for arts' sake but as distinct commercial and marketing stratagem. As Anne Friedberg (1994) points out, the centrality of the mobilised and virtual gaze is a fundamental feature of today's reality. What she calls the 'shoppers' gaze' and forms of visual mobility, which were once solely the stronghold of first world imperial cities, became a framing principle for a global standard of modernity. Friedberg identifies this relationship between sight and bodily movement as developing from the earlier activity of travel. The touristic gaze is the overarching paradigm that also shaped many modern architectural forms, such as the museum or the shopping arcade. Consumerism engendered and encouraged shoppers' gaze and is thus intertwined with the concept of travel and tourism, which became a crucial device in framing proto-cinematic visual culture. Most importantly, this brought artefacts of the world and the past into a virtually tourable present. This is where colonial history shares the legacy with the current post-modern hyperreal (Friedberg: 1994, 1-5).

## From the British Empire to Post-Colonial India

Post-colonial independent India negotiated its representation of itself as a consequence of its unique history and political reality. Indian culture with abstract essentialisms was fitted into this grid of 'primitivism' of sorts, in which authentic India was believed to reside in its villages and countryside rather than in the rapidly modernising urban spaces. Moreover, the overarching feudal politics that ruled the newly formed India, celebrated the glamour, luxury and lifestyle of the erstwhile royalty and princely families that had to abdicate power in order to be formally incorporated in the new geo-political alliance. Immediately after independence, the propagation of the national idea – projected both domestically and abroad – backed by the Government of India, embraced a 'heritage industry' that promoted ethnic jewellery, crafts, textiles and motifs. The paradigm that emerges in such exhibitionary complex is one of a colonially inherited 'aesthetic of primitivism'. This opens up a new debate when Indian fashion is studied through this analytic aperture of 'museology'. If one were to historicise the trend, one would need to travel back in time to take a closer look at the colonial visual culture. The colonial Durbars comprise one such instance of representing the Indian empire to its people and are important for its ritualistic significance.

The three colonial Durbars, with their spectacle and panache were imperial projects aimed at bringing the alien yoke into participation in the celebration of colonial glory. In the exhibitions, which formed the prelude to the Durbar of 1877, an exhibition of Indian Art was held under Lord Curzon's patronage, designed as a showcase of Indian craftsmanship. Within each tent, every item of furniture was 'of native manufacture'. Curzon took the opportunity to lecture the Indian princes, telling them to abandon their predilections for 'Tottenham Court Road furniture' and 'Brussels carpets' and purchase Indian wares instead. The British, in their attempt to usurp the power and magnificence of the erstwhile royalty in India, adopted not only the rituals like the Durbar, but also strove to make the entire visual effect typically Indian: from clothes to pageantry to the shamiyana [a marquee]. This is something that post-Independence India continues to embrace as its favourite cultural self-representation, for example in cultural performances that aim

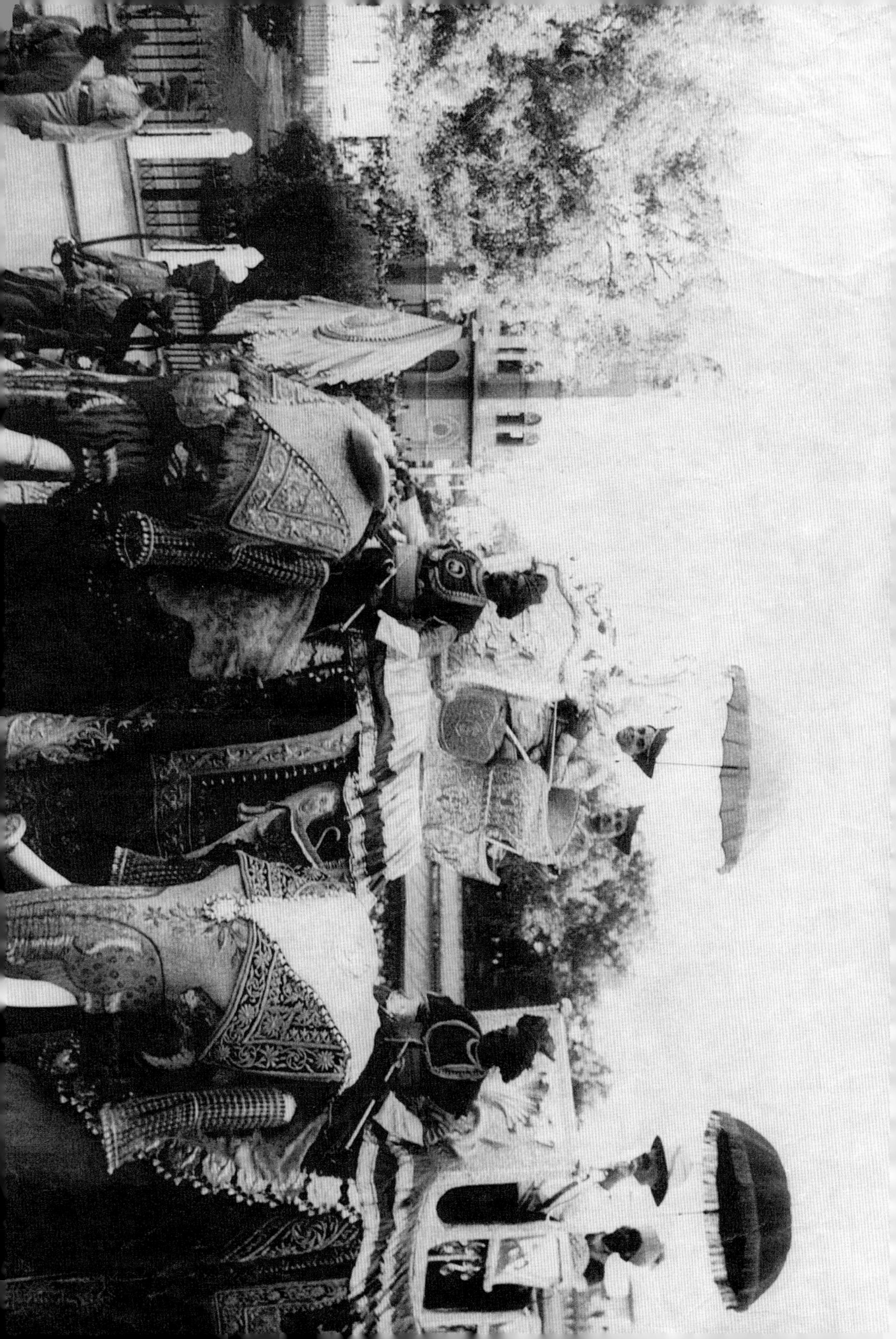

to showcase the nation to both a domestic and global audience.

Sudipta Kaviraj (1998) and Dilip Menon (2004) both point out how in the tussle between tradition and modernity in the initial years after Independence, the new nation drew her symbols from pre-colonial tribal and ethnic culture. The rural landscape, with its autochthonous arts and crafts, emerged as the site of recovery of pristine and essential India in visual culture, such as art and cinema. The village was seen as the repository of authentic cultural past of the modern people, something that needed to be upheld and celebrated. The Gandhian glorification of the village community became the sole metaphor for signifying Indian culture. India's heritage enacted in national spectacles was to be prominently devoid of the urbanity, cosmopolitanism and the present everydayness. All through the fifties, avid industrialisation was never viewed without a degree of suspicion and cultural expressions never whole-heartedly embraced modernisation. Industrialisation, modernisation and urbanisation were issues that were repeatedly debated against a backdrop of ethical socialism. Amidst this debate, the synthetic modernity that evolves is one that is very often backward-facing, at least in the field of aesthetics and culture, where indigenous folk and tribal forms are deemed authentic. The debate generated at the time of Swadesi Movement centring around Gandhi's *charkha*-spun *Khadi* and imported Manchester mill cloth had far reaching impact on the postcolonial consciousness. To quote Menon:

> ... in a rendering of the very idea of the 'people' as a romantic abstraction, their pre-modern 'encrustation' being rendered as popular culture rather than awaiting radical historical transformation (Menon; 2004).

Modernity, as visualised by the post-colonial construction, was an 'already existing, indigenized, and naturalized state of being' (Menon; 2004). This precept was consolidated, as a rule, in national spectacles, spanning the past to the present. Such an exhibitionary impulse, in trying to unearth the tradition of India, ran into another set of problems. India had not yet given up her colonial inheritance and retained the main pillars of colonial practice, such as its police, bureaucracy and education system. (Kaviraj; 1998, 160) An important acolyte for these was also colonial anthropology, which studied the races and tribes of the colonies along with their rituals, customs, religion and habits in order to

Left:
Pooja – state elephants and bullock chariot (Ratha)
The Museum of Cultural History collections

legitimise their subjugation for the sake of their own advancement and benefit. The incorporation of the native within the narrative of European advancement, reason and progress figured in iconographic traditions and anthropometric studies.

Christopher Pinney points out how colonial photographic enterprises like that of William Johnson's *The Oriental Races and Tribes, Residents and Visitors of Bombay: A Series of Photographs with Letter press Descriptions* (1866) and *The People Of India* (1868-75) by Watson and Kaye, often sought representatives of almost all the races and tribes of the Indian continent and islands. Together with this, they were concerned with systems of identification that included physiognomy, bodily marks, costumes and characters. (Pinney; 1997, 28) These anthropological depictions and physiognomic observations, along with their material artefacts, would serve as future indices for identification, not only of these tribes, but also, later, of Indianness itself. Other such exhibitions included Joseph Fayrer's ethnological display:

> 'With typical examples of the races in the old world' in which exhibits would 'sit each in his own stall, and submit to be photographed, painted, taken off in casts and otherwise reasonably dealt with in the interest of science' (Pinney, 46).

Pinney suspects that in some cases the emergent modernity of some tribes was erased and some were coerced to pose for photographs in their primitive attire (Pinney, 46-8). The paradigm that emerges through such incidents is an 'aesthetic of primitivism'. This opens up a new debate when Indian national pageantry is studied through this analytic aperture of 'museology' (which Bernard Cohn calls the 'museological mode'). Very often, there is a reiteration of the theme of crafts and craftsmen in an attempt to stabilise regional identities.

## Ethnicities, Crafts and Public Consumption

Quite often, in national festivals and events like the Republic Day procession, one can find states being represented with a distinguished and popular form of handicraft, such as the famous Lucknow chickan of Uttar Pradesh; the bandhni from Rajasthan; the bidri from Andhra; the bamboo or cane handicrafts of Assam; gurjari handicrafts from Gujrat, and so on. In fact, representations have conformed with the fixed grids of identification when it comes to performances and *tableaux vivants*. The flip side of the modernity – tradition and authenticity debate is however often an economic pragmatism. In his essay, 'Nation, Economy and Tradition Displayed' dealing with the Indian Crafts Museum of New Delhi, Paul Greenrough identifies four cross-cutting strands:

> The economic betterment of poor artisans; shifting demands for handcrafted goods; elite practices of cultural revival and preservation; and propagation of the national idea domestically and abroad. (Greenrough; 1996, 220)

Greenrough recounts how these handicrafts, often retailed in government-run emporiums, have paved their way into bourgeois urban homes as fashion and interior decoration. Ethnic jewellery, crafts, textiles and motifs also have significant markets outside India. These form a part of the world of 'the heritage industry', which includes tourism and travel. In fact, tourism is perhaps the biggest profiteer from ethnic showcases such as fashion shows abroad. As an aside, one should mention the invocation of the old feudal order and royalty in this industry in order to cash in on a sentiment of nostalgia for the past (in the case of erstwhile aristocracy) and a chance to live like the aristocrats (in the case of the *nouveau riche* bourgeoise) (see Kuldova, p. 51-72). On the other hand, it is important to note that the feudal order is not entirely extinct in India and it is due to the veto from large pockets of existing feudalism that modernity, together with avid industrialisation, have been halted and criticised throughout the post-Independence decades. Feudalism still exerts its influence and power in subtle ways: not only having a direct impact on government policies but also controlling the cultural domain in India to a significant extent. Returning to the earlier point, could it be said that the visual pleasure of the spectacle, in a display such as this, ties it up with consumer appetite? According to Arjun Appadurai and Carol A. Breckenridge, the museum experience has recently undergone regeneration in the public sphere by adopting a 'festival form, especially as it has been harnessed by the Indian State in its effort to define national, regional, and ethnic identity' (Appadurai and Breckenridge; 1990, 400). At the same time, one also needs to mention other museum-oriented festivals of India, such as the Republic Day parade or the 'Apna Utsav' or Our Festival, where a vast state-sponsored network is notable for interregional exhibition of art, crafts, folklore and clothing, which, according to them, 'support reinvigoration of museums, on the one hand, and the vitality of exhibition–cum–sales, on the other' (Appadurai and Breckenridge; 1990, 409). These two forms, that is, the ethnic–national festival and the exhibition–cum–sale, have characterised the public world of goods in contemporary India. The boundaries that divide commerce, pageantry and display happen to be porous, encouraging permeation of one into the other.

Induced by this museum-based consumerism, there is a shift towards objectifying culture. Objects of religious and ritual significance that were uprooted from their spaces of origin or establishment when transported to spaces such as the museum or exhibition hall, lost their earlier value and were thereafter merely seen as artefacts with aesthetic significance. Tapati Guha Thakurta mentions the instance of the iconic Yakshi (a figurine of a semi-divine being or tree spirit), which was first deported to the Patna Museum and subsequently to the Indian National Museum. In so doing, the icon worshipped as a goddess by the locals was decontextualised, divested of its everyday customary practice and transformed into a mere piece of art (Guhahakurta; 1998, 98). As Dipankar Gupta points out, 'culture is enlivened in space such that without space there is no clear conception of cultural membership' (Gupta; 2000, 20). On the other hand, what he calls the 'non-spaces', such as the 'airports', 'national highways' 'supermarkets' and 'apartment complexes' are insensitive to cultural 'root metaphors' (i.e. culture that emblematises roots) and do not arouse passionate membership in the way that cultures do with their spaces. The stage of the fashion pageant, one can argue, as with shopping arcades, malls, markets, museums or exhibition halls, is such a non-space where traditions lose their ritual meaning in paying homage to capitalism-generated adoptive categories of showcasing cultural and racial differences.

Similarly, the cinema industry in India, which contributes while at the same time borrowing from the international fashion industry, was also built on the premises of oriental spectacle. The first Indian film to be viewed in Britain dates back to 1926, when King George and Queen Mary held a command performance of *Prem Sanyas [Light of Asia]* (1925) at Windsor Castle (Dudra 2006). Needless to say, the film was viewed as an oriental spectacle enabling a creation of a fantasy space, complete with a host of multifarious cultural markers, such as clothes, ornaments, jewellery, architecture and identifiable 'spiritualism' associated with India. The Mumbai film industry to this day conforms to this grid, determined long back by the colonial masters. However, this is not to say that experiments with self-fashioning have not occurred. The particularised 'screen economy' and practices in the movie entertainment in India today shed light on a spectrum of film product as a site-specific and clearly identifiable fashion culture, consumed by both resident Indians and diasporic audience abroad. In tracing the linkages between the image-sound-design elements and the wider economy of perception, one can not only identify the market impulse but also trace, as has been my central focus in this chapter, a pre-colonial and therefore a pre-national quality in the national representation. In the wake of massive post '90s globalisation, rapid industrialisation has, together with drastic revamping of urban landscapes, inaugurated a new urbanism in Hindi cinema, which tends to uphold the idea of a 'global nation' rather than a 'territorial nation', resulting in a cultural amalgam between the local and the global. (See Vasudevan; JMI, 7) Indian fashion and its spectacles too, often choose the global arena to showcase local cultures addressing both kinds of audience: ones who are aware but alienated from that local culture and those who are completely foreign. The encapsulation of the past in the name of 'tradition' within the modern globalised visual grammar ensconced in a well-established market economy is a trademark of Indian fashion spectacles on world forum today. As explained earlier, this is an outcome of a long-standing debate between 'modernity' and 'tradition' resulting in a synthetic 'invention of tradition' (Hobsbawm; 1983). The resounding themes of 'incredible India' and its 'rich diversity' reverberate throughout these performances painting an image of a unified and harmonious ethne.

## Conclusion

I have thus crossed three significant junctures in Indian history, namely, colonial; post-independence; and post-liberalisation, whereby I have tried to show how specific representational strategies are adopted at various times, dictated by various power constellations. Fashion shows and pageantry, which I read as simply another form of theatrical production, closely follow these representational strategies, having a shared history in the colonial past, along with Indian art and cinema in the global arena. I see this colonial past as being fraught with multiple socio-economic dynamics that contribute to the culture of spectacle emerging in the nineteenth century. A whole gamut of innovations in the realm of visual and performance cultures, like the exhibitions, museums and department stores, as a result of the new formulation of urbanity tied to consumerism in the latter half of the nineteenth century (which must be commemorated as the first onslaught of globalisation), still persists to this day. The valorisation of cultural and ethnic differences arising out of disparate geographical locations is an oft-repeated trope embellishing such performances, entertainment and exhibitionary culture and space. Therefore recreational space almost always banks on 're-created space'. Bodies become bearers of that distinct geo-cultural identity.

India was once again placed in the cross currents of history and its desired future course when the foundation of the nation needed to be rethought after it gained its independence. A synthetic modernity configured through the debates on what was considered to be India's 'tradition', based on regional differences, and what was generally thought to be a more Western course of 'progressive' modernism (which was deemed to be inevitable but was viewed with suspicion by many as the perpetrator of centuries-long colonial oppression of its native people).

The rural and folk forms and arts were, in this case, distinctly chosen by the state to represent the nation. Straddling two opposing tendencies, the aristocracy is still alive in certain pockets, re-emerged as an important symbolical entity intended to represent glamour and tradition of an imaginary antiquarian India in the post-liberalisation decades since the '90s, which could compete in style with the Guccis and Diors, and other such international fashion brands. India now needed to be seen as a vast market for consumption and had to make its forays into markets abroad. The erstwhile aristocracy, which still exerts considerable control over rural India and over a collective imagination of India, became (much like the colonial state) the flag-bearers, connoisseurs and protectorate of Indian arts and crafts, which were thought to carry the distinct essence of 'real' India or India's heritage. In the world fair, this India could be represented, reproduced and consumed.

## Bibliography

Appadurai, Arjun and Carol A. Breckenridge. 'Museums are good to think: Heritage on view in India', David Boswell and Jessica Evans ed. *Representing the Nation: A Reader. Histories, heritage and museum*, London: Routledge, 1999.

Adorno, Theodor and Max Horkheimer. 'The Culture Industry: Enlightenment as Mass Deception', *Dialectic of Enlightenment*. U.S.A.: Stanford University Press, 2002.

Backett-Milburn, Kathryn and Linda McKie eds. *Constructing Gendered Bodies*. United Kingdom: Palgrave, 2001.

Banner, Frances et al eds. *Imagining Women: Cultural Representations and Gender*. London: Polity, 1995.

Baudrillard, Jean. *Seduction*. Montreal: New World Perspectives, 1990.

Benjamin, Walter. *Illuminations*. London: Fontana, 1973.

Benjamin, Walter. *Illuminations*. Pimlico: United Kingdom, 1999.

Braudel, Fernand. *Civilisation and Capitalism, 15th -18th Centuries,Vol. 1: Structures of Everyday Life*. London: William Collins and Sons, 1981.

Bruzzi, Stella and Pamela Church Gibson eds. *Fashion Cultures: Theories, Explorations and Analysis*. New York: Routledge, 2000.

Buckley, Reka and Stephen Gundle. 'Flash Trash'. In Bruzzi eds. *Fashion Cultures: Theories, Explorations and Analysis*. New York: Routledge, 2000.

Butler, Rex. *Jean Baudrillard: The Defence of the Real*. London: Sage, 1999.

Cannadine, David. *Ornamentalism: How the British saw Their Empire*. Oxford University Press: Oxford, 2001.

Costa, Janeed Arnold ed. *Gender Issues and Consumer Behaviour*. New Delhi: Sage, 1994.

Cranny-Francis, Anne et al eds. *Gender Studies: Terms and Debates*. United Kingdom: Palgrave, 2003.

Entwistle, Joanne. *The Fashioned Body: Fashion, Dress and Modern Social Theory.* United Kingdom: Polity, 2000.

Friedberg, Anne. *Window Shopping: Cinema and the Postmodern.California*: University of California Press, 1994.

Greenrough, Paul. 'Nation, Economy, and Tradition Displayed: The Indian crafts Museum, New Delhi', in Carol A Breckenridge ed. *Consuming Modernity: Public Culture in Contemporary India,* Delhi: OUP, 1996.

Guha-Thakurta, Tapati. 'Instituting the Nation in art'. Partha Chatterjee ed. *Wages of Freedom: Fifty Years of the Indian Nation State.* Delhi: OUP, 1998.

Gupta, Dipankar. *Culture, space and the Nation State: From Sentiment to Structure,* New Delhi: Sage, 2000.

Gundle, Stephen. *Glamour: A History.* Oxford: Oxford University Press, 2009.

Hobsbawm, E.J. And Terence Granger. *The Invention of Tradition.* Cambridge: Cambridge University Press, 1983.

Kaur, Puneet. 'Fashion and Indian Women'. <http://www.indianest.com/women/0061.htm>

Kaviraj, Sudipta. 'The Culture of Representative Democracy' Chatterjee, Partha. ed. *Wages of Freedom: Fifty Years of the Indian Nation State.* Delhi: OUP, 1998.

Keenan, William J.F. *Dressed to Impress: Looking the Part.* New York: Berg, 2001.

Koh, Aaron. 'Politicising "the popular"'. <http://ec.hku.hk/kd2proc/default.asp>

Konig, Rene. *The Restless Image: A Sociology of Fashion.* F. Bradley trans. London: George Allen and Unwin, 1973.

Leitch, Vincent. "Costly Compensations: Postmodern Fashion, Politics, Identity". *Modern Fiction Studies,* vol. 42, Spring 1996, p. 111-28

Mann, Doug. 'A Secret History of the Liquid Body: Image and Counter-Image in Twentieth-Century Culture'. <http://home.comcast.net/~crapsonline/Library/body.html>

Menon, Dilip M. 'The Plebeians Rehearse Citizenship: Radical theatre in Kerala, '1950-1960', This paper was presented at the Conference on Theatre Politics in Asia and Africa, SOAS, London, 14-15 May, 2004.

Pinney, Christopher. *Camera Indica: The social life of Indian photographs,* London: Reaktion Books, 1997.

Steele, Valerie. *Fashion and Eroticism: Ideals of Feminine Beauty from the Victorian Era to the Jazz Age.* New York: Oxford UP, 1985.

Tarlo, Emma. *Clothing Matters: Dress and Identity in India.* New Delhi: Viking, 1996.

Vasudevan, Ravi. 'The Meanings of Bollywood', *Journal of the Moving Image,* 7. www.jmionline.org.

White, Nicola and Ian Griffiths eds. *The Fashion Business: Theory, Practice, Image.* New York: Berg, 2000.

Wilson, Elizabeth. *Adorned in Dreams: Fashion and Modernity.* London:Virago,1985.

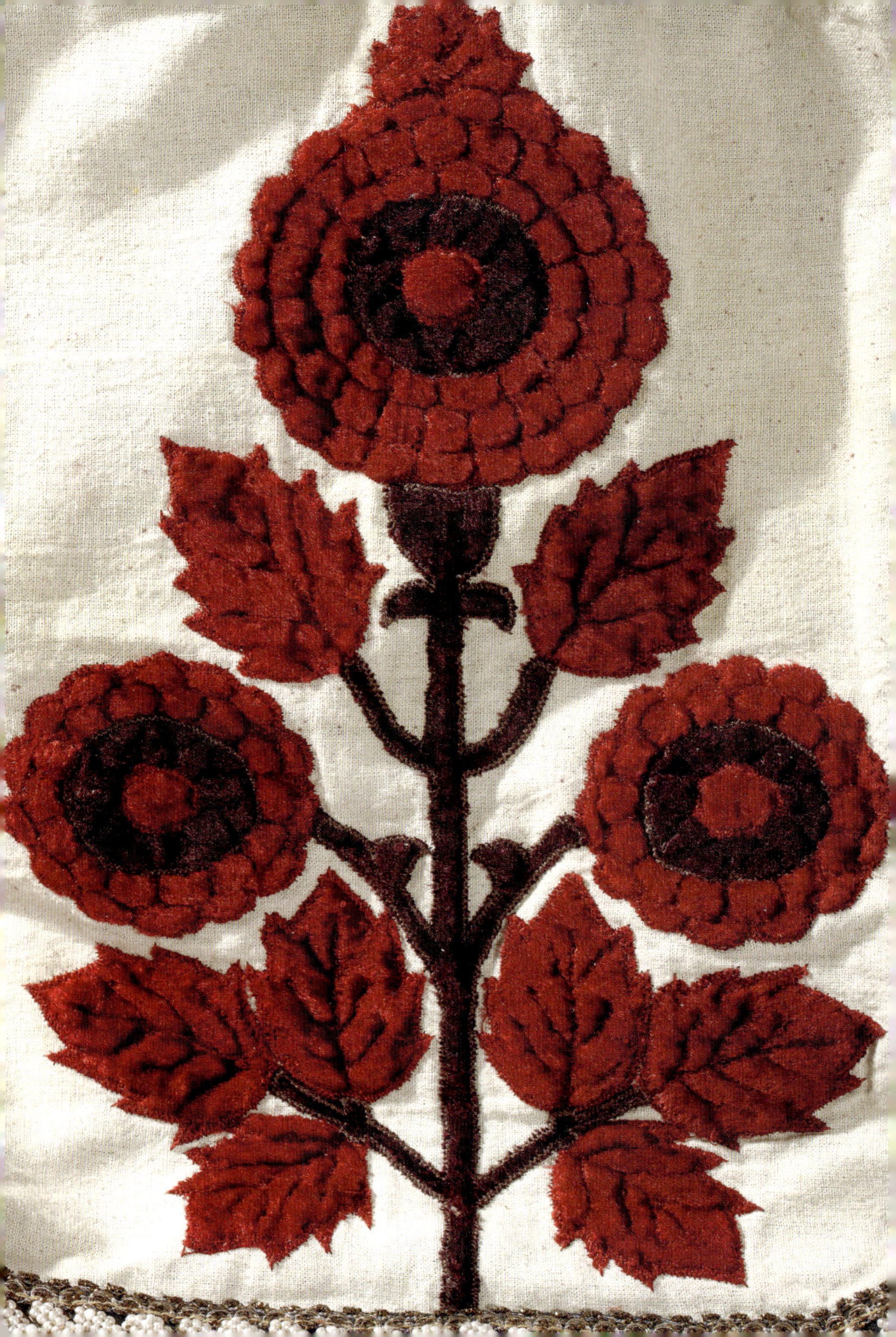

# When the Local is in Fashion
## How to spend a few hours waiting for a delayed flight in the middle of the night at the Delhi airport and receive an ethnographic enlightenment
Paolo Favero

This chapter is based upon an exploration of the Indira Gandhi Airport in Delhi that arose, somewhat by necessity, during the spring of 2012. One night, on my way to Europe, I became caught up in a succession of serious delays and was therefore compelled to keep myself entertained for several hours. So, I started wandering between the many shops, bars and attractions available in the newly refurbished departure lounge. The 2010 Commonwealth Games had entailed a complete renewal of the airport. Thus, compared to my previous visit a few years earlier, I suddenly found myself in an entirely different place.

Observing and photographing the architecture of the space, as well as the products and aesthetics on display, I realised that this lounge mirrored the narratives of cultural change which I had followed with my research in Delhi during the last decade. The lounge spoke of the prominent on-going strive towards 'Indianness' that I addressed in my work on Delhi as a constitutive part of the process of globalisation (cf. Favero 2003 and 2005). Waiting in this airport, a period that would otherwise have been characterised by boredom and idleness became a creative opportunity to reflect anew upon topics that I had worked on for many years. In a way, this chapter is therefore an ode to the act of waiting. In line with the ancient Greeks' cult of '*otium*' [idleness] as a productive activity, I used the slow pace and aimlessness of the act of waiting as a resource, as a tool for discovering new perspectives on places, people and situations that I had thus far treated as familiar. In order to further nurture this connection, this chapter was predominantly written in different waiting situations: in airport lounges; coffee shops; and, also, in the waiting room of an emergency department in a hospital. However, this is not where this paper will depart from. In order to begin this narrative, I will in fact have to invite the reader to take a step back in time with me to the Delhi of the mid-1990s.

During my first stays in Delhi, as a backpacker in 1995 and a fieldworker in 1997, I developed a curiosity for the conspicuously absent souvenirs of the city. Souvenirs branding Delhi were largely unavailable. The closest item I managed to find that in some manner depicted the city as a specific location, rather than just as a natural prolongation of 'India', was the standard postcard booklet sold by the tourist touts hanging out at the entrance of the India Gate, the Red Fort or the Jantar Mantar.

Over time, I discovered how this absence indeed mirrored the on-going discourses on Delhi among backpackers, tourists and foreign visitors at large. Most visitors, at that time, seemed to consider Delhi as nothing more than a necessary stopover on the way to, or from, the country. The guesthouses of Pahar Ganj were full of unaware backpackers who had been dropped off there in the middle of the night by a taxi driver assuring them that this was the nicest area in town (no wonder most backpackers were never particularly keen to return to Delhi after that!). Waiting to leave for other destinations, these people were rarely interested in Delhi as such. After all, Delhi was not really known for anything in particular, except for being the capital of India. Bombay embodied modernity, Varanasi religiosity, Bangalore the new cyber economy, and Calcutta, a (to the Western eye charming) blend of poverty and intellectual life. Yet, what was Delhi about?

Nevertheless, the tourists, respectfully maximizing their travel experience, made their tourist 'duty' here too. They would embark on the urban trail that would take them from the exotic charms of Chandni Chowk, Jama Masjid and the Red Fort in Old Delhi to Connaught Place for a taste of cosmopolitan 'westernized' India and for enjoying a soothing snack at Nirula's, the famous Indian fast food chain. They would then proceed to shopping in Janpath's Tibetan market, and, finally, pay a visit to the India Gate in South Delhi (the monument erected in 1933 to commemorate the Indian soldiers who had died fighting for the British). A few particularly dedicated visitors, would on occasion also venture further south to see the Bahai Temple or the Qutub Minar. However, for the majority of the travellers that I met during my time in the city, a visit to Delhi roughly coincided with the trail I have described thus far.

The 'place-ballets' (Edensor 1998) of the tourists that I had the opportunity to observe between 1995 and 2002, indeed symbolically divided the city into four sections, defined by two main axes. One axis ran from North to South (along an imaginary line connecting Old Delhi to Rajpath), the other from East to West (from India Gate to Rashtrapati Bhavan, the official residence of the President of India). This rather violent reduction and mapping of Delhi, one of which left out many other (primarily metropolitan but also historical) types of attractions caught my attention. Coupled with the notion, popular among backpackers, that Delhi is not really a place worth visiting, this map provided me with some interesting insights regarding the politics of representation of India among foreign visitors. Such reflections, however, also had the side-effect of further binding me to Delhi as such. I too had initially experienced this city as a fairly dull and difficult place to be in. Yet, over time this Delhi evolved, in my eyes, to a fascinating and dynamic place, bearing most of the transformations that were characteristic of a globalising India. With its many facets and its multi-layered history, along with its lack of any well-defined public identity (expect for being India's key political centre), Delhi seemed to me an ideal place for an ethnographic study on cultural identity. After all, Delhi looked like a city in search of its own identity.

So my search began. For my PhD I decided to enter Delhi's urban rhythm by focusing on young, middle-class men. I faced difficulties in preparing myself for such fieldwork: there was scant literature available on the city (with one, for me, very important exception indeed, see below); films did not provide me with any great insight into the city either. My first interviewees were of no great help in these concerns. One of my first interlocutors, a young medical doctor called Manish, shared with me, during a nightly car ride across the city, his perplexity regarding my choice of middle-class Delhi as a topic and site of research. While discussing the meaning of middle-class culture in India, Manish suddenly stopped the car in the middle of the road and, pointing to a group of barefoot peasants who were most probably entering the city, stated: 'Look at them Paolo, that's India, that's the real face of this country! You are an anthropologist, you should study them, not people like me!' Basically, for Manish, I was in the wrong place and I was also focussing on the wrong people. Nevertheless, I remained content concerning where I was and found the contradictions that surrounded me utterly stimulating.

## Delhi: A multi-layered city

It is now time to give the reader some more insights into Delhi and its history. In *Delhi: a novel*, famous writer Kushwant Singh, through a number of short stories, offers us one of the most intriguing descriptions of the city. One of these stories in particular is dedicated to Bhagmati, an alluring yet intimidating *hijra* (a transvestite or eunuch) that somehow embodies Singh's own relation to his city. Singh writes:

> I have two passions in my life: my city Delhi and Bhagmati. They have two things in common: they are lots of fun… [a]nd they are sterile… Having been long misused by rough people they have learnt to conceal their seductive charms under a mask of repulsive ugliness (Singh 1990: 3 and 1).

When I first encountered this book, I was impressed by Singh's original manner of giving Delhi's ambivalent identity such a human feature. *Hijras* are social characters that most inhabitants of Delhi encounter daily on the streets of the city as beggars. Delhi'ites may, however, also come across them at matrimonial ceremonies. In such occasions, *hijras* suddenly appear at the party only to then be chased away by celebrants afraid that these flamboyant characters may cast an evil eye on the bridal pair. This gesture therefore becomes a blessing for the couple. Singh's choice of letting Delhi be narrated through the body of one of these ambivalent individuals promotes an idea of Delhi as a frail, disputed, ambiguous city, used by all and loved by few. This is a stimulating and provocative perspective in terms of addressing the transformations that the city was, and still is, undergoing.

During the 1990s Delhi was rapidly changing. Becoming the poster child of post-1991 India[1], the city was a crossroad of new and old interests. Increasingly presented by the press as India's 'New Boom Town' and 'the epicentre of the country's economic modernisation', Delhi was undoubtedly becoming India's most attractive metropolis, a new terrain to be conquered, in particular for multinationals and emerging businesses. The presence of governmental structures and offices, combined with the (theoretically unlimited) potential for expansion (Delhi is surrounded by barren land) were turning the city into a popular goal for Indian and foreign business; real estate agents; newly established private universities; entertainment activities and so on. Statistically, in the late nineties Delhi had the fastest rate of job creation in India and represented the country's most affluent market. The population of the city grew by 43 % between 1991 and 1999, and, according to unofficial estimates, it became a city with 15 million inhabitants. During this period, the city expanded geographically to the extent that it subsumed its surrounding satellite cities of Gurgaon, Noida and so on. The completion of the new subway has recently testified to, and sanctioned, this new cartography of the city.

I often talk of Delhi as a 'starry place' (borrowing from John Berger cf. Favero 2003), a place defined by the meeting 'of an infinite number of lines, as the centre of a star' (Berger 1974:40). The Delhi I experienced and have attempted to describe was (and is) indeed a 'star-like' entity. It is a place where different streams meet, creating new and (at times) unexpected narratives of culture. This capacity to function as a catalyst

---

[1] 1991 is the year in which, sanctioned through the economic reforms of the incumbent president, Manmohan Singh, India officially entered the global market.

for a multitude of varied interests and actors is not new, however. In the 18th century, the famous poet Ghalib described Delhi as follows: 'I asked my soul: what is Delhi? She replied: the world is the body and Delhi its life.' These lines testify to the ways in which the city has always been a place of convergence and condensation of many different influences from all over the world, something that is embedded in the very multi-layered history of the city.

Delhi is, in fact, composed of seven cities all of which have functioned as centres for their respective kingdoms. Initially known as Indraprashta (home of the dynasty of the Pandavas in the epic Mahabharata), Delhi became a capital during the reign of the Hindu dynasty of Tomar (around the year 1000). This prestigious role was maintained throughout the succession of a variety of Hindu kingdoms and endured until the arrival of Muslim conquerors.

The Islamic Mughal period (that started at the end of the 12th century and ended with the arrival of the British) was probably one of the most flourishing periods in the history of the city. Particularly important is the phase that started with the Lodhi dynasty (in the early sixteenth century), which ended with the rule of Shahjahan (from 1627-58), the man primarily known for building Agra's Taj Mahal. In 1638, Shahjahan brought the capital of the Mughal empire back to Delhi and founded Shahjahanabad, which is today the heart of Old Delhi. This period of splendour ended when the British Crown took over Delhi from the East India Company in 1858.

After having ordained Calcutta to be the capital, King George V decided, in 1911, to move the centre of British India back to Delhi and accordingly laid the foundations for expansion of the city. The construction of 'New' Delhi was a grandiose undertaking. New Delhi was designed as a new, Western-style garden city aiming to become the major symbol of the Empire on which 'the Sun would never set'. Clearly detached from the Old City, New Delhi was to evolve as a scarcely populated area, characterised by an incredible amount of open green spaces. Adjustments had to be made in order to achieve this. Upon the arrival of the British, a wall separated the Old city from the rest of the town. Edwin Lutyens (the creator of the Imperial Delhi plan) opposed the idea of demolishing this wall, on the grounds that the latter, as he put it, protected 'New Delhi from the rats of Old Delhi'. Instead, he decided to establish a new square, named after Admiral Connaught, south of the wall. Connaught Place was conceived by Lutyens and the architects of the Raj as a natural divide between Old/North and New/South Delhi and became a topographical buffer zone between the 'Indian' and the 'British': the colonized and the colonizers. Connaught place helped the British, who inhabited the area south of it, to keep a 'safe' distance from the Old City with its high population density; poor planning; lack of housing and sanitation; slums; poverty; and congestion all of which were seen as a potential threat to the order of the city.

After partition, the problems and discordances characterising Delhi were aggravated. By the beginning of 1948, after the exodus of Muslims from India to Pakistan, and of Hindus in the opposite direction, roughly 16 million people lost their homes and at least one million people (according to unofficial estimates) lost their lives. These years were critical in terms of the construction of modern Delhi. Within two months, the population doubled and the planning of the city experienced a drastic change. New 'colonies', the local term for block or neighbourhood, were created to host the thousands of refugees arriving from what had just become Pakistan. The agony of families divided by the tragedy of partition characterised the first steps in the creation of post-independence Delhi.

Today, Delhi still bears traces of this multitude of divides and critical developments. Unequal access to electricity, water supply and sanitation demarcate the differences between different colonies. Furthermore, illegal settlements and slums expand, as an answer to immigration, in the most diverse parts of the city. Different colonies are today characterised by specific lifestyles, incomes and ethnic profiles. Throughout the years, however, the divide between Old and New Delhi has become the most distinguishing trait of the city. While the inhabitants of New/South Delhi consider themselves the most successful and 'modern' inhabitants of the city, the Old Delhi-*whallas* present themselves as more authentic and genuine. According to the Delhi Master Plan too, Old Delhi is indeed full of the fragrances of the past, yet it is also a planner's nightmare, owing to congestion, insanitary conditions and narrow roads. South Delhi, on the other hand, is regarded as the 'modern', 'middle-class' part of the city, evoking the colonial and modern era with its structured streets, flyovers, the spectacle of architecture – ranging from the modernism of the 1960s and '70s to Punjabi Baroque (see photos below) – and to the most recent (post)modernist styles, which, in addition, echo ancient pan-Indian mythologies.

## A Visible Search for Identity

Having been away from Delhi for some years I was quite literally shocked when, in 2012, I landed at the newly refurbished Indira Gandhi Airport. Accustomed to being met by a worn grey decaying building, the airport now offered a rather glamorous arrival. Fitted orange carpets furnished the corridors; through the windows of these corridors I could glimpse a giant Buddha decorating one of the departure lounges (see Photo 1).

Passport control, previously located at the end of a dark corridor, was now immersed in light and situated underneath a wall displaying an array of sculptures representing a variety of different *mudras* [spiritual hand-enacted iconic gestures pertaining to Hinduism and Buddhism] (see photo 2). In a dialogue between essentialised visions of an idealised past and hymns to transnational capitalism, the boots were placed directly in front of the Tax Free Shops. Thus, in the shadow of the *mudras*, while having their passports checked, arriving visitors could, for example, also consider which brand of whisky to purchase for a friend's father.

2

3

"Dhyanalinga - The highest possible manifestation of meditativeness"
Sadhguru

"This life for me is an endeavour to help people experience and express their Divinity"
Sadhguru

"All that a human being considers as wellbeing will be his, if only he earns the Grace of Bhairavi"
Sadhguru

The moments of further ethnographic exploration of the airport came, however, later on. Upon departure from India, I got the opportunity to observe and photograph the various items, shops and decorations that characterised Delhi airport. Delhi airport had been transformed (probably as a result of the 2010 Commonwealth Games) into a gallery representing an idealised, mythical India. Through a vibrant mix of kitsch, pocket spirituality, modern technology and a 'Thousand and One Night' visions (see photo number 3), the airport was introducing visitors to a country consciously and opulently attempting to display (or perhaps even construct) its identity.

As seen on photo number 4, the airport offered a large variety of different environments, each promoting a particular aspect of a local identity. In the India Explore shop (to the left in photo number 4) one may find statues of deities, scents, incense, miniature representations of politicians, and lamps, among other items to "indianise" one's home.

Beside the India Explore shop, a jewellery store (to the right in photo number 4), displayed the widest variety of precious miniatures of Ganesh conceivable (fashioned from Swarovski crystal to gold). Furthermore, in the tax-free shop visitors could find, among other things, a vast array of T-shirts bearing images devoted to India. Among these, I found one T-shirt particularly interesting (in the middle of the photo). Testifying to India's increasing central positioning in the global market, it mocked Westerners' fear of India with a text declaring, 'I survived the great Indian experience!' A few meters away from the t-shirts, the tax-free shop displayed a rich collection of Gandhi-inspired mementoes. Pens, notepads, mugs, miniatures, cardholders and so forth, all celebrated the personality and message of India's great anti-colonial leader (see photo 5). Here, visitors were offered a unique opportunity to bring home a small piece testifying to the long history of encounters between India and the West.

Indeed, the cavalcade proceeds even further with other, perhaps more contemporary, celebrations of Indianness. For example, a shop selling jewels, bags and other design items of foreign brands displayed a customised Royal Enfield Bullet. The formerly British bike which had become the iconic vehicle of the Indian middle classes was now used to attract rich buyers from all over the world.

Finally, and this brings us to the next topic, visitors could also enjoy a beer in the newly opened cricket bar, which, on the wings of the popular Indian Premiere League, celebrates Delhi's team, the Daredevils.

The celebration of Indianness displayed by Delhi airport mirrors the processes that have been taking place in the city at large. A vignette of the city's architecture and décor can be quite instructive, in terms of understanding the way in which Delhi's urban space has embodied a variety of narratives of cultural change.

The city strikes the observer at a first glance with its syncretic character. Lime-washed surfaces of functionalist and modernist character and futuristic experiments live in Delhi side-by-by-side with baroque decorations and Roman details, with Mediterranean/American styled villas (such as the one entitled White House, in the top right-hand corner), and examples of the 'very Delhi' Punjabi baroque style. The latter genre, born in the first post-independence period as a consequence of the upper classes' desire to react against Nehru's austerity rule, was developed by the Austrian architect Joseph Heinz (again a testament to Delhi's long syncretic history).

Contemporary architecture has, over the last decade, developed a counter-stream to the 1950s desire for the importation of foreign symbols and ideas. The most recent trends in private housing design, for instance, demarcate the growing popularity of 'India' and locality among members of the metropolitan elite. Over the last 15 to 20 years, the latter have desired houses that assimilate 'Western' comforts with Indian values. A young architect I interviewed in 2000 related how the expectations of the majority of his clients were increasingly shaped by this very logic, declaring, 'they want houses that merge the best of India and the West'. The house featured in photo number 9, located in South Delhi, is a good example of this phenomenon. A fully modern and equipped villa, it is built with materials and decorated by items (such as the bells above the gate or the little windows that adorn the wall), deriving from village India.

Related to this phenomenon is the growing popularity of Indian furniture and design. Haus Khaz, an urban village built on the remains of a Mughal city, has, throughout the past decade, progressively been transformed into a celebration of this trend. A gallery of 'real, traditional Indian' items, today Haus Khaz is a chain of shops selling Indian fashion and furniture, art and jewellery. Here one may also find a vast array of renowned restaurants as well as Delhi's famous Institute of Fashion Technology. In Haus Khaz, amazing collections of (overpriced) items, such as posters and covers of soundtrack recordings of old Hindi films are also available.

This recuperation of old Indian memorabilia is a growing business at large in contemporary India. In 2009, I met Preksha, a young designer who has specialised in the promotion of old objects and materials (essentially 'junk') shaped into art installations for hotels and shopping centres. During a visit to the junk market with Preksha one early Sunday morning, I discovered the sheer amount of film souvenirs available in the market (see below) and also the number of young, middle-class men and women hunting for such objects.

From Haus Khaz, the step to Dilli Haat, a market for traditional Indian hand-crafts born in the late 1990s in South Delhi, is a relatively short one. Constructed to resemble a traditional Northern Indian rural market, with forms and materials resembling those of Indian villages, Dilli Haat, although seemingly 'touristic', is actually mostly popular among the local middle-classes who flock there, especially during festivities. Similar to other institutions, such as the Crafts Museum and the Crafts Emporium, this market packages and promotes the heritage of rural India, a phantasm of India embodying the logic of consumption. Visitors consume Indian history and culture here. They gather here to shop and have fun, while soaking up the ambience of traditional Indian lifestyles. As one man carrying his young child around the market remarked: 'at' least my son will learn something about India!' Dilli Haat also hosts a number of small street eateries offering specialities from different parts of India. Allow me to use this as a stepping-stone to describe another trend that I observed during my fieldwork. Despite expectations of a progressive 'MacDonaldization' of the world (Ritzer 1996), my interlocutors actively, and quite avidly, sought the best *kebab* in the city. Among the various places they took me to, Zila Kababpur (roughly translated as 'the city of *kebabs*') serves as a good example of a hybrid concept defining and marketing itself through notions of Indianness.

Owing to its exterior design, Zila appeared to be a cosmopolitan eatery. However, it was actually marketing itself though the popular brand of Lakhnawi cuisine (considered to be the heart of Mughlai cuisine). While the servants walked around clad in red and blue mechanic's overalls and baseball caps, the place was replete with small signs of 'India': glass containers filled with different types of legumes; a large poster showing Indian varieties of spices and lentils; a menu consisting exclusively of lentil soups [*daal*], different types of North Indian bread [*roti* and *naan*], and *kababs*. Zila's *kebabs* were served without knives or forks (inducing clients to eat with their hands in the proper Indian manner). The food, however was served on small, smart colourful porcelain plates and trays (rather than metal ones as in regular street-eateries). The place had also adopted the small paper containers which fast-food dealers use to serve French fries, filling them with the raw onions and raw green chillies, which are compulsory in Northern Indian cuisine.

As two of my interlocutors told me when they took me there for the first time, this was one of the 'musts' for *kebab* lovers. During my last year of fieldwork, however, their passion had been transferred to another newly opened restaurant called 'Punjabi by Nature' (ironically the name of a well-known Canadian-based activist movement supporting the cause of a free Khalistan, i.e. an independent state for Sikhs).

This process of localisation progressively defined not only India as a glamorous consumption item but Delhi too. In 2007, I was able to observe how the process of the branding of India gathered further momentum, at the same time as transforming itself into something new. Indianness is, in fact, now coupled with a progressive narrowing and particularisation of local identities. Delhi had increasingly started branding its own identity and history.

At Nirula's, one of Delhi's first Westernised fast food restaurants, the novel celebration of Delhi's identity resembles one of the numerous examples of a later, and more specific, stage in the re-enchantment with, and branding of, locality. Nirula's is an early example of this. Here, bearing images of the Qutub Minar (a key monument of historical Delhi), accompany a white Ambassador (the emblem of all politicians and bureaucrats travelling across the city) and a smiling Sikh (whereby Punjabi culture is employed to epitomise the city). Such decorations echo the Delhi Daredevils pub and, perhaps even more so, the aesthetics of the Delhi bazaar at the airport (see picture 13).

The creation of ambiences, objects and decorations aimed at representing and branding that which is local, bears witness to ongoing attempts to shape an identity for the city: an identity inevitably constructed vis-à-vis the surrounding world. As in the case of the T-shirt described above, such an ongoing dialogue with the outer world can also assume the form of irony. In photo number 15, this process is materialised in the form of a postcard. Playing with stereotypes of Delhi's busy, noisy and polluted street life, this free postcard, which I picked up in a Delhi pub, indeed invites the viewers to use the airport for its real purposes and 'take a break from the city'.

# References

Berger, J. 1974. The Look of Things. New York: Viking Press.

Edensor, T. 1998. Tourists at the Taj: Performance and Meaning at a Symbolic Site. London: Routledge.

Favero, P. 2003. 'Phantasms in a 'Starry' Place: Space and Identification in a central New Delhi market'. In Cultural Anthropology, 18, no 4 (2003). Washington DC, USA.

Favero, P. 2005. India Dreams: Cultural Identity Among Young Middle Class Men in New Delhi. Stockholm: Almkvist & Wiksell.

Ritzer, G. 1996. The MacDonaldization of Society: an investigation into the changing character of contemporary social life. Thousand Oaks: Pine Forge.

Singh, K. 1990. *Delhi: a novel*. New Delhi: Penguin.

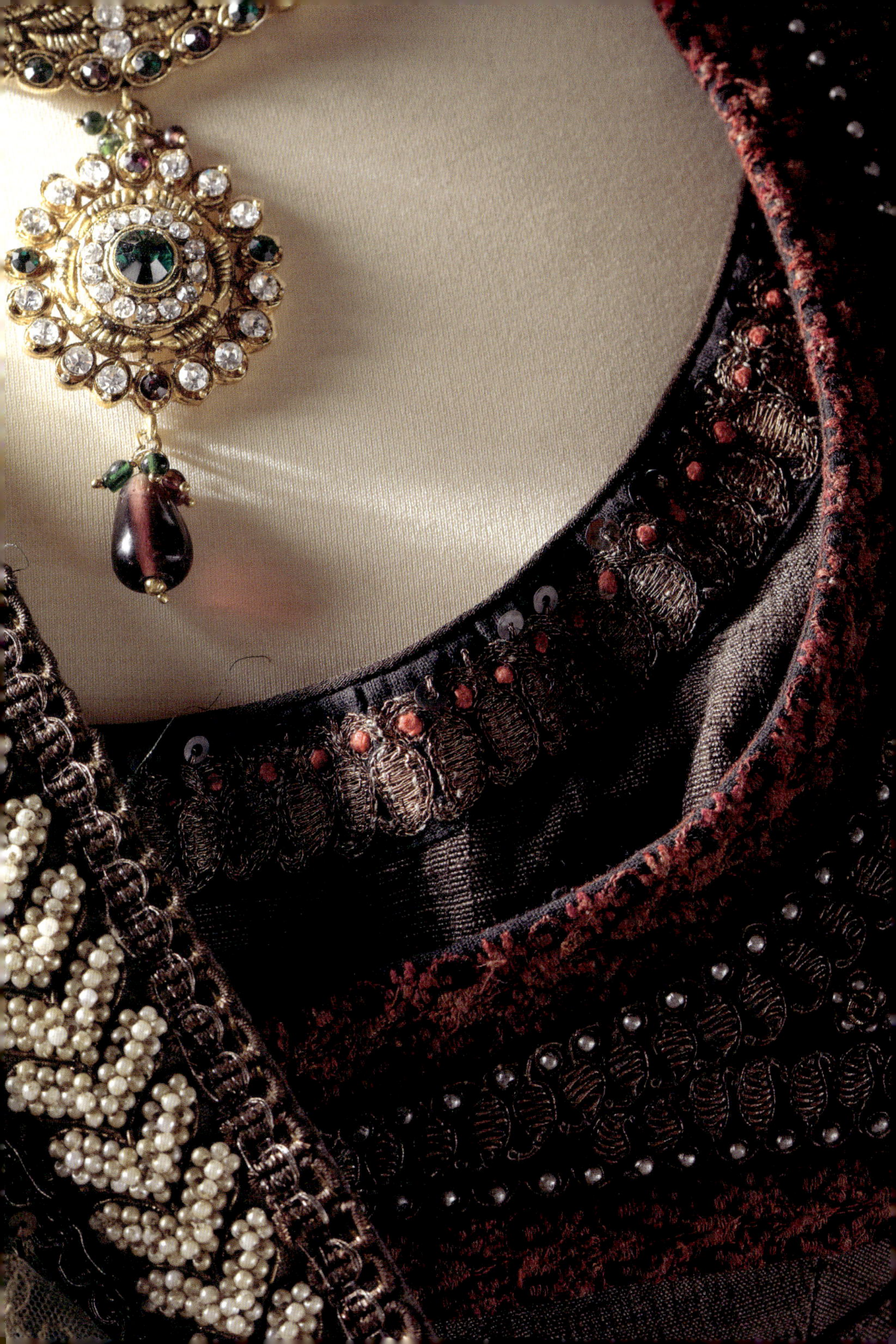

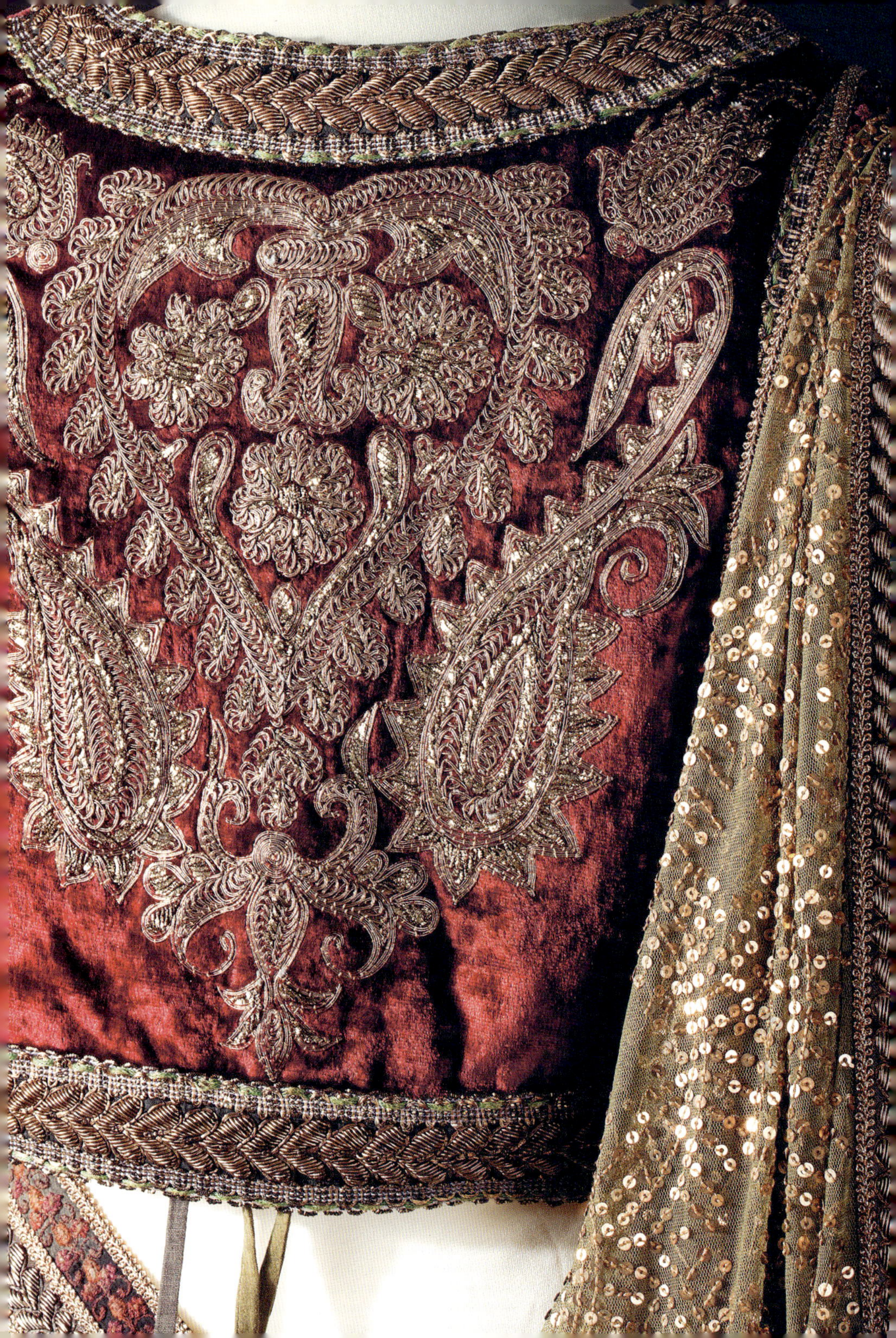

# 'The Maharaja Style'
## Royal Chic and Double Vision[1]
Tereza Kuldova

'Indianness' is the buzzword in contemporary Indian fashion design. Even the most extravagant and artistic designs often claim to express 'Indianness', in one way or another. While during the 1990s, the nascent Indian fashion scene was looking to the West for inspiration – trying to free Indian woman from multiple layers of fabrics and heavy embroideries, introducing the simplicity of cut – in the last decade there has been a shift away from the 'Western', a *back-and-forward* shift towards the 'Indian'. However, this current version of the 'Indian' is not the 'ethnic chic' inspired by the Indian village idealised in the nationalistic discourses that were the trends of the middle classes in the '90s (Tarlo 1996); parallel, at that time, to the seductions of the 'Western style' and big brands entering the Indian market. Instead, this current obsession with showing off 'Indianness' is expressive of the popular discourses and perception of India as being the new global economic power to reckon with. Interestingly, it draws on the royal history of India, playing with the aesthetic referents of the pre-colonial Indian elite, while aiming to visually reconstruct India's greatness by *citing* (see Nakassis in this volume) and recycling the symbolic and material worlds of the rajas, maharajas, nawabs and Mughal rulers and projecting them into the future, into India's anticipated future (and present) as a global economic power.

Problems with poverty, infrastructure, illiteracy, unstable food security and so on notwithstanding, contemporary India likes to see, and project, itself in the media and advertising as confident, buzzing, hypermodern, developed and highly sophisticated. This confident new India is the urban India, the urban poor of which have been expertly photoshopped. This newly confident and powerful India, celebrated in both global and local economic discourse, the *Forbes India magazine*'s version of India, the India of the new (multi-)millionaire class, of the business, corporate and political elite, demands to be taken seriously on its own (i.e. 'Indian') premises (whatever that may refer to in any given context).

---

[1] This chapter is based on my fieldwork in urban North India (2008; 2010-11), when I followed luxury high-quality hand embroidery, from its multi-staged production process in Lucknow to high-end fashion boutiques and workshops of an elite Indian fashion designer in New Delhi. This research resulted in a PhD thesis entitled *Designing Elites: Fashion and Prestige in Urban North India* (2013).

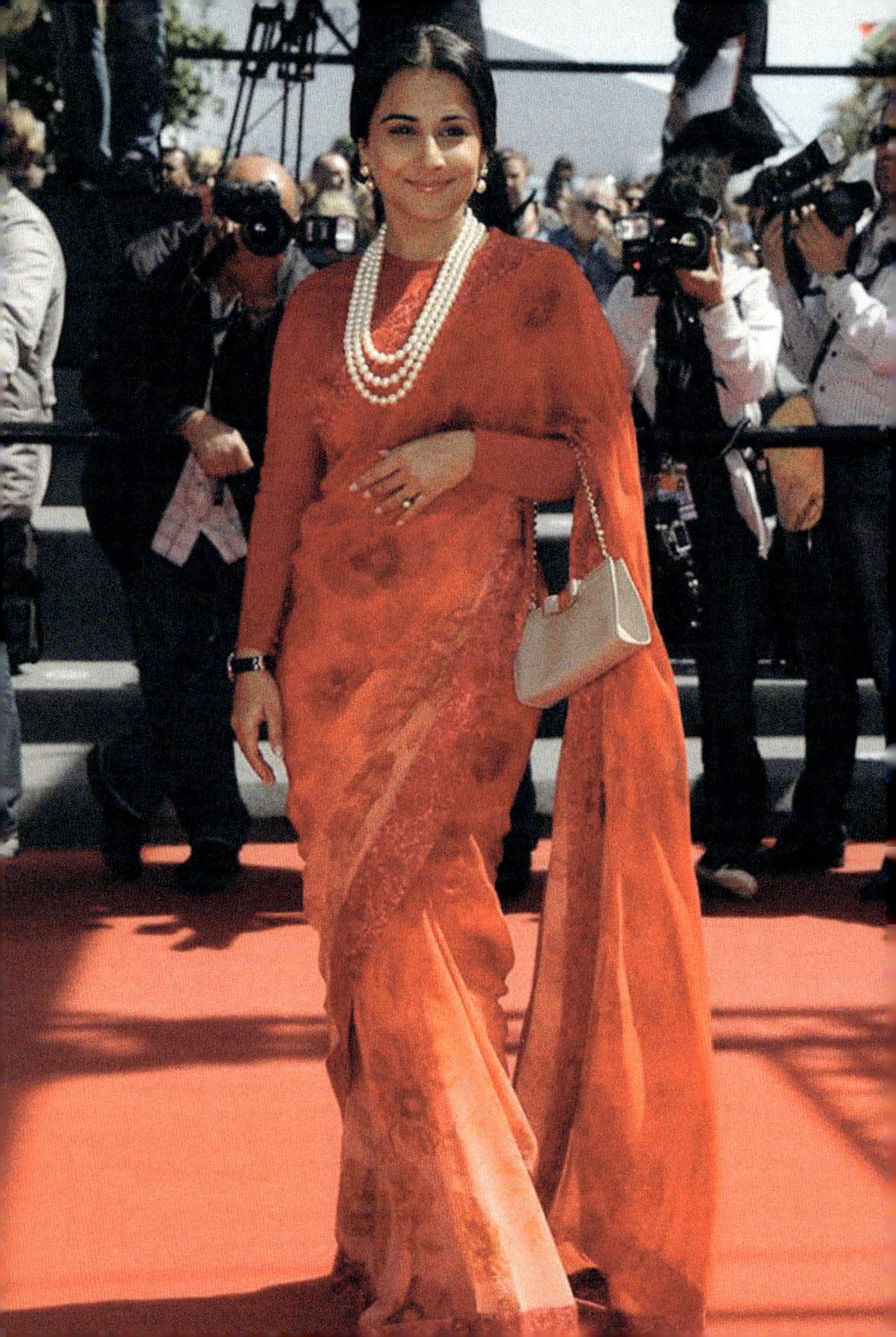

Left:
Sabyasachi Mukherjee's design for the famous Bollywood actress Vidya Balan at the *Cannes Film Festival* 2013 is a clear example of the staging of powerful Indianness that draws on India's heritage.
Courtesy: Sabyasachi Mukherjee

'Staying true to one's Indianness', as one of my elite interlocutors and a prominent CEO pointed out, 'should be at the core of every action and expression of an Indian businessman, be it his way of tackling problems or of dressing for the occasion'. Indian elite now wishes to conquer the world applying its non-threatening 'soft power' (Tharoor 2007): exploiting spectacular and positive 'Indianness' to the maximum (be it food-culture, heritage luxury, fashion or Bollywood), while, at the same time, demanding to be recognised as powerfully Indian, or rather as powerful precisely because of its Indianness, being in tradition.

## Maharaja Dreams and Royal Chic

The thousands of years of culture and 'heritage' are imagined as the source of India's current strength and potency. This heritage[2], an increasingly popular word in the elite circles, needs to be cherished, celebrated, flaunted, and the world around has to be continually reminded of it – or at least, so do many Indian fashion designers instruct their elite clients. The designers' mission is to educate, instruct and dress their elite customers in lavish attires that reflect India's royal and tradition, often by incorporating intricate craftwork on hand-woven fabrics outsourced from across India. The convergence between the emergence of the Indian business elite, the 'monied class' in search to distinguish itself both from 'those below' as much as from its western counterparts, and the increasing emphasis placed on 'Indianness', has led to the boom of the heritage luxury segment of the economy. This segment ranges from heritage luxury resorts flaunting antique furnishing, art and collector's items to high end Indian fashion and interior design, all imitating the lifestyles of the royalty. The heavier, the more embellished, multi-layered, elaborate, and the more reminiscent of royalty, the better. The quest is for unique fashion pieces that cannot be copied, pieces that take the artisans and tailors working for the fashion designer months

---

[2] The contemporary Indian heritage luxury has to be understood here in the context of global proliferation of heritage discourses largely stimulated by the agendas of transnational organizations such as UNESCO, that promote the value of conservation and revival of both tangible and intangible heritage on a global scale. The heritage discourse has been particularly influential in India, appropriated by the government, nationalist discourse and bodies such as the Crafts Council of India or INTACH (Indian National Trust for Art and Cultural Heritage).

to produce, pieces that may themselves be replicas of royal attires dug out of the archives by the designer or pieces that incorporate antique embroideries transposed onto new fabrics. I came to label this trend the 'royal chic'.

The Indian elite's quest for distinction goes beyond brands, logos and trademarks; luxury brands like Louis Vuitton or Prada are good enough as casual wear, but no longer as a marker of 'true' distinction, not for the Indian style connoisseurs claiming their superiority to the 'vulgar new money' that conspicuously devours in western luxury brands and to their Western elite counterparts that are imagined as increasingly lacking culture and heritage to be proud of. As one of my elite interlocutors pointed out, 'our Indian heritage is living, the European heritage is dead; it is only an idea, that culture is gone and whatever is left can be bought (by us)'. Within this logic then, the possession of symbols and signifiers of western modernity is turned onto its head – it ceases to be perceived as running after the West and is turned into possessing the West, while at the same time claiming difference from and superiority to the West. India is re-imagined as conquering the world through the possession of its riches – the fact that luxury sales are higher in India than in the whole of West, or so it is claimed, is stated as a proof of the turning tables. The contemporary Indian haute couture is a materialization of these ideas par excellence, where the theatrical fashion shows manifest a specifically Indian elitist aesthetics. The distinction which is sought by contemporary Indian elites is a striking perpetuation of the *imperial* and *feudal* hierarchical impulses within the realm of the free market democracy, where everyone can potentially reach the top and make it big – or so the ideology of *spectacular capitalism* would have us believe (Gilman-Opalsky 2011).

## Spectacular Capitalism and the Indian Elites

Spectacular capitalism refers here to the dominant mythological understanding of what capitalism is and what it does in the world, i.e. to a 'mythology about capitalism that disguises its internal logic and denies the macroeconomic reality of the actually existing capitalist world' (Gilman-Opalsky 2011:17). The most prominent feature of this mythology

---

Right:
Anju Modi's design for her collection Devi (Goddess) showcased at the *Delhi Couture Week* 2012. The collection was meant as a visual interpretation of the powerful Indian femininity, of the distinctively Indian womanhood – powerful, beautiful and modestly hidden under layers of elaborately embroidered hand-woven fabrics.
Courtesy: Delhi Couture Week 2012

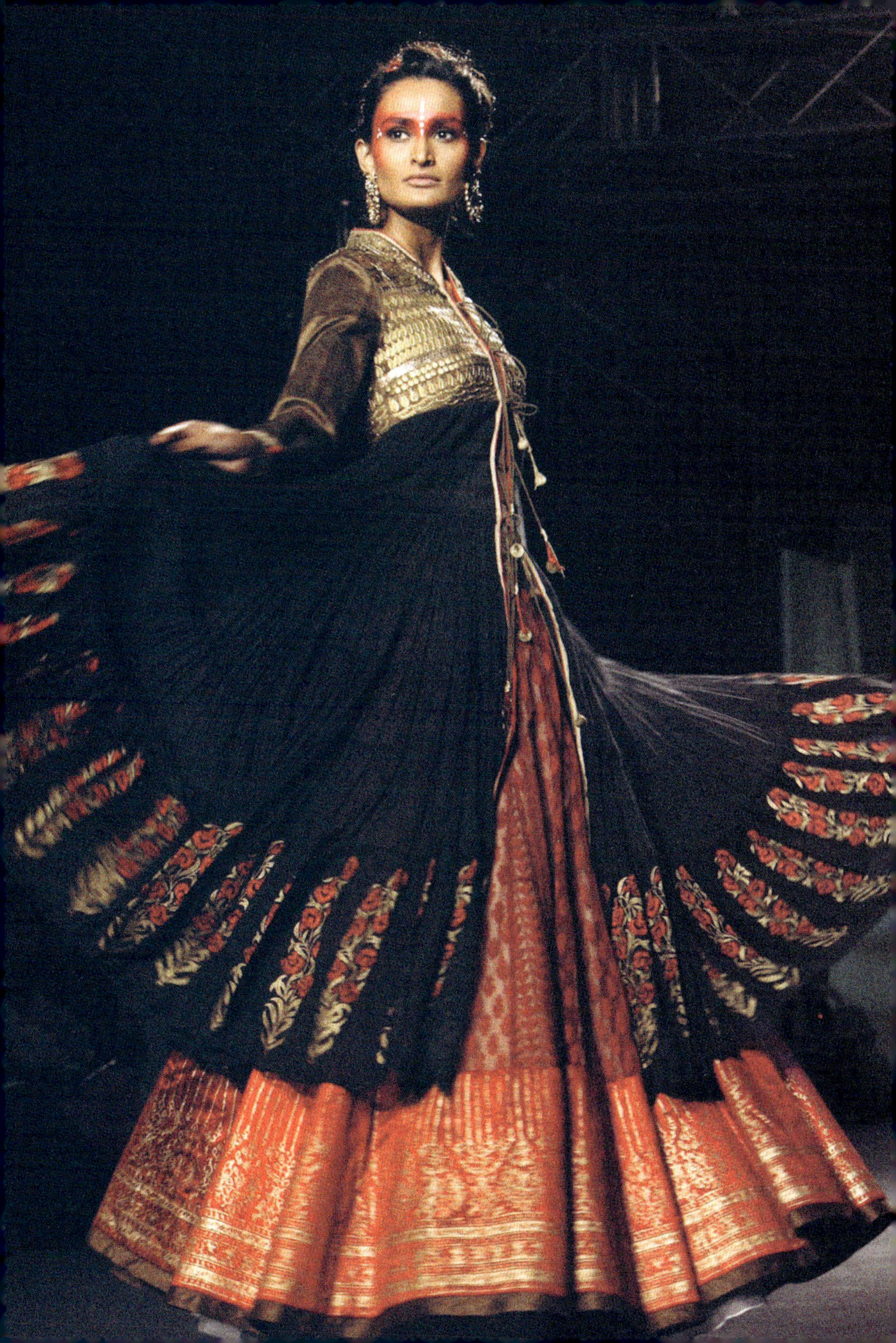

and also for us the most interesting considering the Indian elite's desire for distinction and the simultaneous need to legitimize the source of their wealth, is the ideology of meritocracy. 'Capitalism, the story goes, offers upward mobility for individuals who have the initiative to work hard. Every person can live a comfortable life of relative wealth if they so choose to create such a life for themselves. The main ingredient is ambition. Thus, personal failures and poverty are never due to the deficits in the system, but rather to the human error of individual persons making bad decisions' (Gilman-Opalsky 2011). Another and related assumption is that the spread of free market capitalism leads almost automatically to a spread of democracy – yet, the increasingly successful authoritarian and/or aristocratic capitalist systems, from China via the Gulf to Singapore, certainly prove this myth to have little bearing in reality.

The Indian elites often attempt to reproduce this mythology of spectacular capitalism, legitimizing their wealth by references to their hard work, ambition and commitment (rather than hereditary privilege), while seeking an aesthetic distinction more reminiscent of the feudal hierarchical social structure. As Mehta points out, in contemporary India, 'meritocracy has become part of the self-justification of elites (…) what we are seeing on display is not just greed; it is a society struggling to find measure of worth' (Mehta 2011: 7-11). However, the problem with meritocracy is that it systematically legitimizes social inequality by arguing that success depends on the individual's abilities and talents, while ignoring all together the structural conditions of opportunity in the first place (Jodhka and Newman 2007). Shamus Rahman Khan, in his study of America's elite St. Paul's college, argues that the US lives in an era of *democratic inequality* (Khan 2010). The current processes occurring in India appear to be of the same character. Democratic inequality refers to a state of affairs in which a certain amount of diversity (few publically recognized self-made men) is combined with the dominant narrative of meritocracy thus creating an illusion of an open society, something that obscures the underlying structural inequalities that are being perpetuated. Royal chic in Indian fashion reproduces aesthetically the feudal and royal symbolism, which on one hand is now accessible to anybody who has enough capital, while on the other hand it perpetuates and visually reinforces the underlying hierarchical structure of hereditary distinction. The fashion shows themselves function as myth-making machines of spectacular capitalism, featuring individual designers who have reached the top solely because of their creativity, ambition and innovativeness. All the while the spectacular shows where the credit is given to one creative 'head' effectively cover up the vast amounts of skilled and creative artisans that have actually produced these garments, those who would never be able to receive the same credit for their creativity and skill, no matter their ambition or talent, precisely due to their hereditary (inferior) position within the class structure. And yet these artisans are the key to the aesthetics of powerful Indianness, to the 'Indian essence' that so many designers are eager to express in their designs. The artisans hidden behind the curtain of the media spectacle are the key to the satisfaction of the desire for royal-like opulence; via the designer, they produce luxury for the wealthy elite that imagines itself to benevolently patronize these rural and urban poor and low class artisans along the line of the royals of the bygone era, who patronized the arts and crafts.

Paradoxically enough, these artisans are the key to the elite's distinction, to the elite's Indianness that can be worn on the elite bodies and flaunted. They are the key to the designers' expression of India's position within the global order, not as an imitator of the West but rather as a confident nation and future economic leader. They are the key to the designers' *artistic nationalism* (Winther-Tamaki 2001), one that plays with *retro-futuristic* visions of India and Indianness. Retro-futuristic here implying a play between visions of the future as seen from the past, the past as seen from the future and the *future seen as a recreation of past in futuristic terms.*

## Retro-futuristic Indianness and the Cosmopolitan Nomadic Royals

In 2012, JJ Valaya presented *The Azrak Collection – The Realm of the Sultan at The Bridal Fashion Week.* This collection was inspired by the Ottoman Empire and for its staging JJ Valaya created a lavish stage set, featuring replicas of a lively Turkish bazaar with trademark chandeliers glittering above it, balconies and domes at the backdrop, belly dancers moving through the scenery and aerial dance performed by gymnasts on fabric trails. JJ Valaya is one of the most successful Indian couturiers for whom haute couture is ultimately about the lavish, excessive, royal and potlatch-like Indian wedding – the wedding being the time of one's life when anybody can be turned into royalty. His designs are notoriously steeped in embellishment, ornamentation, texture, detailing, and craft; they are pregnant with uncontrollable references to past and aristocracy that transgress any imagined boundaries of time and space, past and future. As his mission statement proclaims, he is determined to 'show to the world the new India, resplendent with aura of blue-blooded elegance, innovative craftsmanship and modern sensibilities (http://www.valaya.com/home.html). Valaya calls his customers, the wealthy cosmopolitan elite distinguished by frequent international travel and its pluggedinness in transnational networks, the *nomadic royals*. The attires that he creates for these nomadic royals materialize most forcefully the paradox of the continued feudal and imperial logic blended with attempts at democratization and abolition of hereditary hierarchies – at once for everyone, and for selected few.

With the help of haute couture, like JJ Valaya's, the New Delhi's elite attempts to reclaim the city once again as the city of rulers, as the city of modern day maharajas of the new India. The spectacular fashion shows and even more so elite weddings, perfectly crafted by the haute couturiers and teams of interior designers, bear a dramatic resemblance to the royal *durbars*, creating an atmosphere of imperial splendor, wealth and power (see chapter by Nilanjana Mukherjee in this volume). Valaya's work caters to this desire of being part of this retro-futuristic imperial elite, thoroughly nomadic and cosmopolitan.

In this respect it is interesting to review David Cannadine's argument who in his book *Ornamentalism* (Cannadine 2002) points out that the British Empire was not exclusively about race or about the distinction between the superior West and the inferior Orient, but it was even more significantly about *hierarchy that cuts across any division between West and its Other*. The British indulged in what they imagined as traditional India, precisely because they could mirror their own class-based social structure within it, precisely because India still possessed something that they saw as disappearing in the West, the West which they perceived as falling prey to democratic vulgarity – India had the traditional elite, aristocratic security and thus firm social hierarchy. That is why the British happened to a large degree ignore and disregard the emergence of the urban, educated, nationalist and modernizing middle classes. Cannadine points out that 'depending on context and circumstances, both white and dark-skinned peoples of the empire were seen as superior; or alternatively as inferior' (Cannadine 2002: 124). In other words, the English gentlemen had more in common with an Indian maharaja than an East End costermonger, in fact, the British rulers found it utterly amusing that low class white settlers had an unprecedented difficulty grasping the fact that aristocratic breeding cut across any imagined

---

Right:
The Maharaja of Palanpur
The Museum of Cultural History collections

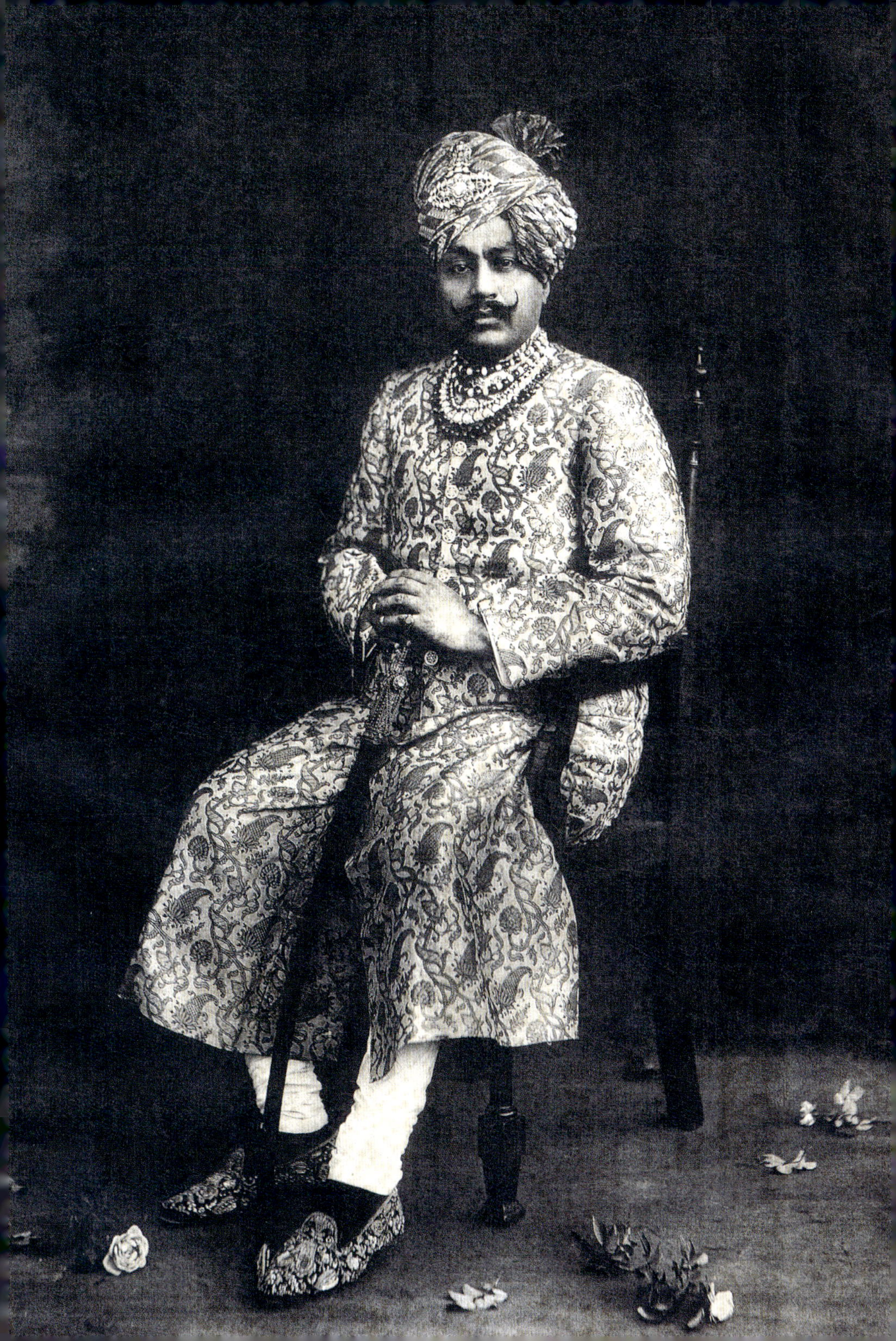

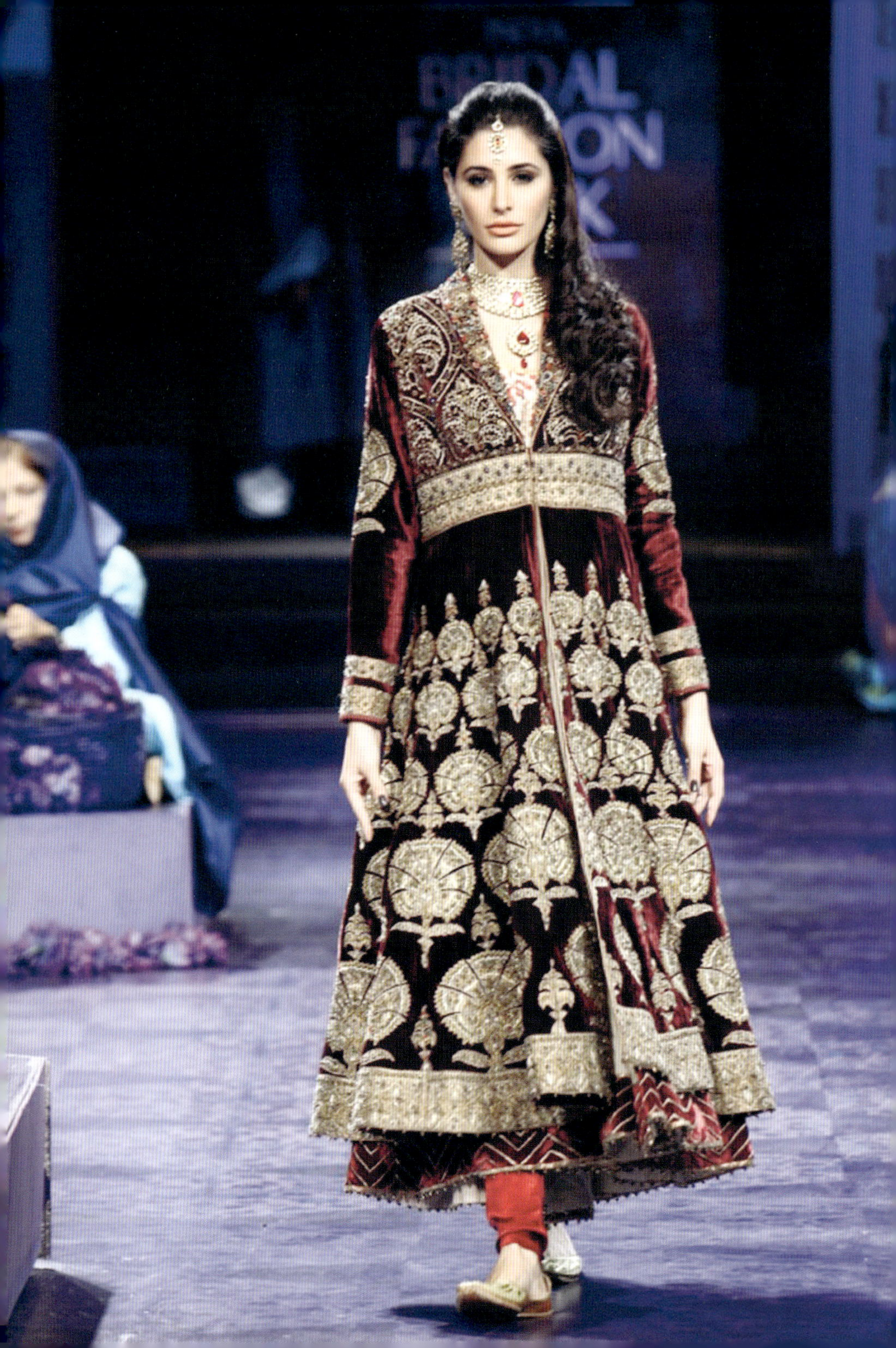
BRIDAL

racial boundaries. The empire was united through its hierarchy, which positioned the chiefly, kingly and royal elite across the empire, against the 'inferior' subjects – individual social status and position within the hierarchy was what greatly mattered. What goes for the empire goes as well for contemporary Indian haute couture that caters to the nomadic royals, it was and is

> about antiquity and anachronism, tradition and honour, order and subordination; about glory and chivalry, horses and elephants, knights and peers, processions and ceremony, plumed hats and ermine robes; about chiefs and emirs, sultans and nawabs, viceroys and proconsuls; about thrones and crowns, dominion and hierarchy, ostentation and ornamentalism (Cannadine 2002: 126).

The independence turned out to be the triumph of the middle-classes and urban-based radicals, so detested by the Raj. 'The matchless splendors of viceroyalty, in New Delhi, and at Simla, vanished (...) the whole ceremonial carapace of durbars and state elephants and loyal toasts and Empire day was swept away' and the rulers of the native states 'lost their freedom and independence, and eventually in 1971, their revenues and their titles, in *this brave new world of post-imperial egalitarianism*' (Cannadine 2002: 156, emphasis mine). However, a way of regaining this freedom in the context of contemporary India is precisely by living out the retro-futuristic visions that materialize themselves through haute couture, a part of larger luxury heritage segment across the globe.

The princes themselves while on one hand consigned to the dustbin of history, on the other eventually turned their palaces into five star luxury heritage hotels, selling the royal experience to anyone who has the financial capital to afford it. Some have turned into businessmen, others into socialites, fashion designers, politicians (most famously Gayatri Devi, who happened to be once named by *Vogue* among the ten most beautiful women in the world) and industrialists, thus retaining the remnants of their power and remaining involved the country's life. However, the liberalisation of Indian economy enabled the emergence of newly monied business elite, which now seeks an equal place on the top and is driven to acquire all possible markers of this newly achieved status. Quite tellingly then, JJ Valaya is patronized by the Royal house of

---

Left:
Showstopper piece of JJ Valaya's Azrak Collection at *The Bridal Fashion Week*, 2012. Notice the women sitting on the ramp, the made up 'bazaar', forming the (poor, ethnic, or low class) contrast to the dressed up model, who thus even more powerfully emerges as an aesthetic manifestation of royalty.
Courtesy: The Bridal Fashion Week, 2012

Jaipur, as much as by the *Glenfiddich* whisky and a number of prominent businessmen and industrialists. Valaya is also an eager art collector, interior designer and art photographer. Valaya's *Home of the Traveler* label features personally hand-picked interior decorations by the designer himself during his travels, where each piece is dated, handmade, unique, appealing to the ideas of ancient dynasties and exhibitions of curated objects. The luxury store is turned into a museum-like display of antique, one of a kind, imperially-charged objects from all over the globe – from India, Siam, and Turkey to Russia. The items sold there, even though placed within the space of his enormous luxury store, are in principle unbrandable and unmarked, reflecting the desire for unique objects that defy branding, ooze value of heritage, culture, royalty and style and at the same time are, following the imperial legacy, maximalist. In order to create the *aura* (Benjamin and Tiedemann 1999), the more, around his designs Valaya not only uses the theatrical stage sets in his fashion shows but also uses people with considerable social power and/or wealth as his models on the ramp, turning actors, actresses, industrialists, businessmen, popular historians, and socialites into models. Choosing real people, with real charisma over generic young slim models, reinforces the power of his garments through the power of the wearer, right there, on the ramp. For Valaya the person needs to match the garment. The garment and the person are thus imagined as empowering each other, creating in their montage an excess, an aura of power. Within this logic the garment needs to be permeated through the body and spirit of the wearer in order to be effective and in order for the viewer to identify with it.

The spectacular visions of the retro-futuristic elite, however, depend in a peculiar way on the existence of their opposite, the poor – aesthetically, physically and economically. The elite can only emerge in juxtaposition to those from whom it aims to detach itself. At the same time, these poor Others enable the elite's existence; the elite can only exist by contrast.

## Lotus Grows out of Mud

The Indian haute couture, because of its devouring in lavishness and ornamentalism, is defined by its ambiguous relation to craft and craftsmen, who are on one hand imagined as the soul of India (Kaviraj 1998), a celebrated and cherished source of national pride and on the other hand tend to be reduced to mere manual workers defined by their poverty and backwardness, a social evil that needs to be dealt with. Designers, who are most often dependent on the production of craftsmen, therefore often go to great lengths to distinguish their individual creativity from the collective creativity of the craftsmen, their ability to innovate from the craftsmen's inability to move beyond repetition. A great number of designer showrooms-cum-studios therefore 'feature' at least a small group of craftsmen (even though most embroideries are done elsewhere), usually sitting one floor below or above in a special room, a room that is visually a striking juxtaposition of the designer's office and sales space. The artisans' space tends to be simple and dim-lit with *paan* (betel leaf) stains on the walls. The designers' space often features luxurious interior, statues of gods, mirrors, art works, book shelves, throne-like chairs, chandeliers, mannequins, smell of incense sticks, suggestive music and so on. The first space is intended to reinforce the inferiority of the craftsman, positioning him as a mere worker, while the second space is intended to reinforce the image of the designer as an expert authority, taste connoisseur and creative *head*. This spatial division and the juxtaposition of these spaces, was also central to many visits of elite customers to such studios. When in the designer's office and showroom, the customers would engage fully with the materials, embroideries, listening to the designer's discourse on connoisseurship, heritage, tradition, that notoriously celebrates the *hands* of the craftsmen, their skill and so on, while trying on the garments and (re)creating themselves in the process as elite by breathing in the atmosphere of luxury as much as the words of the designer. However, their visit would often not end there; they would also pass the workspace of the craftsmen only to *gaze* at them working, while discussing their impoverished state of being from a safe *distance*, never engaging in a conversation with them and often even avoiding eye contact. Gazing at the artisans from distance enabled them to position themselves as superior, as patrons of crafts as much as patrons of the designer, who represented himself as elevating the impoverished artisans. This juxtaposition was necessary for the daily re-creation of the elite.

However, it is not only spaces of designer studios that are defined by this striking juxtaposition of full visual and sensual engagement and of objectifying visual distantiation. The whole of Delhi and Lucknow fashion world appears to be permeated by this logic of intense engagement versus detachment, of luxury amidst poverty and indeed of 'intentional blindness', as one of my interlocutors called this. The world is thus divided into the auspicious and the inauspicious, one which demands intense engagement and the other which demands rehearsed distantiation and detachment, one driven by the desire to merge and possess and the other driven by the fear of the 'evil eye'. The fashion villages in South Delhi – Hauz Khas, Shahpur Jat and the emerging Lado Sarai – all feature fabulously furnished, styled and air conditioned designer boutiques next to craft workshops in falling buildings and amidst piles of garbage, and the allegedly dengue infected mosquitoes and 'dangerous characters', against whom I have been warned on numerous occasions. The 'proper' way to reach these designer studios was by car with a driver, preferably parking as close as possible to the showroom, so that one would not be exposed to too much dirt. Yet, at the same time the desire to gaze from distance at the craftsmen working was still there and trips to the designer's artisan workshops just to 'have a quick look' were quite common.

Even the most popular shopping malls, be it *Select City Walk* in Saket or DLF *Emporio and Ambience Mall* in Vasant Kunj, find themselves strikingly juxtaposed by their surroundings, the first by a slum-like area on the opposite side of the road, the other by the unfinished constructions, dust and migrant workers living along the road. Such contrast and the parallel use of a double mode of vision by my elite interlocutors appear to be necessary for luxury to emerge, the intense engagement versus detachment being crucial for maintenance and perpetuation of class boundaries.

This juxtaposition of poverty and luxury has also become a controversial issue in contemporary fashion photography. Interestingly, there is an increasing amount of fashion photographs in magazines such as *Vogue*, which feature luxury brands against an impoverished background. In 2008 *Vogue India* featured a series of photographs in which urban and rural poor modeled *Hermes* bags, *Burberry* umbrellas and where for instance an old and visibly poor woman missing her upper front teeth held a child wearing a *Fendi* bib worth 100$. Pakistan has experienced similar public outcry about photographs featuring a beautiful model posing in front of poor coolies with Louis Vuitton luggage. Even though cases like these at times provoke public debate, going through fashion magazines reveals that such photographic and commercial juxtapositions of poverty and wealth are more common than their media coverage would suggest.

However, interestingly, once turned into art, such photographs rarely lead to public outcry and are instead celebrated as striking works of art, the case in point being the designers' JJ Valaya's art photographs

---

Right:
Designer Samant Chauhan with a model dressed in his creation posing in a village with a family of one of his weavers in the background.
Courtesy: Samant Chauhan

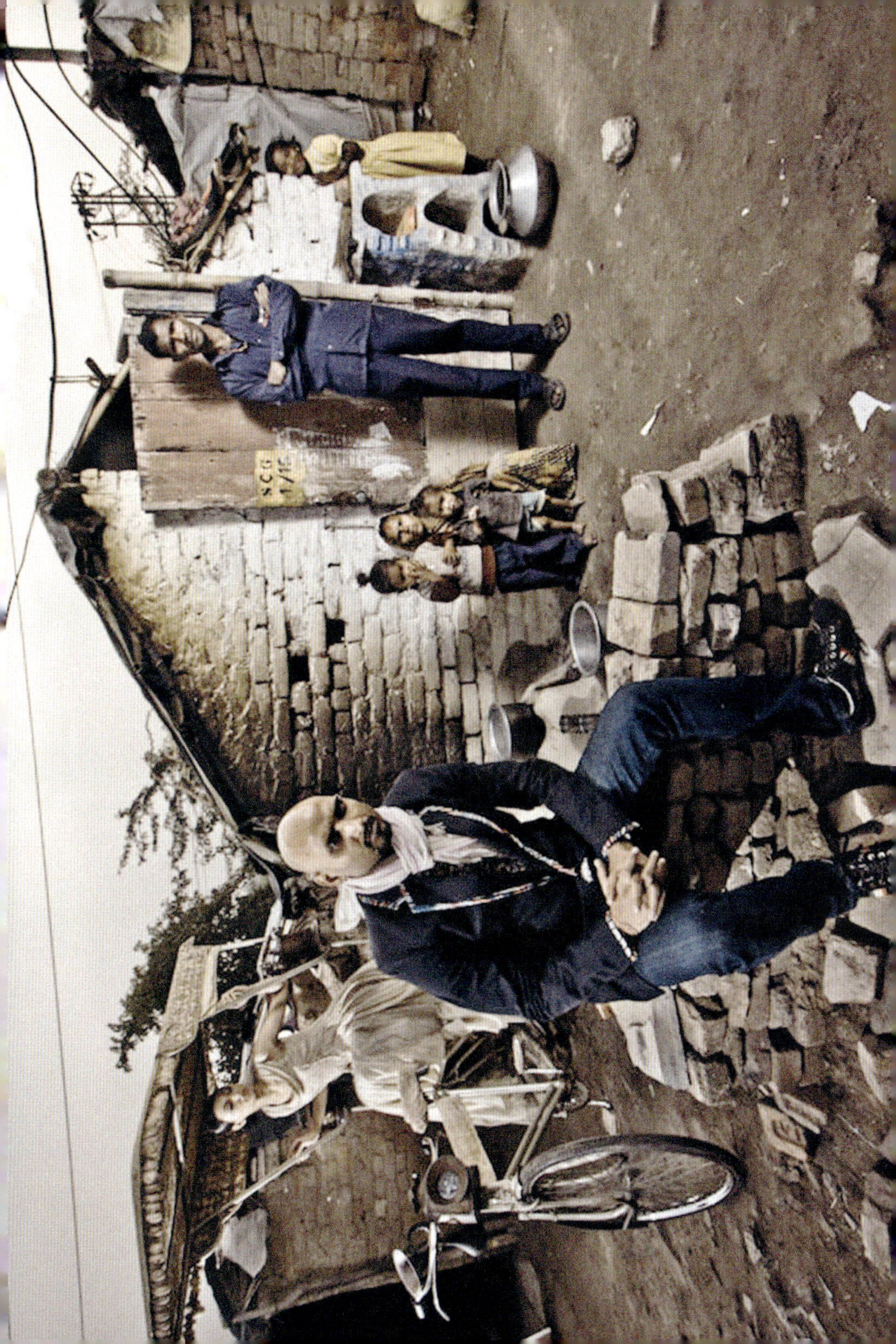

created under the patronage of *Glenfiddich*, the Scottish whisky brand, and published in a coffee-table book tellingly called *Decoded Paradox*. Through these photographs Valaya seems to intend to reestablish Delhi as the city of rulers, drawing on its royal past and juxtaposing it with modern-day New Delhi – strikingly a modern-day Delhi of the urban poor. The photographs feature 'real' characters from the past dressed in recreations of the wardrobes of Mughals and Rajputs (*Vintage Valaya* collection). Modeling these 'real' characters are members of contemporary Delhi's elite, such as for instance a famous artist Subodh Gupta or Aman Nath, a historian and owner of *Neemrana hotels*. Aman, dressed up as a Maharaja, stands proudly in the middle of an abandoned road in Sarai Kale Khan, with a street dog, garbage, provisional tents and low caste boy in the background. The modern-day Delhi of Valaya, onto which these mock-Maharajas are juxtaposed, is again one of poor neighborhoods. The same logic was used during the aforementioned fashion show of Valaya's aforementioned Ottoman inspired couture collection. The ramp was populated by seated female street-sellers covering their heads, while the royally dressed up models were passing through – again, in order to create the atmosphere of elite luxury it appeared to be necessary to draw in the impoverished Other – the montage needed a clear juxtaposition in order for the impact of aristocratic aesthetics with its promise of sovereignty to be complete.

## Double Vision
When perceiving contemporary India through the elite's eyes a double vision is necessary. On one hand, there is the idea and vision of the brave new urban India from which the urban poor are photoshopped, an idea of India in which the elites completely immerse. On the other hand, there is the India of urban poor, an India of the craftsmen, villagers, artisans, the India which is *kept at a distance*, but which is at the same time constitutive of the desired 'Indianness'. There is a dynamics of distantiation and immersion at play here. The vision of the elites is capable of perceiving and not perceiving poverty at the same time, of forcing poverty into the background (like on the fashion photographs) only to emerge in the foreground as *the* elite.

The elaborate theatrical stage sets produced at fashion shows and the designer showrooms and perfected to minute detail, intend to produce a total atmosphere in which the audience and consumers would immerse, using *sensory branding* to its utter limit (Lindstrom 2009). Within these total spaces, the aesthetic force penetrates the bodies of the viewers, becoming an undeniable part of the experience of the objects located within its boundaries (Entwistle 2009, Böhme 1993, Biehl-Missal and

Saren 2012, Pritchard 2009, Kapferer and Hobart 2005). And yet, the inclusion of references to the poor artisans within these spaces and atmospheres – the artisans at once celebrated as the very lifeblood of India while positioned as oppressed, in a state of constant need of rescue, thus turned into perfect objects of patronage – stimulates the opposite, distantiated mode of vision. This paradoxical and yet productive juxtaposition that keeps both the elites and the poor 'in their place' become interestingly a part of "the creation of display and staging values" and is turned into 'a new type of use value, centered around the manufacture of semblance, aura, atmosphere, illusion in relation to people and things' (Roberts 2003: 88).

## Designer Guru

This double vision becomes even more obvious if we consider the interactions between elite Indian designers and their most loyal customers. As I have experienced, such encounters can take on a form of *darshan* (visions of the divine), thus transgressing the boundary between the sacred and the profane. Hindu worship is all about seeing, touching, tasting, smelling and hearing and as such is a material and sensuous practice that connects the believer to the deity and the spiritual (Eck 1998), while the deity is imagined to be present in the image. However, *darshan* in contemporary India goes beyond the realm of religious practice and often penetrates into public culture. The *darshan* of a wide variety of people is thus being sought, from holy persons, sadhus, sannyasins, gurus, politicians and activists via Bollywood celebrities to, as I would argue, fashion designers. Female customers often tended to boast about their favorite designers, passing on comments such as 'we are here to *see* you', 'we have to go see our darling, our fashion guru', 'whenever I go *see* him, I *feel* instantly awesome', and so on. The female customers often commented on the *need* they have to see the designer, which related both to their desire for his knowledge and to the feeling and sensation connected to being in his presence and indeed to the empowering atmosphere of his boutique. Some designers were even perceived as capable of removing negativity and obstacles (a phrase strikingly reminding of *Ganesh* – the remover of obstacles) both through their often comforting and empowering discourse and through their products. Designer studios and boutiques thus not only appeal to the *darshanic* understanding of vision in India – the importance of seeing and being seen (usually connected to the deity), but they also most powerfully appeal to the tactile vision that operates in an expanded sensorial field. This desire to see the designer and to be exposed to his presence, to the interior, to his products and to let oneself be overwhelmed by this engagement, stood in a stark juxtaposition to the engagement with the artisans. While the designer was the auspicious one, a guru of fashion connoisseurship, the artisans were inauspicious, observed only from a distance, talked about but not talked to, turned into object-like feature of the all-pervading atmosphere of power. When I inquired into this, many women admitted their fear of involving themselves too much with the craftsmen, expressions like 'you sort of see through them' or 'you learn to see them but not see them, it is necessary' were very common, pointing towards a conscious distantiation by means of vision and intended reification, necessary in order to keep their own world intact and undisturbed by the poverty, which at the same time enabled their own existence in many ways.

## Conclusion

Contemporary Indian haute couture is indeed a strange continuation and re-imagination of the imperial and hierarchical impulse projected into the future and placed within the logic of neoliberalism and spectacle of globality, where it suddenly also has to cater to the increased desire for staging of a *back-and-forward* looking authenticity and distinct identity. What is at stake in Indian haute couture is the negotiation of the position of elites, as distinctively Indian elites within a global space. The fashion spectacles produce a mythical space, which is marked by plays with temporality and timelessness, by excess of multiple referents, by blends of incongruous elements, and juxtapositions of styles, which all lead to a point where search for origins becomes meaningless, where origins are erased and can, to the contrary, only emerge from this mythical space. Such mythical spaces are synthetic and dynamic, they are a montage of things, people, ideas that take on axiological features – they become carriers of value and expressions of the ways in which values are shared or not, an expression of ways in which people create divisions. When we are confronted with the work of the designers we perceive this mythical space, the totality of the configuration. This totality can be approached through a double vision, one of corpothetic immersion, the other distantiating, creating alliances and hierarchies that separate the elite from those below. What we perceive are relations and things in proportion to each other, and it is in this totality of the constellation of often incongruous and anachronistic elements that a particular atmosphere emerges. This atmosphere is then something, following Gernot Böhme that 'proceeds from and is created by things, persons and their constellations'. The atmosphere is neither objective or subjective but rather 'thinglike, belonging to the thing in that things articulate their presence through qualities – conceived as ecstasies' and subjectlike, belonging 'to subjects in that they are sensed in bodily presence by human beings and this sensing is at the same time a bodily state of being of subjects in space' (Böhme 1993: 122). With the shift of the economy towards valorization of aesthetic labor and towards production of aesthetic value, the designers' work becomes increasingly one of creation of atmospheres that impact and have a subtle social power. The creations of the leading Indian haute couturiers are thus in their form symptomatic of the increased aestheticization, which 'represents an important factor in the economy of advanced capitalist societies' (Böhme 2003: 72). As the marketing gurus teach us: 'goods and services are no longer enough to foster economic growth (...) to realize revenue growth and increased employment, the staging of experiences must be pursued as a distinct form of economic output (...) the greatest opportunity for value creation resides in staging experiences' (Joseph and Gilmore 2011: ix). The designers also promise, in line with contemporary economic logic, the customers' transformation through the garment (the customer can effectively be turned into royalty by way of dressing up). This is again symptomatic of our contemporary economies, in which the customer is turned into the product and where the transformation of the individual becomes the mission of the business. Such an economy is dependent on the creation of the *more* and of the atmosphere that transcends the object being sold and establishes an affective relationship with the subject (Anderson 2009); this *affective* relationship again relating to the corpothetic engagement with the staged objects and images. The atmosphere is what penetrates the body, gives aesthetic pleasure but at the same time is equally capable of aesthetic manipulation and as we have seen also separation and distantiation – atmospheres can be manipulated so as to appear as atmospheres of shared values and alliances as much as their opposite, atmospheres of poverty and oppression, demanding distantiation. The Indian haute couturiers are ultimately in a business of creating retro-futuristic imperial atmospheres, where utopias 'not only offer an arresting vision of future possibilities, but because they tend to be written in the past narrative tense, also imply that their depiction of the good life, an ideal world, is eminently attainable. The future is past.' (Brown and MacLaren 1998: 279).

## References

Anderson, B. 2009. 'Affective Atmospheres.' *Emotion, Space, Society*, 2, 77-81.

Benjamin, W. & Tiedemann, R. 1999. *The arcades project*. Cambridge, Mass.: Belknap Press.

Biehl-Missal, B. & Saren, M. 2012. 'Atmospheres of Seduction: A Critique of Aesthetic Marketing Practices.' *Journal of Macromarketing*, 32:2, 168-80.

Brown, S. & MacLaren, P. 1998. 'The future is past.' In S. Brown, J. Bell & D. Carson (Eds.) *Marketing Apocalypse: Eschatology, escapology and the illusion of the end*. New York: Taylor & Francis.

Böhme, G. 1993. 'Atmosphere as the Fundamental Concept of New Aesthetics.' *Thesis Eleven*, 36, 113-26.

Böhme, G. 2003. 'Contribution to the Critique of Aesthetic Economy.' *Thesis Eleven*, 73, 71-82.

Cannadine, D. 2002. Ornamentalism: *How the British Saw Their Empire*. Oxford: Oxford University Press.

Eck, D. L. 1998. Darśan: *Seeing the Divine Image in India*. New York: Columbia University Press.

Entwistle, J. 2009. *The Aesthetic Economy of Fashion: Markets and Values in Clothing and Modelling*. Oxford: Berg.

Gilman-Opalsky, R. 2011. *Spectacular Capitalism: Guy Debord and the Practice of Radical Philosophy*. New York: Minor Compositions.

Jodhka, S. S. & Newman, K. 2007. 'In the Name of Globalization: Meritocracy, Productivity and the Hidden Language of Caste.' *Economic and Political Weekly*, 42:41, 4125-32.

Joseph, P. & Gilmore, J. H. 2011. *The Experience Economy*. Cambridge, Mass: Perseus Books Group.

Kapferer, B. & Hobart, A. 2005. 'Introduction: The Aesthetics of Symbolic Construction and Experience.' In B. Kapferer & A. Hobart (Eds.) *Aesthetics in Performance: Formations of Symbolic Construction and Experience*. New York/Oxford: Berghahn.

Kaviraj, S. 1998. 'The Culture of Representative Democracy.' In P. Chatterjee (Ed.) *Wages of Freedom: Fifty Years of the Indian Nation State*. New Delhi: OUP.

Khan, S. R. 2010. Privilege: *The Making of an Adolescent Elite at St. Paul's School*. Princeton, NJ: Princeton University Press.

Lindstrom, M. 2009. *Buyology: How everything we believe about why we buy is wrong*. Great Britain: RH Business Books.

Mehta, P. B. 2011. 'Meritocracy and Its Discontents.' *NUJS Law Review*, 4:5, 1-13.

Pritchard, M. 2009. 'Directions in Contemporary German Aesthetics.' *The Journal of Aesthetic Education*, 43:3, 117-27.

Roberts, D. 2003. 'Illusion Only is Sacred: From the Culture Industry to the Aesthetic Economy.' *Thesis Eleven*, 73:May, 83-95.

Tarlo, E. 1996. *Clothing Matters: Dress and Identity in India*. London: Hurst & Company.

Tharoor, S. 2007. *The Elephant, the Tiger and the Cell Phone: Reflections on India in the 21st Century*. New Delhi: Arcade Publishing.

Winther-Tamaki, B. 2001. *Art in the Encounter of Nations: Japanese and American Artists in the Early Postwar Years*. Honolulu: University of Hawai'i Press.

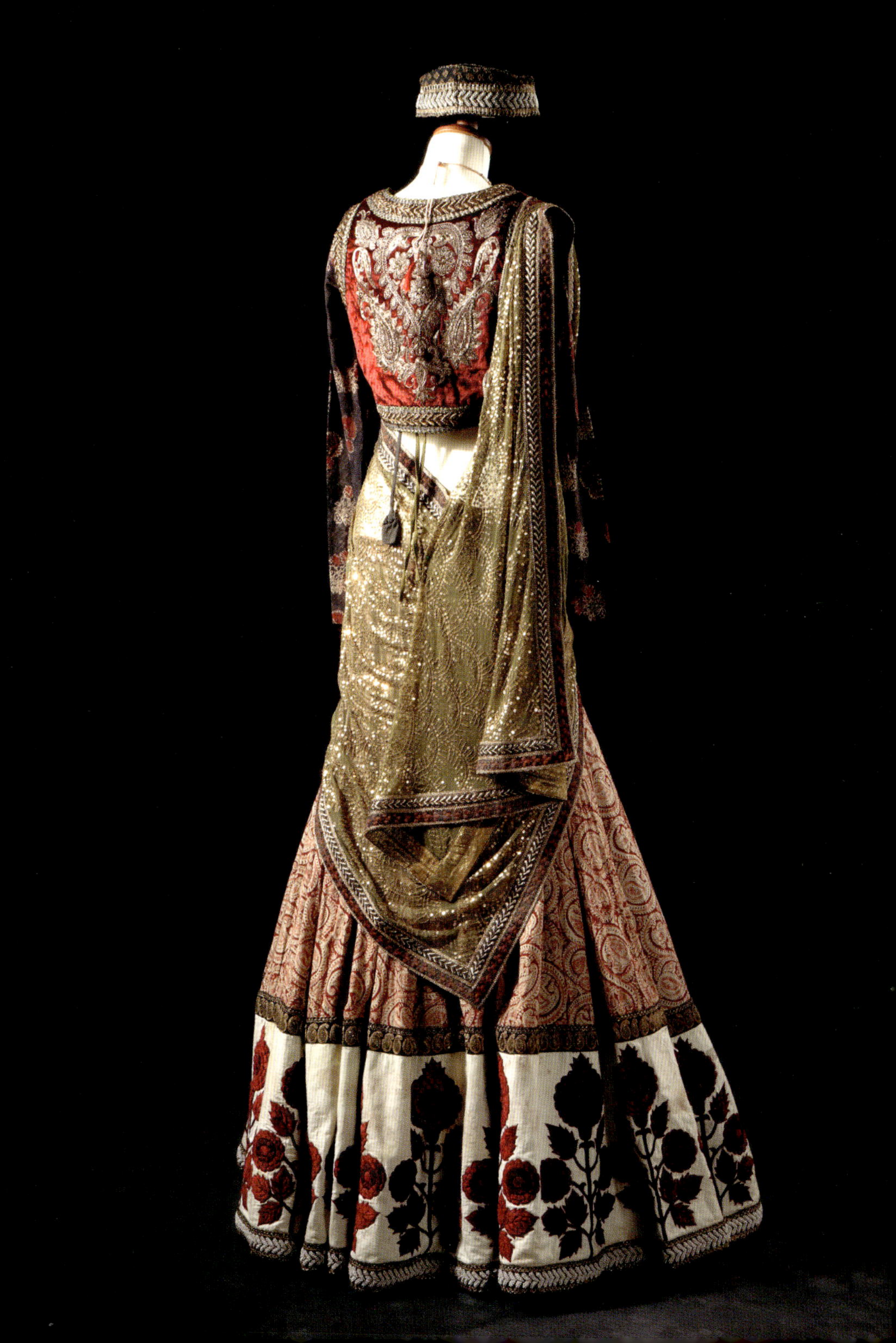

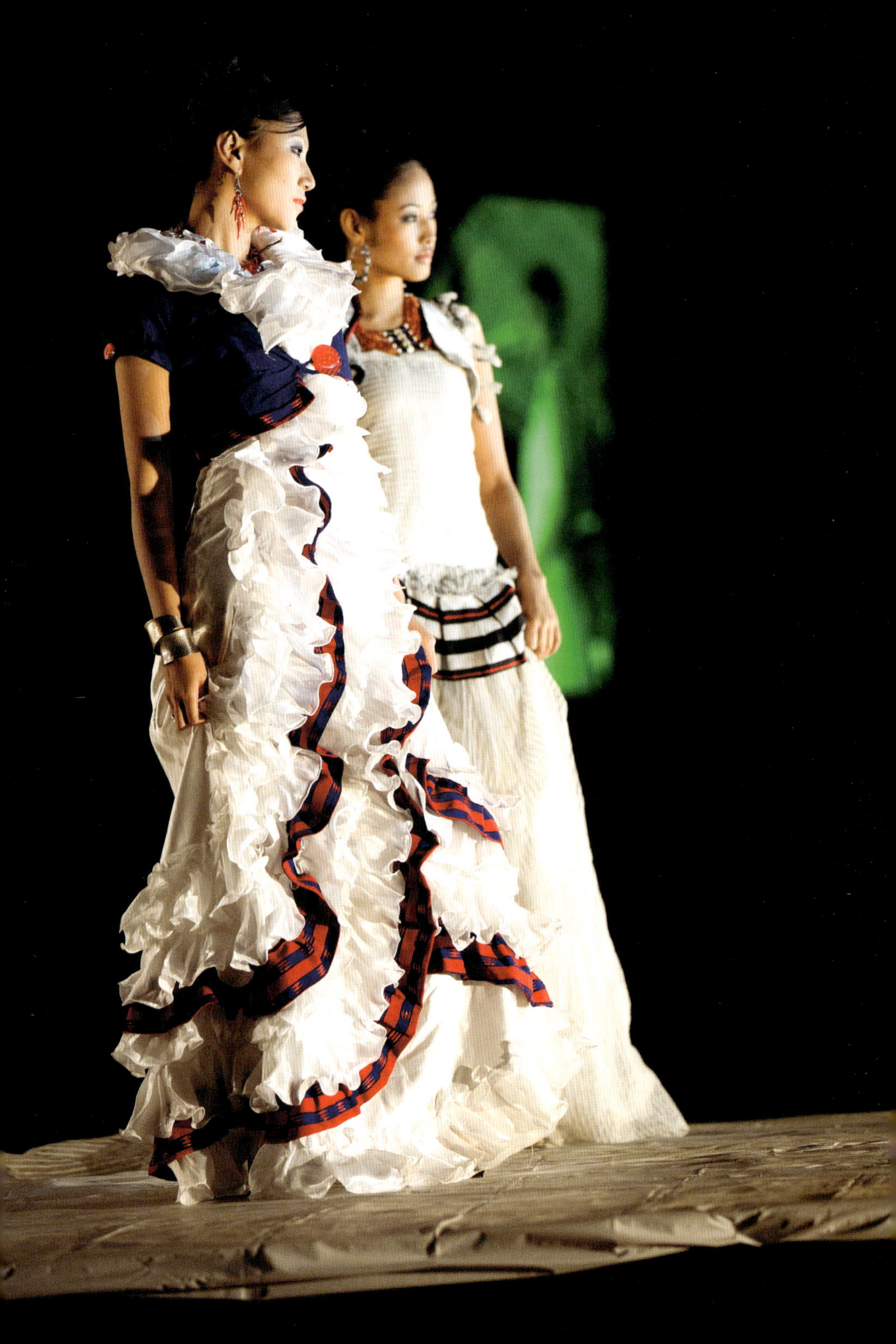

# Fashion Zeitgeist in Northeast India

Text: Marion Wettstein
Photographs: Alban von Stockhausen

> It is a widely accepted fact that Fashion and Northeast India are synonymous. ... It is a well-known fact that in the Northeast, one gets to see very well dressed and elegant girls and also boys sporting the latest hairstyles. In fact, fashion in the Northeast is not just a modern trend but it has been present since a long, long time. This is due to the fact that in the Northeast itself we have more than 400 communities – each unique and magnificent in its own way, in fact, giving an identity to Asian Fashion worldwide. ... So, it's only understandable that we carry on the legacy passed on by our forefathers. ... People nationwide appreciate and acknowledge our efforts. Be it our bloggers, designers, models or fashion photographers – we have a super scale range of talent in terms of Fashion.

This is the appraisal of the situation by Yanam Waghe in one of her internet blogs (Waghe 2012), a young woman from Northeast India in her mid-twenties, living in New Delhi. The self-confident and self-evident manner in which this young woman, who is present on the internet in the form of several fashion statements on LookBooks, Twitter and the like, perceives and represents the fashion scene of Northeast India, is no exception among the Northeast youth of today. In the last decade, a general notion that Northeast India is a hub not only for trendy fashion, but also for contemporary ethnic looks, has been established. This self-image of Northeast India is not restricted to the fashion-conscious youth or a handful of enthusiasts; a nearly identical notion of the fashionability of Northeast India can also be found among middle-aged members of the administrative and political establishment. On the official website of the Government of Nagaland we can therefore read that:

> The present generation of Nagas have ventured into fashion designing in a big way, reproducing fabrics that represent the ancestral motifs blended with modern appeal. Indeed, it is a beautiful mix of the past with the present... a paradise for those who are into fashion designing. This is an affluent fashion station of the East.
> (Government of Nagaland 2013).

## A Legacy of the Forefathers

The Nagaland referred to here is one of the 'seven sister' states of North-

---

Left:
Evening wear designed by Akala Pongen, Nagaland. The blue-red striped fabric intersected to the white frills in the dress in the foreground stems from a traditional Ao Naga woman's dance skirt, while that of the dress in the background is taken from an Angami Naga woman's skirt. The blue bolero jacket is manufactured from a very common shoulder shawl worn by men and women among the Ao Naga.
Hornbill Designers Contest 2010, Kohima, Nagaland.

east India, along with Arunachal Pradesh, Assam, Meghalaya, Manipur, Mizoram and Tripura. In territorial terms, Northeast India is only connected to 'mainland' India via a narrow corridor of land, and, for a large part of the 20$^{th}$ century, it was known as a zone of ethnic turmoil. Closed for decades to foreigners and Indian visitors alike, it has seen many open, armed conflicts that were barely noticed outside of India. In 'mainland' India, the people of the Northeast were largely perceived as combative, exotic 'tribals' or 'dangerous terrorists'. The self-perception of the great diversity of ethnic groups in the region was, for many decades, defined by freedom fights and a political notion of self-determination or separatism. These conflicts mainly originated in colonial times, although were also rooted in a long history of local kingdoms fighting for power and influence especially in the Brahmaputra valley, and wars and battles between local small-scale communities in the surrounding hills, in which the honour and splendour of 'the warrior' was held in high esteem. Taking the example of the Naga groups, prestige and status could mainly be gained by two means in ancient times: through success in war and through feasts of merit that were arranged by individual families for the whole village. When the British colonizers started to become more interested in the region, in the middle of the 19$^{th}$ century, they encountered a highly ritualised court culture in the plains of Assam and war-like tribes in the hills. These people were striking not only for their practice of head-hunting, but also by their incredibly splendid material culture and dress. In fact, the jewellery, head-gear, textiles and weapons of the Nagas were so appealing to the British that a substantial part of the object collections in the Pitt Rivers Museum of Oxford University – one of the largest ethnographic museums in the UK – stems from the Naga region of the beginning of the twentieth century (see for instance Jacobs 2012, Oppitz et al. 2008).

Consequently, the remarkable shift that has recently occurred regarding the image of Northeast India reorienting from that of a dangerous war zone to a lively fashion hub is, as stated by our young blogger, not entirely based on new ideas. In certain ways, the fashion scene in Northeast India does 'carry on the legacy of the forefathers' – indeed, in multiple ways: an important aspect of the current fashion scene is the manifold fashion shows, 'model hunts', beauty pageants and designer

---

Right:
Evening wear designed by Boney Darang, Arunachal Pradesh. The embroidery is traditionally applied to a background cloth with more patterning and structure. The style to wear a rectangular, uncut piece of cloth as wrap skirt with a matching shawl is very closely oriented at traditional wearing styles. Hornbill Designers Contest 2010, Kohima, Nagaland.

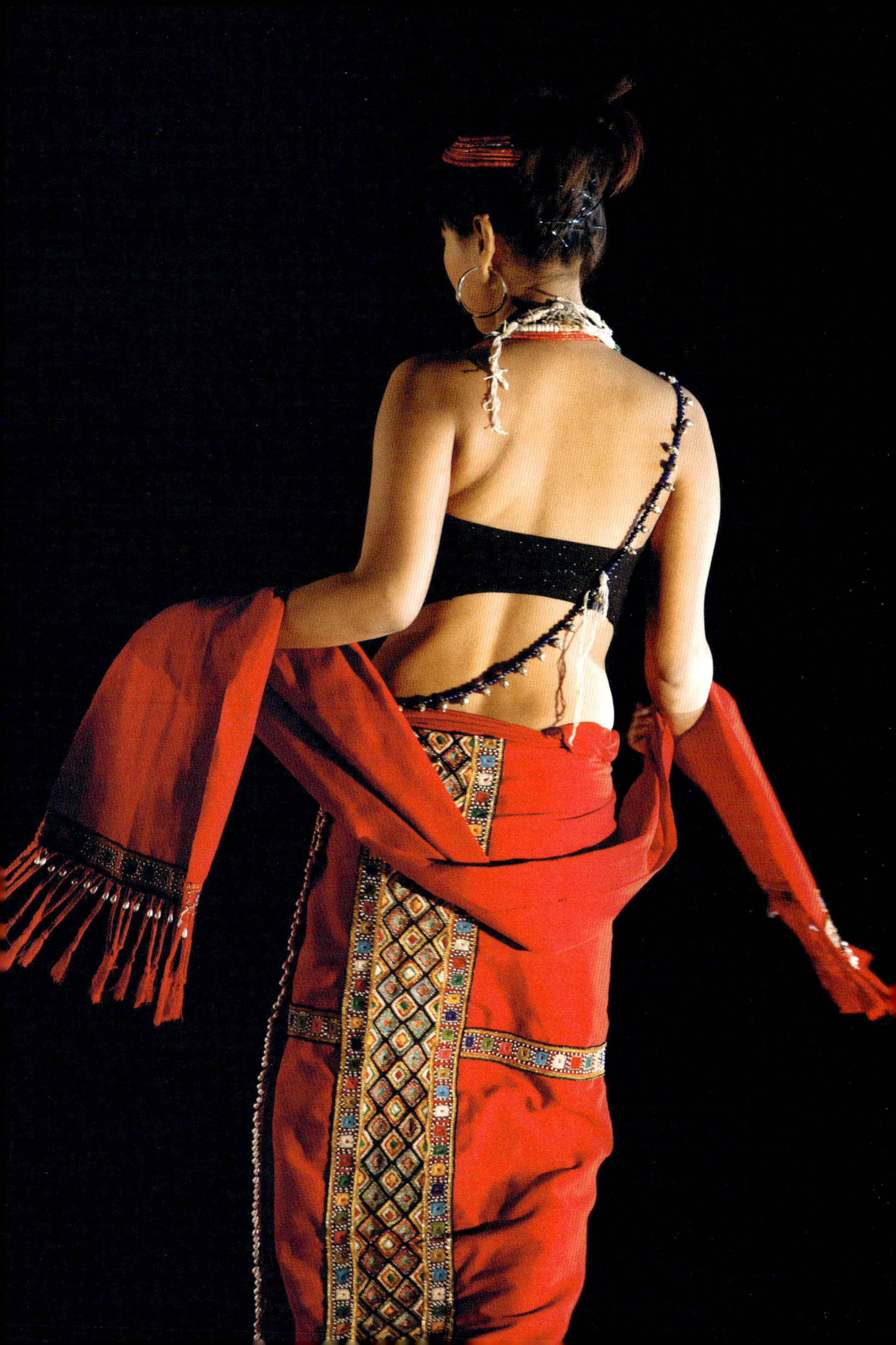

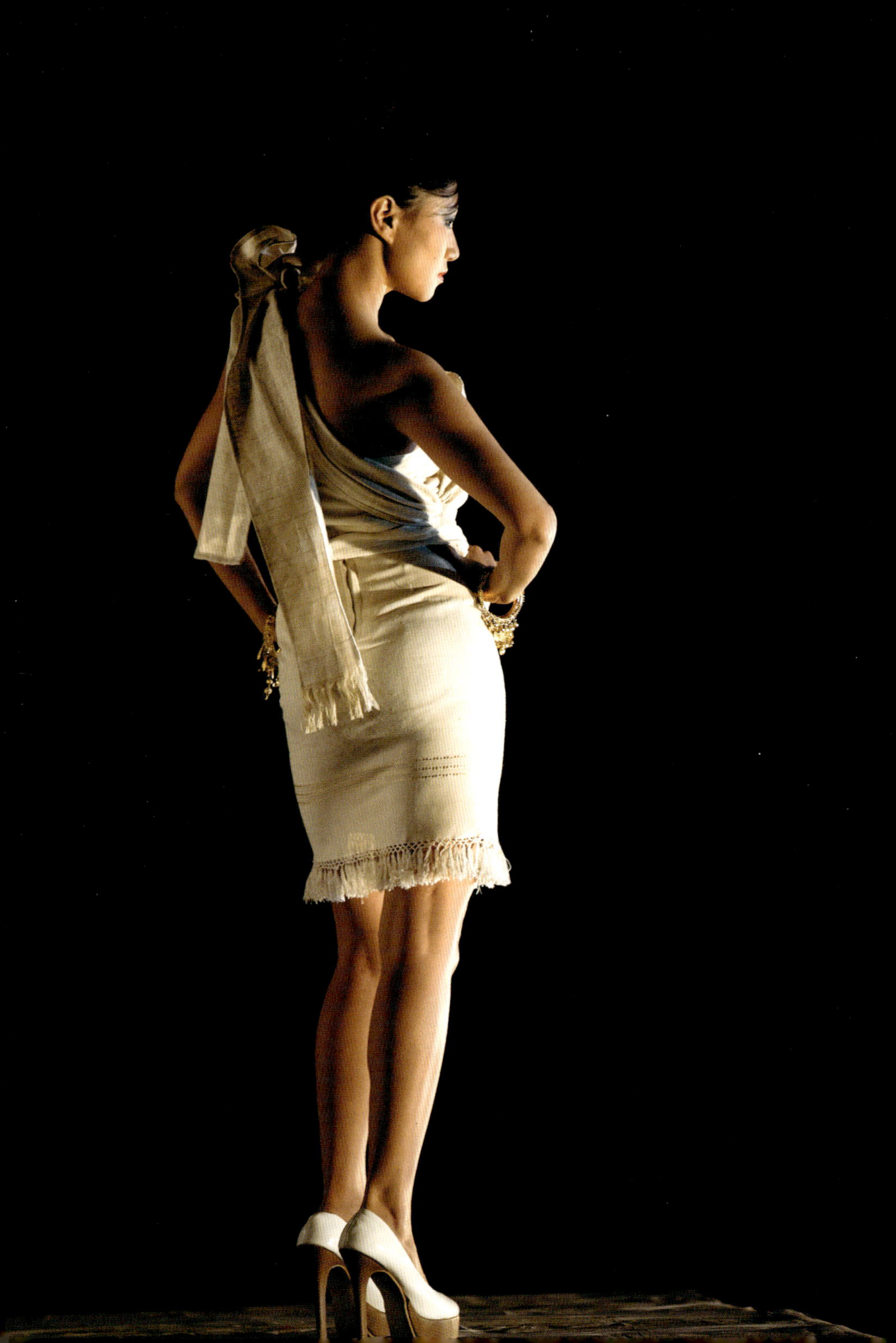

contests that are specifically held for 'ethnic fashion' and largely sponsored by the local governments of the seven sister states. Examining such events, one can find links and parallels to a notion of dress and fashion with a long history. The fact that the designs presented on stage use traditional ornaments and textile patterns is the most obvious connection. The show environment used to present fashion – which is often not worn in everyday life or 'on the streets,' and tends to be dominated by a modern Korean style in the hills or the kurta *sarval/sari* mainstream in the plains – can similarly be linked to 'shows' in ancient festivals and rituals held on occasions of feasts of merit or head-receiving ceremonies, to take the Naga example once again. In these celebrations, the village people were resplendent in their best outfits and, when the feast or ceremony was over, the splendid ornaments and intricately woven textiles were stored away again, ready for the next occasion. The governments of the states, in the guise of particular representatives responsible for the events, have taken on the function of sponsorship – an analogy to the feast-givers of ancient times – and, in this way, have the opportunity to accumulate personal status among the spectators and visitors, as well as through the local media.

This also means that the local ethnic fashion designers in Northeast India, especially in the tribal hill states, are often not dependent on making a living from their sales, as a considerable proportion of their shows and the expenses incurred are covered by the government funds. They do not have to promote their labels among the general public to generate sales. This also means that they give little attention to making creations that are suitable for everyday use. Thus, ethnic fashion in the hill states is more closely tied to governmental programmes of identity-building than to economics, leaving the designers with a great deal of freedom in terms of artistic creativity (see also Wettstein 2013).

A slightly different overall picture can be found in the plains of Assam and Manipur: in some cases, the notion of tribal dress is not as sharply distinguished from other clothing styles. The Assamese *mekhla chadar*, for example, a women's garment in three pieces (blouse, skirt and a long shawl) that superficially looks like a sari when worn, is seen very much as an ethnic garment, especially when woven from the local *muga*, *pat* or *eri* silk. In its simple variations, it is also used widely in everyday life.

---

Left:
Evening wear designed by Daniel Shiem, Meghalaya. With the effects of the simple, uni-colored, cosmopolitan elegance and the use of lesser known local raw materials like for instance the mix of cotton and eri silk, Shiem's designs won the contest in the category of evening wear. Hornbill Designers Contest 2010, Kohima, Nagaland.

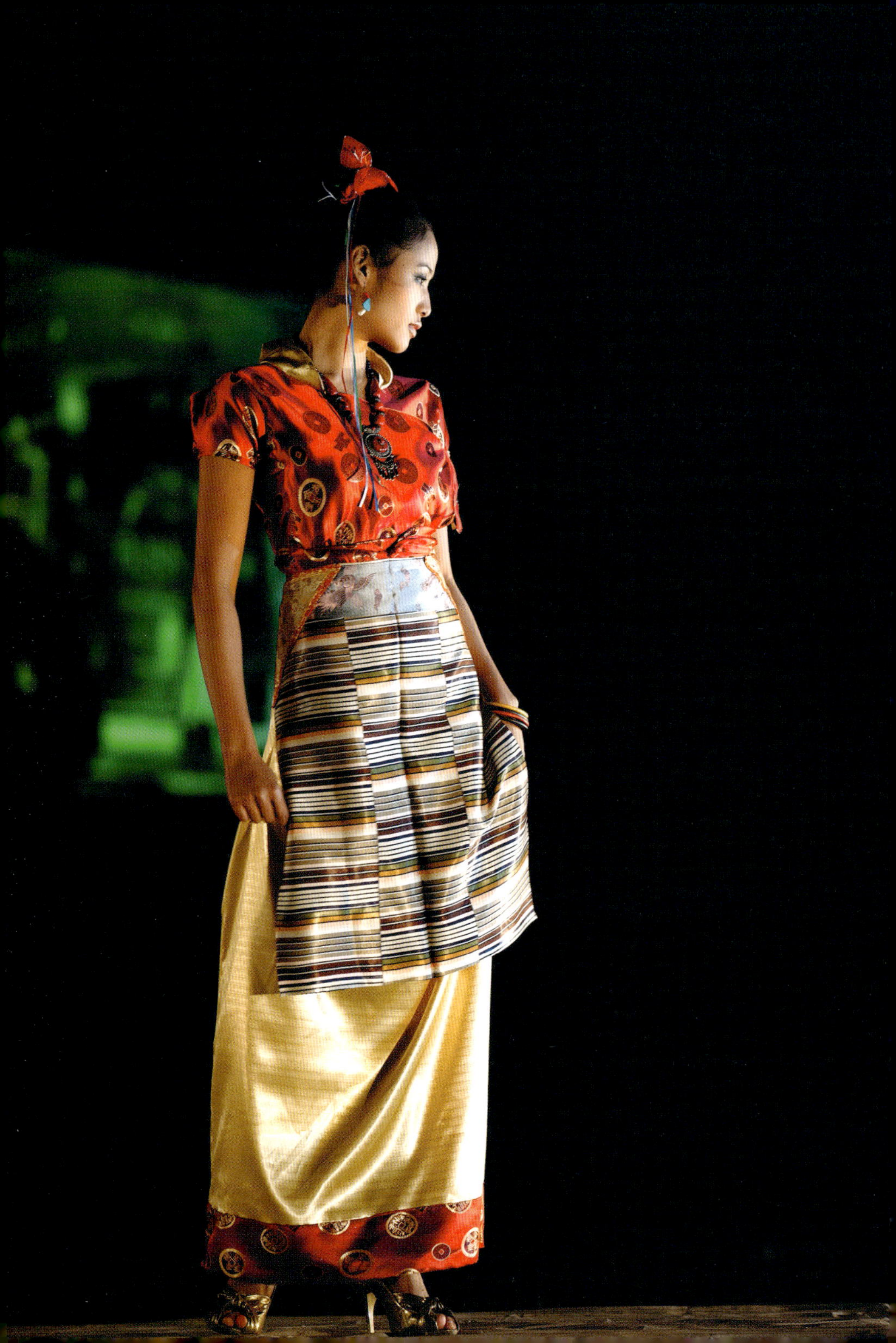

## Ethnic Glamour and Tribal Chic

As far as the hills of Northeast India are concerned, one can clearly distinguish a trend to link contemporary tribal, ethnic fashion with notions of glamour and chic, rather than with a down to earth 'eco' or alternative lifestyle, as is the case in so many other parts of the world. As stated elsewhere (Stockhausen & Wettstein 2008), the notion of 'extravaganza' has established itself since some time in the vocabulary of fashion in Nagaland, and the trend has been bolstered throughout the Northeast – as can be gleaned, for instance, from the *Manipur Fashion Extravaganza (MFE)*, held on January 6$^{th}$ 2013, which was explicitly organised 'to promote the existing sense of glamour and beauty of Manipuris since antiquity' (*Eastern Mirror* 2013). Similarly, the *North East Fashion Fest* held in February 2013 was praised as 'all set to bring you a thrilling juxtaposition of fashion, glamour, Bollywood, beauty and elegance' (*The Times of India* 2013). Yet what exactly does ethnic glamour from Northeast India look like? How is this new notion of the over-arching image of the region conceptualised?

As an example to illustrate Northeast Indian ethnic glamour and tribal chic, we can take a closer look at an event that took place in December 2010 in Kohima, the capital of Nagaland: *The Hornbill Designers Contest*, with the motto 'traditional fashion of Northeast India'. This contest was held within the larger framework of the annual *Nagaland Hornbill Festival*, usually scheduled in the first week of December, showcasing 'traditional' dances, costumes, games, cuisine and other activities for an entire week. In 2010, several other events were scheduled alongside the festival, such as a fashion night, a night bazaar, a photo contest, the *Miss Nagaland Beauty Pageant*, a motor rally, and the aforementioned designers contest. During the preparations, one fashion designer from each of the seven sister states of Northeast India was selected as a representative, in most cases once it had been assured that the designer's main centre of activity was in the state they represented and that they were not already established nationally or internationally. The contest was thus conceived of as a competition between the states rather than primarily between specific ethnic groups – of which there are too many in the region for all of them to be represented in such a show. In my view, this specific conceptualisation of the contest connotes two important polit-

---

Left:
Evening wear designed by Tenzin Tsering and Riya Payang, Sikkim. In these designs featuring blouses made of Chinese 'silk' and aprons of three horizontally striped lengths of cloth we can recognize the strong influence of Tibetan traditional dress that is predominant in the very northern borderlands of Northeast India.
The Hornbill Designers Contest 2010, Kohima, Nagaland.

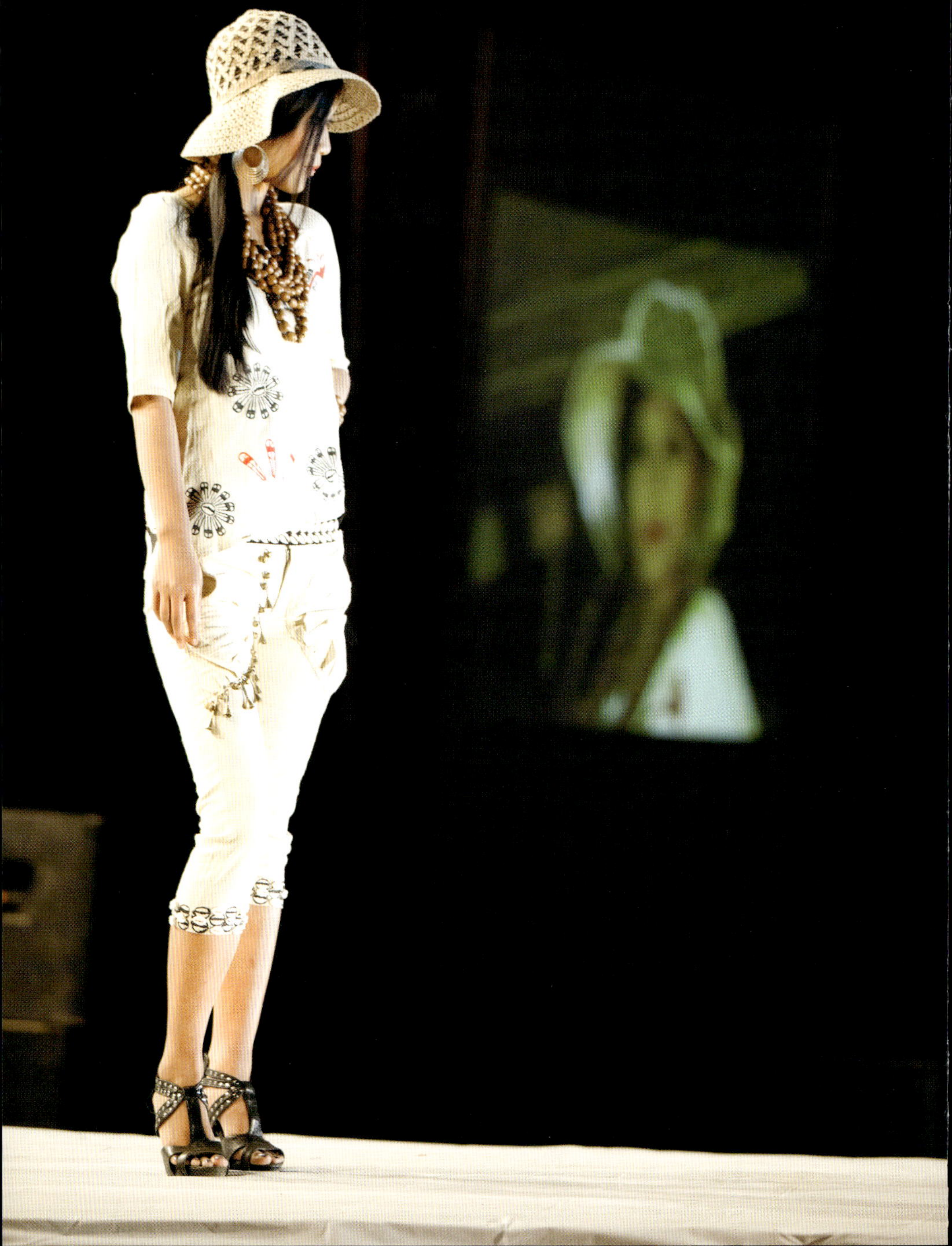

ical messages in its subtext: Firstly, it clearly tries to avoid rivalry and jealousy between individual ethnic groups. Tribalism and armed clashes between ethnic groups in Northeast India have continued to occur up until quite recently, so the politico-cultural establishment supporting such contests and shows attempts to alleviate tension from all notions of tribalism. Secondly, the concept reinforces the administrative notion of the Indian Nation being subdivided into union states, thus confirming the integration of these states into 'India' and thereby diverting attention from separatist ideas. At the same time it strengthens the notion of Northeast India as one single cultural unit and thus gives it more weight as a whole within India. Incidentally, these tendencies can be observed not only in the emerging fashion scene, but also in ventures in such fields as tourism, agriculture and small-scale entrepreneurship.

To return to the designers contest, however: the participating designers were explicitly requested in advance to use traditional ethnic elements in their garments. They were given two rounds of presentations to win over the audience and the judges: one for 'street wear' and one for 'evening wear'. As an incentive for the collections they produced, they each received a subsidy of 10,000 INR [Indian rupees] (approximately 160 euros or 215 US $). However, as in the case of the Naga representative, this subsidy was insufficient to cover the material costs for the collection. Even if the designer choses lower quality traditional textiles for the show, the investment for the basic materials alone will be appreciably higher. Likewise, the materials used by other designers doubtless far exceeded this incentive, considering, for instance, the cost of *muga* silk. But the awards in the different categories were substantial by Northeast Indian standards: Zothanpui Puite, the representative for Mizoram, won the prize for 'Best Hornbill Traditional Designer' (50,000 INR) and 'Best Street Wear Designer' (30,000 INR), while the prize for 'Best Innovative Designer' went to Akala Pongen representing Nagaland (30,000 INR), and for 'Best Evening Wear Designer' to Daniel Shiem representing Meghalaya (30,000 INR). The other participants in the event, which was sponsored by the Government of Nagaland and the Music Task Force of Nagaland, were Prashant Singha (Manipur), Tenzin Tsering and Riya Payang (Sikkim), Boney Darang (Arunachal Pradesh), and Dhiraj Deka (Assam).

---

Left:
Street wear designed by Akala Pongen, Nagaland. In this outfit the designer shifted the notion of Naga dress from using actual ethnic textile design to applying general Naga symbolism to a plain cloth. The wheel of hornbill feathers usually worn as a traditional male headgear and the sign of the mithun (local buffalo) are considered essential symbols for 'Naganess'.
Hornbill Designers Contest 2010, Kohima, Nagaland.

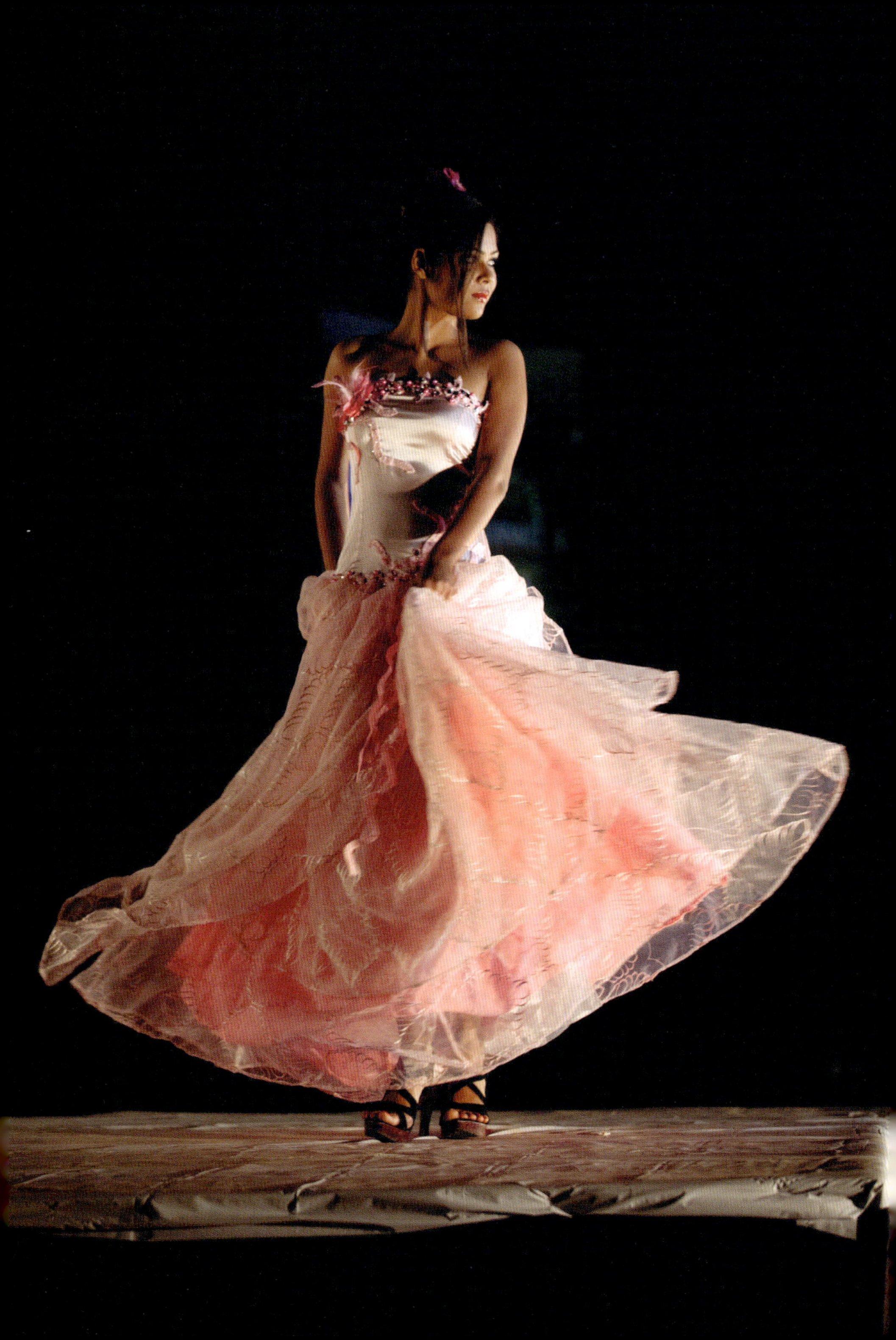

The range of dresses presented by the designers at this event extended from those with a distinct ethnic background to such strong fusions of traditional design or materials with mainstream, mostly Western styles that an 'ethnic' touch could only be recognised by people with significant background knowledge. Akala Pongen and Boney Darang certainly made the strongest and most obvious use of traditional textiles in their designs. The majority of their garments were directly based on traditional cloths or patterns, adapted and cut to shapes familiar to the Western fashion world. But while their creations are of the kind that can scarcely be worn outside the catwalk, and can thus rather be considered as wearable art, the creations of the main winner, Zothanpui Puite, who also made strong use of ethnic textiles, were more moderate in appearance and evoked the clothes that could, in fact, be found locally during weddings or special church services. (Christianity is the dominant religion in the hill states of the Northeast, while the plains are mainly Hindu influenced).

The fact that the main award went to Puite's collection may indicate that the judges acknowledged the balance she achieved in her dresses – deftly incorporating a touch of everything: ethnicity, a little glamour, although not too much for an interested customer, a good mix of traditional and Western colours, and, last but not least, a realistic opportunity of local marketability. After all, we must remember that the Northeast of India does not (as yet) have a super-rich upper class able to afford pure luxury, in contrast to many urban areas in the rest of India. Any fashion designer who genuinely wishes to survive at home on the basis of his or her profession, must have a good sense of intuition concerning how much glamour is socially acceptable away from the catwalk. When comparing the evening-wear collections, many visitors may have wondered why Daniel Shiem's collection won ahead of others that were, in the eyes of visitors, far more glittery and captivating. In this case the honour was awarded due to the very simple elegance evoked by straightforward, clearly cut sewing patterns and the naturally dyed, locally produced fabrics. Shiem can certainly be regarded as one of the designers in the competition who skilfully, and yet discretely, applied local materials and ethnic patterns, just like Prashant Singha, another

---

Left:
Evening wear designed by Zothanpui Puite, Mizoram. This dress has nothing whatsoever to do with the ancient traditions of Northeast India, but it mirrors a contrasting contemporary fashion trend. There is hardly a Northeast girl that doesn't dream of a pink, shiny western style princess dress. And evening gowns like this can be increasingly found swishing the ramps of Northeast India nowadays.
Hornbill Designers Contest 2010, Kohima, Nagaland.

Evening wear designed by Dhiraj Deka, Assam. Among the traditional and ethnic fashion styles of Northeast India the Sari-look of Assam has the highest marketability also in 'mainland' India. Especially mugha silk is already known as a trade mark nation-wide.
Hornbill Designers Contest 2010, Kohima, Nagaland.

award-winner, who transformed the stripes found in traditional Manipuri textiles in a manner fitting a young, modern style, with seemingly no recognisable ethnic feel. Ultimately, however, it is probably the silk tradition of Assam and its closeness to the mainstream Indian sari look – in this competition represented by Dhiraj Deka – that will convince the rest of India that the Northeast should henceforth be regarded as a fashion hub instead of being feared to be a hotbed of insurgency.

## Conclusion: A national agenda for a fashionable Northeast
What can be recognised underlying an event such as the *Hornbill Designers Contest* is a national political agenda to integrate the whole of Northeast India in friendly, artistic, creative competition, in keeping with the administrative framework that the Indian nation state has outlined. By focusing such events on backgrounds that evoke positive emotions – beauty, creativity, craftsmanship, show atmosphere, the limelight, music, and so on – tension and energy is distracted from destructive and militant notions of separatism and internal tribal fights. The idea behind

Street wear designed by Daniel Shiem, Meghalaya. In many regions of Northeast India ancient local textile fibers like cotton or nettle have been replaced by chemically colored, machine woven rayon or synthetics. Some designers actively support the reactivation of original fiber production with their fashion.
Hornbill Designers Contest 2010, Kohima, Nagaland.

---

this is to bestow Northeast India with a new image of fashion and glamour. This is clearly part of the national Indian agenda, which can also be gleaned from several other fashion events that took place recently. In late 2012, for example, the Ministry of Textiles at the Government of India announced via the Fashion Design Council that Northeast India would be the special focus region at the renowned *Wills Lifestyle India Fashion Week* 2013 in New Delhi. Alongside many other designers, a special place on the catwalk was given to internationally-working Atsu Sekhose from Nagaland. Having designed for some years for the Spanish fashion label Zara, Sekhose has recently launched his own label 'Atsu', which is renowned for its elegance. For the *Wills Fashion Show*, he created a collection specifically referencing Northeast India that was positively recognised and received nation-wide.

Another event that attests to the new public image campaign was the *North East Fashion Fest 2013* held in one of the few five-star hotels of

Guwahati, Assam, and attracted several thousand people. It was funded by, among others, the Home Ministry of India, the Department of Tourism of India, the Bodoland Territorial Council, and the Department of Handloom Textile. Here, the strategy for gaining national attention was to include Bollywood actors and actresses in the shows. Soha Ali Khan could be enlisted to act as an ambassador for the festival and several other actresses and actors were engaged to walk the catwalk for the featured designers, drawing on 'big' fashion events in mainland Indian metropolises as a model. Time will show whether the image campaign for a fashionable Northeast will bear fruit in the long run and succeed in gradually overcoming the violent experiences and memories and the nation's inner enemy stereotypes of the past, and whether, through fashion, the perception of Northeast India can be changed, so that the people of the Northeast will no longer have to face discrimination and negative prejudices in India.

## References

*Eastern Mirror.* 2013. 'Manipur Fashion Extravaganza (MFE) 2013'. http://www.easternmirrornagaland.com/entertainment/item/5789-manipur-fashion-extravaganza-mfe-2013.html. (Last accessed 10th April 2013).

Government of Nagaland. 2013. "About Nagaland". Nagaland.nic.in/profile/history/about.htm. (Last accessed 10th April 2013).

Jacobs. 2012 (1990). *The Nagas: Hill Peoples of Northeast India - Society, Culture and the Colonial Encounter.* Extended new edition. London: Edition Hansjörg Mayer.

Oppitz, M., T. Kaiser, A. von Stockhausen & M. Wettstein (eds). 2008. *Naga Identities: Changing Local Cultures in Northeast India.* Gent, Zürich & Wien: Snoeck Publishers, Völkerkundemuseum der Universität Zürich & Museum für Völkerkunde Wien.

Stockhausen, von, A. & M. Wettstein. 2008. "'Cultural extravagance' and the Search for Identity in Presentday Nagaland". In R. Kunz & V. Joshi (eds) *Naga: A Forgotten Mountain Region Rediscovered.* Basel: Museum der Kulturen Basel and Christoph Merian Verlag, 180-187.

*The Times of India.* (01/04/2013). "Tracing the Silk Route in the North East". http://articles.timesofindia.indiatimes.com/2013-04-01/designers/37436688_1_silk-fashion-festival-fashion-textile. (Last accessed 10th April 2013).

Waghe, Y. (05/11/2012). "Fashion and Northeast India is synonymous". http://sevendiary.com/fashion-northeast-india-synonymous. (Last accessed 10th April 2013).

Wettstein, M. (currently in print) 2013. "The Ethnic Fashion Scene in Nagaland". *Archiv Weltmuseum Wien* (61-62).

---

Right:
Street wear designed by Prashant Singha, Manipur. Some of the textiles of the Meithei are based on alternating thin same-with stripes, especially in the colors yellow and red. The design here is a very abstracted interpretation of an essentially traditional cloth design. Hornbill Designers Contest 2010, Kohima, Nagaland.

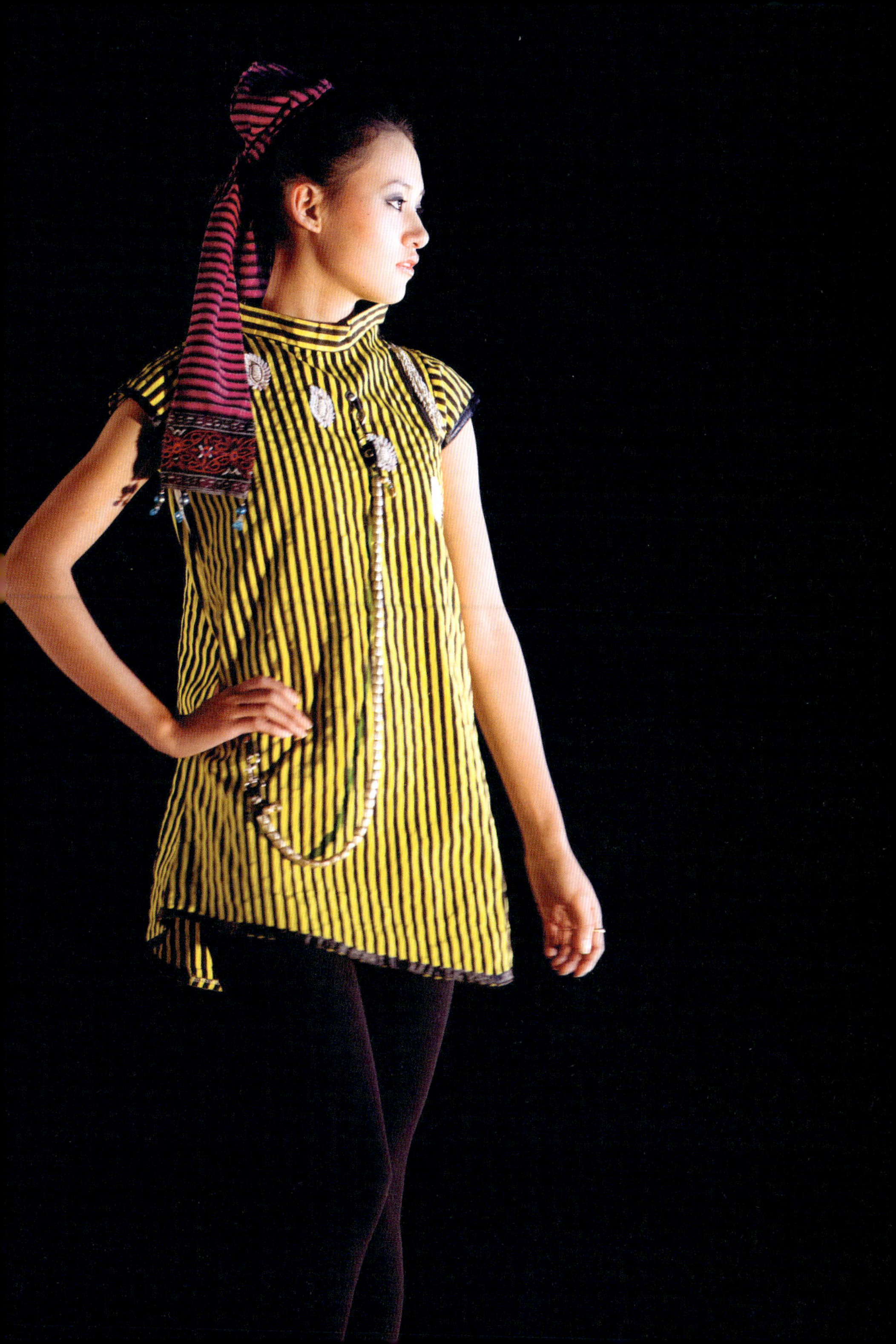

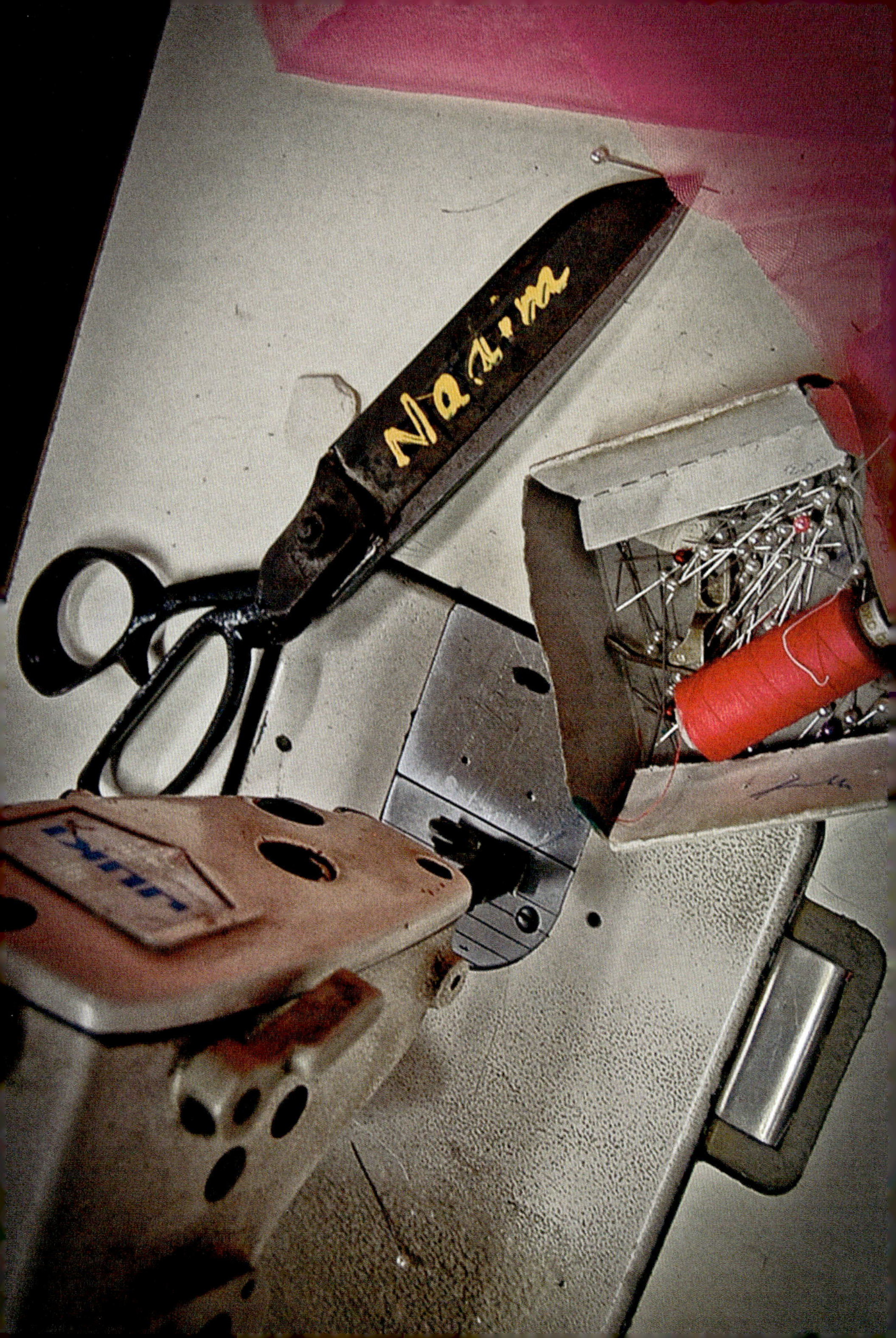

# Seamingly known
## A Photoessay
Meher Varma

These photographs were taken in New Delhi and Noida between 2012 and 2013. They are part of a large portfolio of documents that have informed my ethnographic research on designers and tailors working in the Indian fashion industry.

## The Place of Names Series

### Scissor-Hands
This series of scissors captures the importance of naming tools in the factory space. There is a clear division between tools that are shared and those that are reserved for personal use. I found that inscribing a name on to a tool is important in terms of claiming exclusive ownership over it. This photograph shows how owning and marking the tool of a scissor is a privilege that corresponds to the hierarchy between tailors and masters. A key difference between masters and tailors is that tailors do not actually cut cloth. Therefore, the master position, which is often bolstered by the respect-endowing suffix 'ji,' suggests a mastery over a certain set of production skills in the factory space, most important of which is the ability to cut.

In my interview with Masterjis, they expressed many times that scissors became embodied with a certain kind of enabling power. This was a power that was imagined as customised to the tailor's hand. The expression 'is se haath theek chalta hain' [my hands work well with this] is an expression commonly used by a Masterji when he is referring to the unique development of his process. I suggest that the link between the hands and scissors is one of the ways in which workers expressed the relationship between themselves and their tools as sometimes inseparable.

## The Body Brand

This series also sheds light on the politics of branding in relationship to the idea of a signature. While Masterjis work extensively on the creation of designer products and their names are marked on the tools that go into the making of the brand, the finished product itself is never directly stamped with their name.

This photograph features a bodice that is plastered with gaurav gupta factory tape. It represents the ultimate packaging of the body though the brand. Each product in the gaurav gupta studio is finished with this tape, which, literally and metaphorically, seals the brand signature.

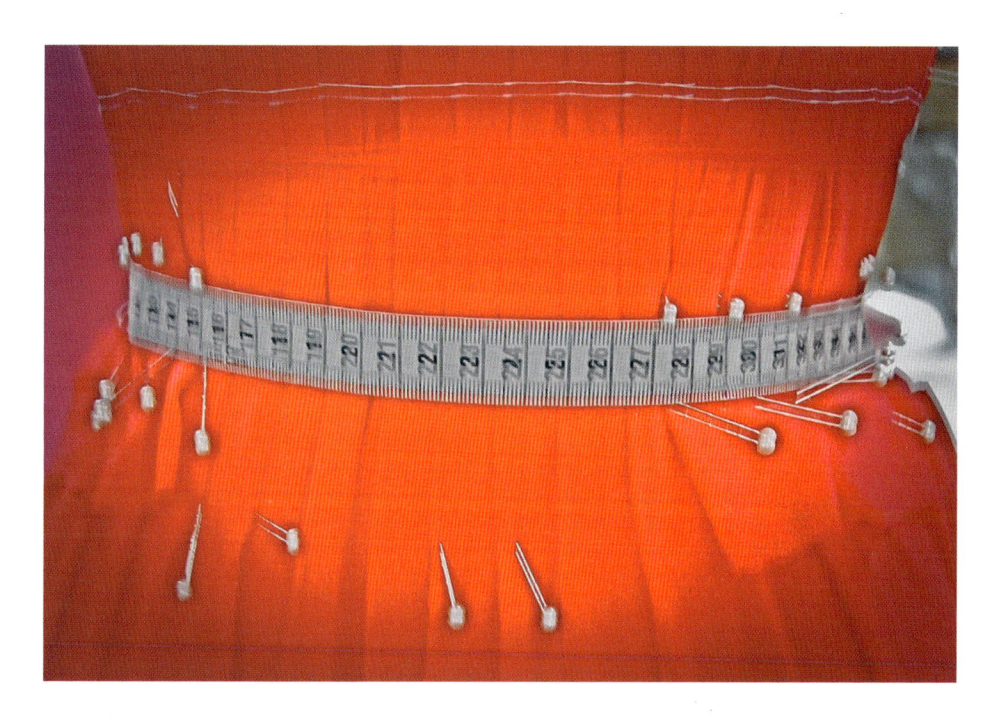

## Politics of Size

Feminist scholars investigating business of fashion have often argued that the industry demands and perpetuates a strict disciplining of women's bodies while often being made in their name.

However, I choose to present this photograph as a deliberately blurry representation of this idea. By specifically highlighting a fuzzy notion of measurement through this photograph, I am not suggesting that the industry has no role in disciplining women's bodies. Rather, I am illustrating that there is an unfixed, unclear relationship between ideal standards of size and acceptability as cultivated by the Indian fashion industry.

One example that evidences this unstable relationship is elucidated in looking at the discrepancy between projected model sizes shown on the ramp and client orders. During my year of working in a high fashion design factory, I was surprised to learn that the maximum numbers of orders for garments pertain to sizes XS (extra small for models) and XL (extra large) more than any other sizes. Furthermore, during the period of my ethnography itself, the measurements that corresponded to a standard M (medium), standard S (small) and so on were also revised.

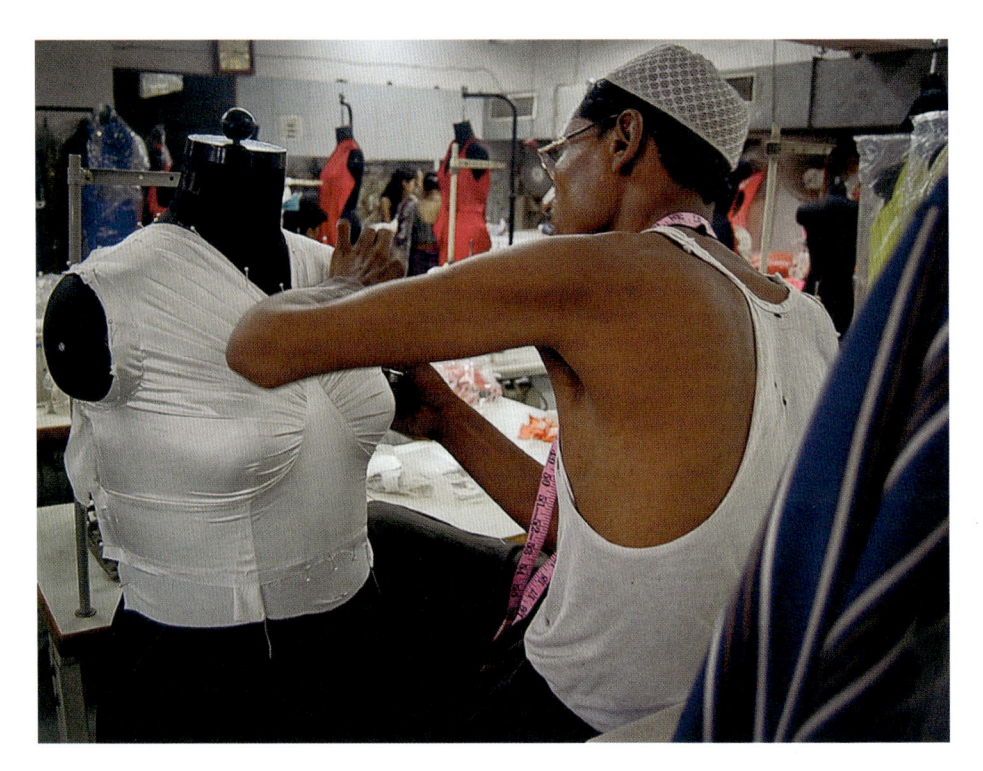

## Custom-Fit
Moreover, I found that through the extensive focus on customisation especially for Couture clients, the success of the garment can often times be dictated by how well a client fits into the dress rather than how well the garment fits the client. This image of a tailor with a measuring tape around his neck captures a production process that is being customised to suit the exact fit of a particular client. This can often take several sessions and I observed that many designers who I worked with consider this a priority.

## Neon Shoes
These shoes belong to Gaurav Gupta's Spring Summer 2013 collection titled 'In a Cathode.' The shoes were made in collaboration with manufacturers Gupta Overseas who are based at Agra, Uttar Pradesh. Neon played an important part in Gupta's summer 2013 collection, inspired by the designer's journey to the Sequoia forests in California. This series explored the relationship between the magnitude of the world and the smallness of ourselves, structure and sensuality.

I particularly enjoyed the chunky neon heels that seemingly had the power to draw attention to the collection from several miles away. This photograph was taken backstage, a few hours before the final show and the models are not yet outfitted. However, the simple adorning of the neon shoes already imbued the trial session with a spectacular feel and allowed the choreographer and designer to play with the order and feel of the show.

From observing the entire production process of the show, I learned that it was in the hours before the show when many important decisions concerning the final production in fact took place. The mood of the show would often come together through decisions about music volume, light, pace and line-up. These spontaneous choices would often be the defining moments in which the designer's personal sense of personal taste would come through and mark the collection.

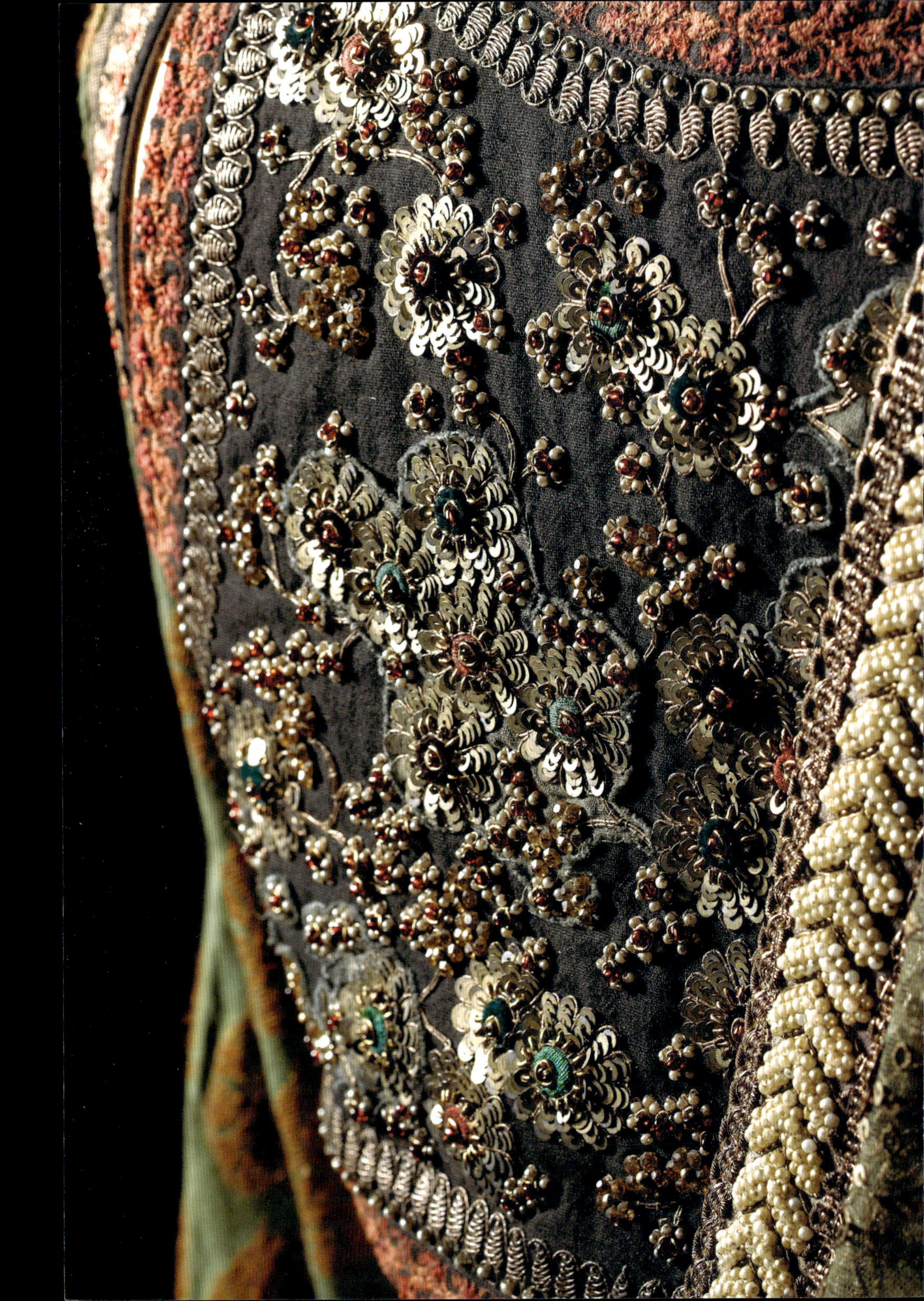

# Dressing India Anew
## Fashion Designers Betwixt and Between
Janne Meier

> India is going through a cultural revolution now, even as we speak, you know, because, finally, after many, many years, India is beginning to realise how powerful India really is: we are realising that the rest of the world is looking at us. Why should we bow down to them? So, a lot of people are rejecting foreign clothing traditions and coming back to Indian clothing. I want to present the real India to the world. You know, India has so much refinement when it comes to textiles, embroidery and handicrafts. I think India is really badly represented by Indians to the West. I don't think the best of India is really ever shown because many people don't know how to manipulate the best of India. There are lots of handicrafts in India and a lot of textiles, which people don't even know of, Indians don't even know about. That is the kind of refined India that I want to show to the West. Because otherwise, you know, India will always be regarded as the sourcing country where you can get cheap clothes. But that is not true of India; India has some of the most luxurious things ever...
>
> Interview with designer, October 2011[1]

Clothing practices in India have always been sites of intense moral negotiations and controversy. They are essential to identity politics and mirror socio-economic change, visualise socio-economic boundaries, manifest power, hierarchies and status.

The general pride, enthusiasm and optimism inherent in the opening statement by one of India's internationally renowned designers must be understood as part of a wider range of interlinked contemporary narratives about the emergence of a brand 'New' India (see Kuldova, p. 51-70). This 'New India' is routinely branded, through public private partnerships, initiatives and campaigns[2] by the government and India Inc. as an emerging superpower and economic force to be reckoned with – a proud, powerful and ancient civilization, as well as a booming economic and cultural force on the contemporary international stage.

The rhetoric of this 'New' India's 'rise' to power and increasing self-confidence is also reflected in the story of Indian fashion where craft and textile traditions are seen as India's 'unique selling point' in a global, competitive industry. Dress, identity and nation are being re-imagined, re-narrated and configured in a 'New' India, where the categories of

---

[1] Interview conducted by the author in Delhi.
[2] The biggest effort in this vein is the Incredible !ndia campaign by the Ministry of Tourism. It was launched in printed and digital media worldwide in 2002 and has since been a steady feature at high profile international events like the World Economic Forum's annual meeting in Davos (http://www.incredibleindia.org/about-us).

'Western' and 'Indian' continue to be meaningfully juxtaposed on the sartorial battlefield.

This makes the field of fashion a fascinating one – and fashion in India, a country where dress, cloth and textiles have always been powerful political tools, spectacularly so.

Models on the ramp, Bollywood stars and celebrities on the front row at the Rohit Bal Finale Show, Synergy One *Delhi Couture Week,* July 25th 2011:

> The PCJ Delhi Couture Week 2013 is attended by the who's who of the Capital and Indian fashion from business honchos, industrialists, retailers, editors, social celebs, and film and television actors…Top Indian designers through a series of riveting shows will make these five days a blend of contemporary art and modern aesthetics as models gear up to celebrate a season of luxe style. The Week celebrates India's everlasting love for luxury and fine taste in high-end couture, a legacy carried forward since the days of Maharajahas.[3]

The Delhi Couture Week is a celebrity event mainly aimed at the Indian wedding and trousseau clientele. It was clear from the behaviour of my fellow audience members and the photographers that the front row guests were scrutinised and photographed almost as much as the outfits and models on the ramp.

---
[3] http://www.fdci.org/Event/EventDetail.aspx?EventID=40

This chapter is based on periods of intense multi-cited, anthropological fieldwork and (participant) observations in the field of fashion in India: at fashion weeks/events and at designer studios, coupled with career and life-history interviews with designers[4] and other fashion professionals and intermediaries, mainly in Delhi[5] but also in Mumbai, during the period of 2009-2012. I trace the links between the evolution of an institutionalised field of fashion in India and a governmental development strategy based on export-oriented growth, 'new economy' policies aimed at supporting 'creative' and 'cultural' industries and conscious nation branding. Consequently, I will map the evolution of the industry and look at how independent fashion designers – a new category of creative professionals – make sense of the figured world of fashion in India and their place in it.

## Fashion Nation: The making and framing of an industry
### From Khadi to exports and back

The economic and symbolic role of textile during India's struggle from colonial rule, and the subsequent development of the modern Indian nation, has been well documented (Tarlo 1998; Trivedi 2007; Cohn 1989; Mohsini 2011). Gandhi and the nationalist movement placed the textile industry at the heart of colonial contestation and elevated *khadi*, the traditional hand-spun and hand-woven cotton cloth worn by peasants and artisans in pre-industrial India, to a key symbol of an independent nation – a national fabric with quasi-sacred properties (Ibid, Barley 1986). Gandhi proclaimed the sacredness of *khadi* and saw in its revival a revival of India herself. A return to *khadi*, and a rejection of imported British cloth could, according to him, unite the nation and save not only India's textile industry (which had declined as the import of cheap British cloth caused widespread poverty) but also save India from losing it's 'spiritual and cultural essence' in the face of Western developmental agendas.

---

[4] This chapter focuses on designers who have independent labels and must simultaneously manage being business entrepreneurs as well as design professionals. I also conducted interviews with designers employed by brands, export houses and successful Indian design houses.

[5] Delhi is, by most people in the industry, the accepted 'Fashion Capital' of India, although this is highly contested by the Mumbai fashion industry with its Bollywood connections. As one informant put it 'Mumbai is fun and glamour, Delhi is serious work'. This sentiment was echoed by most of the industry professionals I encountered in the field. Most designers have their studios and factories in the Delhi area, which is he main sourcing hub for fashion materials, trims, fabrics and accessories. Another important factor is that property prices and therefore rents are lower than in Mumbai and there is a large population of immigrant labour; tailors and embroiderers from the states of Bengal, Bihar and Uttar Pradesh.

"Be Proud Indian Buy Khadi and Gift Khadi"

KHADI GRAMODYOG BHAVAN
KHADI AND VILLAGE INDUSTRIES COMMISSION
Ministry of Micro, Small & Medium Enterprises, Govt. of India
24, Regal Building, Connaught Place, New Delhi-110001

The Ghandian message to the nation is still flying high outside the iconic Khadi Gramodyog Bhavan (Khadi Bhandar) at Connought Place in Delhi. Established in 1957, the Khadi Bhandar was envisioned to 'radiate the message of the Mathatma' and 'work for a non-violent, non-exploitative social order as envisaged by Mahatma Gandhi. Towards attaining our objectives of relieving the rural people from their existing poverty, Khadi & Village Industries sales is being stepped up steadily to provide employment to the rural masses.'[6]

Since independence, the textile and craft industries continue to enjoy a unique symbolic status. Governed by the powerful *Ministry of Textiles*, the industries are seen as vital to Indian economy and pan-Indian identity. Until the mid 1980s, under India's import substitution policies and closed market, they were mainly geared towards the domestic market and defined as a priority sectors to be nurtured for national development, job generation and growth (Tewari 2006, 2008; Venkatesan 2009). From the mid 1980s, India gradually departed from strict economic policies favouring self-sufficiency and import substitution and adopted neo-liberal policies focussed on export-oriented growth (Srinivasan 2011). In this period, 'new economy' policies increasingly placed 'creative' and 'cultural' industries at the heart of national development, not only in India, but also globally.

---

[6] http://www.khadigramodyogbhavan.com/profile.html. See also Trivedi (2006).

In the mid 1980s, the Indian government started actively promoting export in key sectors, including textile and clothing. This led to an initial surge in exports mediated by small buying agents and small-volume exporters: mainly of fashion items in women's wear, supplied initially to the EU and subsequently to the US.[7] Significantly – in contrast to countries such as China, Bangladesh and Sri Lanka, along with other Asian countries – India's export sector developed with a very low foreign direct investment and without the involvement of Indian manufactures in major and dominant global low-price buying chains. State regulation was instrumental in establishing an export sector dominated by locally-owned domestic firms. This sector grew from a 900 million dollar affair in 1985, 9.2 billion in 2004 and to 12 billion in 2012. After the removal of quotas under the Multi Fibre Agreement in 2005, India's exports jumped 43 % between 2004 and 2006 (Tewari 2008: 52-55). It is precisely the strong textile base – 90 % of all clothing manufactured in India employs local fabric – along with the legacies of the licence raj, which resulted in a fragmented, small scale and cotton-based industry linked to the craft sector.

Neo-liberal economists and commentators saw these conditions as limiting India's ability to take advantage of the de-regulation of international trade and become deeply embedded in dominant global supply chains. However, the institutional legacies of the import substitution era, together with a strong Indian state's, continued support of craft, coupled with the development of creative professions, can be seen as instrumental in India's development as a 'fashion nation'. The nurturing of the craft sector, together with design development and an export sector dominated by small and medium exporters cemented India's reputation as a sourcing country for speciality garments with fashion value . This set-up which is well suited to the developments in the international fashion supply chains, which, since the 1990s, have seen an increased value addition, specialisation and segmentation into smaller runs of greater variety and customisation.

---

[7] 80 % of India's exports are still to the EU and US. The recent economic crisis in the US and the Eurozone has made the Indian government focus on identifying new emerging markets and on nurturing the huge domestic market (Ibid).

To promote India as a sourcing destination for foreign brands, the Ministry of Textiles, under the aegis of the Apparel Export promotion Council and the four biggest apparel export organisations have been hosting the India International Garment Fair (IIGF) since 1988. The Fair, like the Wills Lifestyle India Fashion Week, is hosted in the exhibition grounds, Pragati Maidan in central Delhi. In recent years, the fair also runs a fashion show schedule where exporters can show their products. The difference in aesthetics between the two events to any visitor is striking.

## A 'Fashion Nation' for Development

Fashion, Wilson argues, speaks of capitalism (1985). In India, the institutionalised fashion industry, and fashion design as a creative career, developed alongside the liberalisation of the Indian economy in the late 1980s and 1990s (Roy 1998, Tewari 2006, 2008). Its development was supported by the state and has followed the now-hegemonic institutional blueprint for manufacturing fashion value, which emerged in 19th century France[9].

Löfgren (2003, 2005) argues that the technologies of launching 'newness' invented in the French fashion industry (and now adopted by

---

[8] 50 % of India's apparel exports are in the fashion segment and include craft techniques such as embroidery and other embellishments.

[9] The French institutional blueprint; techniques of manufacturing fashion value and the birth of an organised and protected *Haute Couture* [fine-tailoring] industry, along with the framing of the desiger as 'creative genius' and artist is attributed to Charles Frederic Worth (1825-1895). In 1886, he established the organisation *Chambre Syndicale de la Confection et de la Couture pour Dames et Fillettes* in Paris. This institutional set-up effectively patented ideas and ideals of fashion, equating Paris fashion with high fashion par excellence, a move that was made possible due to Paris's affluence, coupled with the availability of cheap labour along with its status as an international hub of art and artists (Palmar et. al 2006; Breward 2003; Craik 1994; Steele 1988;).

nations worldwide) has spread to the economic sphere in general throughout the 1990s: creating a global 'catwalk economy' in which a clearly defined aesthetic and national identity becomes an important parameter for competitiveness and status (Ibid, Palmar et. al. 2006). On the global catwalk, cultural and creative sectors play an increasingly important role in national development policies and nation branding efforts. In this context, a national design policy and an institutionalised domestic fashion industry projects an image of the nation as 'modern' to domestic and international audiences and investors (Skov & Riegels Melchior 2011; Jones & Leshkowich 2003). Fashion is used as an important signifier of urban modernity and world-status (Craik 1994). 'Each nation has a vested interest in being recognised as a place of creativity and aesthetics. We might call this "dressed power" a consequence of the catwalk economy' (Reich 2011: 71).

The mapping of a country's 'fashion DNA' is seen as vital for making it relevant to both national consumers and international buyers, who are sought after visitors at fashion weeks held around the globe. While competition is fierce, the traditional Eurocentric bias and hierarchies of fashion are slowly but surely fading, along the lines of global economic power shifts and turns. While newcomer nations in the fashion week hierarchy attempt to establish themselves as relevant 'Fashion Nations', Paris, and to some degree London and New York, have become globally relevant as *international* fashion nations: capable of attracting the shows of foreign designers. When the Indian designer Manish Arora holds shows in Paris, he places India on the map as a Fashion Nation, but, equally important, he simultaneously confirms Paris's status as a place of international fashion.

## Educational Framework: Linking fashion, design and craft
In 1986, the Ministry of Textiles, in 'technical collaboration' with the Fashion Institute of Technology, New York, set up the National Institute

---

[10] In 1985, the 'Ministry of Textiles' was carved out of the old Ministry of Commerce. NIFT is seen by the industry professionals I interviewed as the most prestigious fashion design institution in the country. It now has fifteen educational institutions in India, (http://www.nift.ac.in/theinstitute.html). Before NIFT was established, courses in sewing, pattern-making and so forth were held at a number of polytechnics in the major cities. In 1993, the private institute, Pearl Academy of Fashion, was established by the export house in Delhi. It is the oldest and most famous of a growing number of schools and institutions offering fashion design and other fashion industry related programmes of varying quality. By 2005, there were ninety-three institutes in various Indian cities offering at least one program in fashion (or apparel or textile) design (Khaire 2011: 353). Amongst the people I encountered in the fashion industry, NIFT was viewed as the most prestigious owing to its strict tests and entry procedures.

of Fashion Technology (NIFT) in Delhi[10]. While the fashion design programme was the first to launch, the stated aim and goal of NIFT was to provide the newly reformed export sector with skilled technical and creative labour, which could aid the growth and competitiveness of the textile industry. As one member of the founding NIFT faculty explained:

> The Industry was getting professionalized, and they [exporters] understood that if they have these trained people it makes a difference to their productivity, it makes a difference to their image also when they are interacting with international buyers and things like that. So I think we could safely say that it was a pleasant, let us say... a fortunate coincidence that the industry's growth and NIFT's development coincided.

In this quote, my informant equates the industry's growth with the development of a field and market for designer fashion in India, something which NIFT consciously nurtured from the outset:

> We were not just producing people to cater to the industry. We were trying to create professionals who could be future entrepreneurs, because that is how the industry grows. If you have, if you create that vision, then you are able to expand the industry in a different way. But if you only create workers and people who could just manufacture, then you are very much limited in your development.

On the website, the opening of NIFT is described as a 'turning point in the Indian fashion industry'[11] and, as far as I am aware, it is the first time the term 'Indian fashion industry' is used in India in an institutional and official context. The focus on design and design competences as a governmental development strategy was, however, not born with NIFT. In 1958, the government commissioned Charles and Ray Eames to write a report on how best professional design education could be established in India in the aid of small-scale industries, in order to upgrade quality, which was seen as deteriorating with the increased industrialisation. The report, which was based on a three-month fieldtrip around India by the Eames', resulted in the government setting upinstigating the National Institute of Design (NID) in Ahmedabad in 1961, under the Department of Commerce and Industry. While NID offered courses in textile design, there was no focus on fashion, or fashion design[12]. The focus of this institution was to upgrade industrial, product and textile design and to showcase, mainly to a national audience, India's modernisation. Many of the first faculty members at NIFT were graduates from NID's textile design programme, and the framing of design as an aid to small and micro industries is echoed in the ethos of NIFT and its support of the handloom and craft sectors (Khaire 2011).

---

[11] http://www.nift.ac.in/delhi/
[12] Recently, due to the growth of the fashion industry, NID has started offering courses in apparel design. The word 'fashion' is, to date, not used in the NID prospectus.

NIFT served both to legitimise and professionalise the burgeoning Indian fashion industry and firmly establish the role of the designer as 'creative genius' and author, not to be confused with widely used and popular *darzee's* (the colloquial term for small shops offering custom tailoring). NIFT's desire is to produce professionals who can compete in a global fashion industry. In the words of a visiting professor from Fashion Institute of Technology in New York, who was advising the government and providing technical assistance in the setting up of NIFT: *'We want them to have this Indian heritage, this Indian feeling. But we want the clothes to be international'*[13]. In other words, Indian designers should be 'Indian' but make 'international' fashion.

As traditional garments were largely unstitched, fashion designers were taught Western patternmaking and took their cues from the Western industry. In terms of cuts and silhouettes, the 'Indian' element was largely limited to *kurtas, churidars, sherwanis, lenghas, salwar Kameez* and *sari* blouses. During my interviews, many interviewees expressed that, for a designer trained in Western patternmaking (which is all about fits and cuts), Indian-wear can be unchallenging as it is mostly about surface embellishments. Also, many saw the flourishing *darzee* industry, with its skilled tailors, as masters of occasion wear and were not initially motivated to enter a segment that their design education had not trained them in. Pursuing Indian wear in the early days of NIFT was by many considered uncreative and therefore perceived by most students and the faculty as low-status, unserious and 'not really fashion'. This framing of 'fashion' as 'international' and therefore not a term applicable to Indian wear was echoed in the narratives of many of the designers I interviewed. Often, they framed the custom-made garments they made for the highly lucrative wedding and trousseau market – the fastest growing segment of the designer fashion industry[14] – as boring and treated this segment as a survival strategy that compromised their 'professional and creative identity'.

This points to an initial tension between cosmopolitan ideals of fashion as international and the perceived creative limitations of Indian styles and fashion markets. While academics often have a tendency to see this tension as the result of larger structural, inherently Orientalist bias, within the industry, which actors internalise (as does Nagrath (2003) in her review of the Lakme Indian Fashion Week, for example), I propose

---

[13] http://www.nytimes.com/1989/06/21/style/new-fashion-school-in-india-draws-from-a-rich-heritage.html
[14] The Wedding and trousseau segment is estimated to be worth 38 billion dollars (Amed 2013).

that we take a deeper look and actually engage with the reasons and strategies the actors themselves put forward. The designers I encountered were all highly aware and self-reflexive about their often-precarious and unstable role as 'Indian' designers, poised between their own creative ambitions and global and national fashion and identity discourses (See also Skov 2003 for a rare study of designers' positions in new fashion centres).

## Designers as Revivalists and Socially Responsible Citizens: The craft story

The 'Indian' elements of 'Indian fashion' were initially established by NIFT and early designer framings. Indian textiles, preferably handloom, and the use of indigenous craft techniques and elements in a revived and contemporised form became synonymous with fashion value in India. NIFT encouraged the link between fashion and craft by making 'Craft Documentation'[15] a mandatory part of the curriculum and by offering a final show[16] award for the best use of traditional craft. In the words of a founding faculty member:

> ... apart from the very industry oriented curriculum, we introduced craft documentation because we felt India's craft base is very strong. It is almost... sort of intricately woven with our lives, with our lifestyle, with what we do and what we wear. So, craft documentation will be important for them to know what their culture is. They may know what fashion in Paris is, what fashion in New York is, or what business internationally is. But if you do not know what your country can offer, then again, your knowledge and understanding is very superfluous. And the whole idea for us, to have these designers, these professionals was that they should be holistic, that they should know the strengths of their own country, they should be visionaries.

By putting 'Craft Documentation' on the curriculum in fashion education, the government signalled their commitment to link the new insti-

---

[15] In the early years of NIFT Craft Documentation took place in the first year while the second year had an industry internship and the third year had students prepare their final collections. The practice of Craft documentation is also followed at most of the private schools offering fashion education.

[16] Until 2003 the government sponsored a fashion show for all graduating designers. As it was the only official fashion event until 2000, the show was a high profile event. At the show awards were given for 'Best design collection', 'Most creative collection', 'Best use of traditional crafts', 'Best Mens Wear', 'Best Womans wear' and an academic award on the overall performance during the three years. The jury at the NIFT award ceremonies consist of industry professionals, well-established fashion designers and people from the art world. The awards are often part or fully sponsored by industry players. After 2003, with the opening of more NIFT centres budgets were cut and students had to find their own sponsors for the show whereas in the earlier years the cost of the show was borne by NIFT and the student had to cover the cost of developing a collection or find their own sponsors. In 2003 the 'North East Award' was introduced.

tution to the cultural model of 'craft for national development' and the values of post-independence national development goals. This link also justified the development of an elite institution, one berated by critics as having no legitimacy or relevance in a poor and developing country. Through this link Fashion could work *for* the Nation.

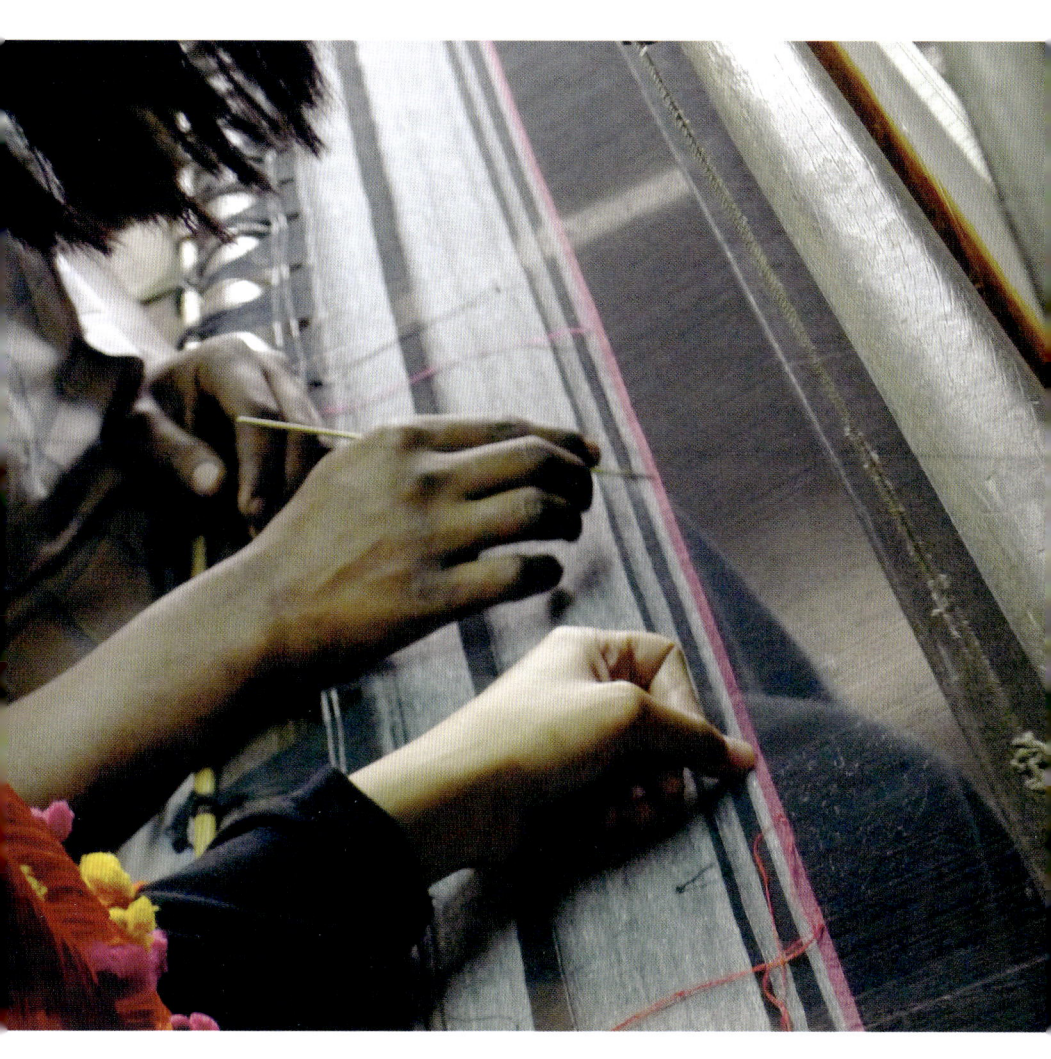

A designer is working with weavers in West Bengal on developing unique fabrics for her collection. For many designers, unique hand-woven fabric is an important selling point. The fact that they can also, in this way feel, connected to Gandhian ideals of craft revival makes the activity even more meaningful. This designer is developing Jamdani. There is a faint white outline of a pattern (butti) on the black warp. Based on this, the weaver inserts an extra weft on area inside the outline, which will form the design. It is a time-consuming technique, which renders both sides of the fabric smooth and free of floats.

Government support in developing a fashion industry by educating creative workers to harness and enhance national crafts and textile traditions as a project of national development should not be underestimated. In many of my interviews with designers concerning their education and careers, craft documentation was mentioned: both as an educational experience and also, for those with an urban upbringing, as an eye-opener regarding the living conditions and life-worlds of fellow Indians. In my interviews with NIFT and Pearl faculty, craft documentation was seen as instrumental in shaping designers aesthetics and giving them a sound ground knowledge of India's competitive advantage in the international fashion industry. In 2006, the Parliament passed the National Institute of Fashion Technology (NIFT) Bill 2005. The bill granted NIFT statutory status and empowered the institute to award its own degrees and other academic distinctions. Furthermore, it put NIFT on the Parliament of India's coveted list of 'Institutes of National Importance': *'With the passing of the Bill, NIFT will get a statutory status and will formally recognize the contribution and pre-eminent role played by the premier institution for its leadership role in the fashion industry, business and crafts.'* (Press Information Bureau, Government of India, 22nd May 2006)[17].

Fashion, craft and business are discursively linked and the understanding of their mutual relevance and interdependence – for fashion professionals, the media and consumers – rests on the enduring salient cultural models of development, national identity and responsibility rooted in Gandhi-Nehruvian ideas of stewardship and patronage, along with the value of creative authorship anchored in the role of the (Indian) designer.

Detailed shot of a dress by the designer Sabyasachi Mukherjee. He is known for his signature mix of a variety of hand-worked surface embellishments; here, embroidery, appliqué and kantha. In the 2013 edition of Delhi Couture week, the Sabyasachi show opened the event.

---

[17] http://pib.nic.in/newsite/erelease.aspx?relid=17995

Detailed shot of a dress by the designer Sabyasachi Mukharjee. He is known for his signature mix of a variety of hand-worked surface embellishments; here, embroidery, appliqué and kantha. In the 2013 edition of Delhi Couture week, the Sabyasachi show opened the event.

## Fashion's Eco-system

Initially, the category of 'designer fashion' was introduced by entrepreneurs in pre-NIFT Delhi in the early to mid-1980s and was used to refer to Indian and Indo-Western styles. The self-taught designer Ritu Kumar was the first to set up a boutique shop under her own label in India. Her extensive work in documenting Indian costumes and dress, as well as her revival and use of craft traditions, coupled with the international recognition of her work, has made her a role (and business) model for many younger designers I spoke to. She is well known by everybody in, and beyond, India's fashion world, where she has attained status as 'the Mother of Indian fashion'. Many of these 'early entrepreneurs' were, like Ritu Kumar self-taught designers, although some of them had received a design education, or worked in the fashion industry abroad and set up studios and retail spaces on return to India. In 1989, Hauz Khas Village, an urban village in South Delhi, was becoming one of the trendiest and most expensive shopping areas for designer clothing and boutiques.

Fashion shops at Hauz Khas Village. A lot has changed since Hauz Khas Village became a designer hub in the mid-1980s. Some of the original fashion boutiques opened are still there, and new ones have surfaced. Now the village is an enclave of cafes, restaurants and bars and a variety of shops selling trendy accessories.

Haus Khaz Village is also only a couple of kilometres away from where NIFT was inaugurated in 1987, so students could easily visit the new hub of designer fashion and browse through the offerings. For the first fashion designer pioneers, it was important to distinguish themselves from the local *darzee* establishments, which offered custom-made outfits. They had to establish their authority as fashion experts and personal style consultants, which they often legitimised by their links to foreign fashion industries or markets.

While many Indian men had adopted Western styles of clothing during colonial times, the *sari* or *salwar kameez* were still the most common attire for Indian women in the late 1980s. At this time, the retail landscape consisted of local *darzee* tailor shops where most women bought sari blouses and *salwars* stitched of fabric that they had bought at fabric shops, craft *melas,* handloom exhibitions or *Khadi bhandars.* The market for 'off-the-rack' was almost non-existent and consisted mainly of export rejects of Western styles, until the emergence of the first multi designer stores, like Ogaan (the first to offer ready-made designer fashions). The practice of buying fabrics and saris, and having outfits made from scratch meant that many women were knowledgeable about fabric qualities and weaves, the cost of materials, and the labour processes involved in creating both everyday wear and the extensively adorned outfits made for weddings and occasions. This elaborate wedding and occasion wear was often inspired by outfits worn by Bollywood actresses in films and fashion tips printed in women's Magazine's like *Femina* (published in English from 1959) and *Sarita* (published in Hindi from 1945). While there was no dedicated fashion magazines or press in India until the early 1990s, Femina started covering designers and their boutiques in the late 1980s as well as publishing an annual book on fashion.

The fact that the consumers were often well-informed of the processes of garment production posed a challenge to the early designers; it was difficult to justify 'designer prices' before the role of the designer as a 'creative genius' and the value of fashion design as an industry and creative field became firmly established and widely shared. To foster this development, NIFT faculty, together with industry professionals and a group of alumni from its fashion design department took the initiative to establish the Fashion Design Council of India (FDCI)[18] in 1998. This move was motivated by a perceived need to organise the disparate fashion design industry and aid it in achieving separate industry status and

---
[18] http://www.fdpc.in/, http://www.fashionfoundation.in/about_ffi.php
[19] An industry thrived on designer 'knock-offs' and copies/ interpretations of Bollywood costumes in cheap fabrics.

recognition. It was important for designers to distinguish themselves from the growing low price, 'off-the-rack' domestic garment industry[19]. In the 1990s, independent fashion designers hosted individual fashion shows and events in order to attract the bourgeoning fashion press; potential costumers, and establish themselves as 'real' designers. While the network of fashion professionals and cultural intermediaries was slowly growing and becoming increasingly organised (i.e. the fields of modelling; styling, fashion photography,; fashion journalism, and dedicated fashion magazines) it was difficult and expensive for designers to mobilise these scattered networks of professionals.

Modelled on the Parisian institutional platform, the mandate of the council was to use the Fashion Week format as a means of promoting the business of independent fashion design in India: aimed at both domestic and international buyers and audiences. The creation of the Council enjoyed the support of the Ministry of Textiles, again based on the premise that nurturing this field would help revive and support handlooms and crafts and create employment.

The Fashion Design Council of India thanks the Textile Ministry of the Indian government for support on billboards displayed at the Wills Lifestyle India Fashion Week in Delhi, Spring 2012.

In 2000, The FDCI hosted the first ever Lakme Indian Fashion Week, in cooperation with the media firm IMG,[20] in a five-star hotel in Delhi. In 2005, Lakme and FDCI parted ways. Lakme aligned itself with IMG to host Lakme Fashion Week in Mumbai; while the FDCI continued as organiser of India Fashion Week in Delhi. The FDCI is seen by industry actors as having been instrumental in developing and legitimising the field of high fashion and establish the founding designer members as industry pioneers.

---

[20] IMG is the world's largest producer of fashion events and involved in organising New York Fashion Week (http://www.imgworld.com/about/default.sps). Having a global industry player like IMG organising the first ever India fashion week helped legitimise the event.

The FDCI's Fashion Weeks, along with the Lakme Fashion Week in Mumbai, serve both a very practical purpose, in affording designers an organised 'one-stop' platform from where to launch their collections and establish positions, and also as an important sense-making arena in the fashion world. These events are seen by designers as the place to network; pick up the latest insider information, and as instrumental arenas for the nurturing of networks with peers and 'support personnel' (models; stylists; the media; fashion buyers, and, indeed, the FDCI staff).

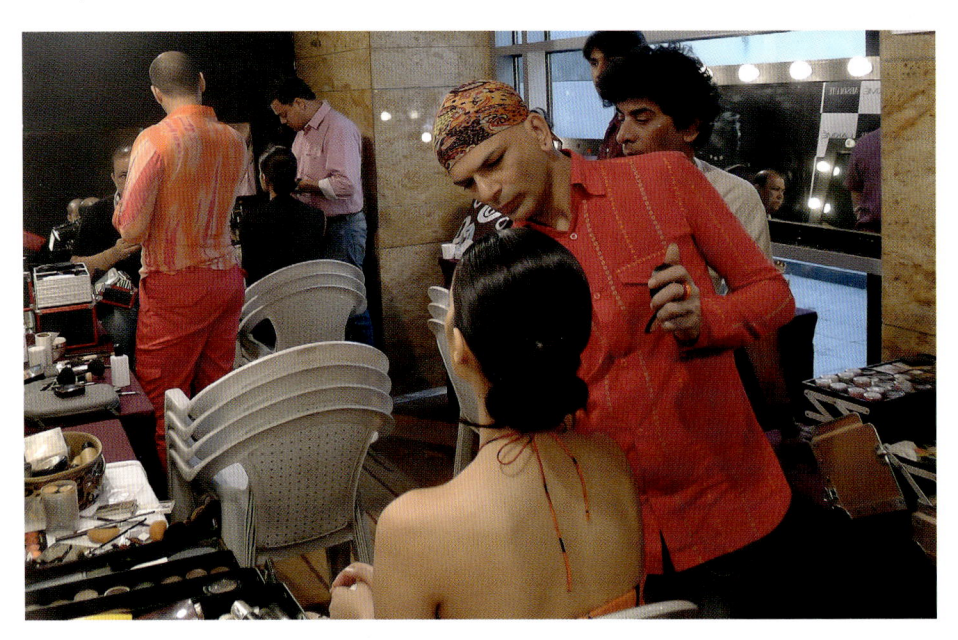

Backstage at Lakme Fashion Week, the support personnel of the fashion world; stylists and models at work: Lakme Fashion Week Winter/Festive 2011. Lakme Fashion Week has adjusted its format and now has two seasons: Winter/Festive and Summer/Resort. This format is intended to be more retail friendly as it shows fashions, which, for the most part, can be supplied by designers within a few months. The Winter/Festive Fashion Week takes place in August and shows designs for the Winter/festive season, which starts around the beginning October, from when the majority of weddings typically start. Most marriages in India take place from October/November until around February and the biggest festival, Diwali, also takes place in October or November.

As one designer put it at Lakme Fashion Week: *'This is where I see the industry and what's happening and show them where I am at. It is not just about sales and the show. Being here makes me feel connected to fashion and gives me a feeling that I know what is going on.'*

For younger designers, participation in Fashion Week launched their careers and positioned them as legitimate industry members, worthy of press attention and as members of the design fraternity. Many started at the subsidised shows, the High Five (in Delhi) and Gen Next (in Mumbai), which provide a platform for new designers. Participation in Fashion Weeks was also seen by the younger designers as a way to learn how to manage the all-important networking game and how to attract the attention of the press. As one designer recalls:

> I reach there for the press-con, which was 5-6 days before the fashion week began, and I get to know that I don't have a publicist, and damn, there is nobody talking about me. But thankfully, my work was good and the press was there, but you have to have somebody. I mean, people will look at your work, but there are so many people, the journalists get confused. There has to be somebody who can go to them and give them the right information. So you need to be chaperoned. And that is the way it is done. So I did not have anyone. I came back, and I was like, 'hey I need to have a publicist.' So I went to somebody, who charged me the earth, because again, they knew that I knew nothing about this. I paid a bomb, for just that one week of work. And trust me, I took over the entire fashion week.

The FDCI, together with different sponsors, now hosts bi-annual prêt weeks for women's wear, the Wills Lifestyle India Fashion Week, which, together with the Lakme Fashion week, are the main fashion weeks. Here, the show schedule is coupled with a trade section of designer stalls, where designers can present their collections to buyers and peers.

Wills Lifestyle India Fashion Week SS/2012. The event is hosted by the Fashion Design Council India and sponsored by Wills Lifestyle, a domestic multi-brand fashion retailer. Wills Lifestyle also invite a handful of designers to collaborate on pieces that are then retailed from their shops. In this way, they promote their image as a fashion-driven retailer and make designer fashions available to mall shoppers across the country.

In 2009, FDCI launched a dedicated week for men's fashion: the Van Heusen India Men's Week. Since 2010, the annual Synergy 1 Delhi Couture Week has also been added to the annual fashion calendar. The Couture Week is mainly aimed at the vast and growing wedding and trousseau market and is a celebrity event, dedicated to Indian occasion wear. While the other fashion weeks are open to fashion design members of the FDCI, and Lakme has their own application procedure, this event is by FDCI invitation only. The participating designers are well-established industry veterans who use the event as an image-creating and networking platform, rather than as a direct business opportunity. Renaming this segment for Indian occasion wear 'Haute Couture' is a clever move on the part of the FDCI as it associates the event with high fashion and sets it apart from the countless commercial Bridal expositions, which cater to this market.

Bollywood star Arjun Rampal flirting with the press wearing a T-shirt with the writing 'SHOW STOPPER' at the Rohit Bal finale show, Delhi Couture Week 2011. Showstoppers are Bollywood stars or high profile celebrities who walk the ramp, usually at the end of a fashion show, creating a media and audience frenzy. The T-shirt is a pun on the whole 'show stopper' tradition and thus allows the designer to critically comment on this while still adhering with the industry convention and giving the audience what is expected.

A lot has changed since the 1980s. While the *sari*, the *salwar kameez* and the CKD[21] continue to be extremely popular and the most widely used garments by Indian women in general, the ready-to-wear and 'off-the-rack' designer fashion market for Indian clothing has taken off and developed. Foreign fashion and luxury brands have entered the Indian market in a steady stream and a great many young and urban Indian women are freely mixing Western, Indo-Western and Indian styles. Fashion, as a market segment, creative field and highly-mediated figured world, has made the role of the designer well established. The fashion eco-system, complete with support personnel, twelve dedicated fashion magazines, including Vogue – which entered India in 2007 along with a fashion press, fashion TV and fashion news and page 3[22] in national newspapers, has evolved at an impressive speed. The number of fashion shops has increased dramatically and gained a presence in cities and towns across the country. E-tailing, fashion blogs and bloggers and social media as industry tools have also appeared on the scene. However, where do these changes, fostered by the institutionalisation and professionalisation of the field of fashion in the wake of economic reforms, leave the independent designer? How do designers position themselves and devise workable strategies at the intersection of this 'new' India fashion landscape? How do they draw on industry scripts and shared cultural models to manage the precarious balance between the values of fashion as a creative field, business success, and their role as mediators – of fashion and of national responsibility - with the power to dress the nation anew.

The designers I interviewed drew on a shared industry story of the role of the designer in India's field of fashion. The vast majority of them related their own biographies to the master narrative of the designer as a self-made entrepreneur who, by hard work and creative vision, has managed to take advantage of the opportunities offered in a 'New' India in a socially responsible manner (as epitomised in the story designer Ritu Kumar). The role of the designer as 'creative genius' is so important to the understanding of fashion that all designers use their name as the label. One NIFT designer told me that he had applied to both FDCI and Lakme with a brand and was refused: they suggested that he re-applied with the same collection but under his own name instead of a brand name.

---

[21] CKD is the term used for a set of *Churidaar, Kurta and Dupatta*.
[22] Page 3 in the biggest newspapers in India has gossip and celebrity news and often features coverage of designers and fashion related news. Page 3 has become a colloquial term for celebrity news.

Apart from the famous designers, whose factories are generally located in the industrial areas of Okhla or Gurgaon, most of my informants have smaller studios in the Shapur Jat or Lado Sarai areas of South Delhi, close to NIFT. Here the rents are manageable and there is an infrastructure of dyers, shops selling trims and materials, printers, embroidery units and so on, which is well suited to cater to the production of the relatively small quantities that most designers work with. The fact that these areas have become 'designer hubs' also allows designers to create support networks with their peers to better cope with the many challenges that running a studio presents, like the occasional sharing of resources and sometimes even labour. The cost of setting up an independent studio is relatively small, a fact that was framed as a competitive advantage for Indian designers. A NIFT faculty explains:

> We are very fortunate. We have access to tailors, we have access to fabric, we have access to embroideries, and our design students can actually start small, with very small budget. And many of our designers have done that. For instance, many studios which are doing extremely well today, started so small that the designers, because they didn't have funds, started their own cutting, with maybe one tailor who did their stitching, they did their own PR, small studio workshops, in very, very, let us say, backward little market places. Because they did good quality work, they got noticed, and the business grew from there. So you need talent.

While it was undoubtedly a lot easier to get noticed when the industry was new and competition limited, the shared stories of the humble beginnings of most of the successful designers motivates many young designers to start their own independent businesses. Some designers start labels in their own names, backed by export houses. Many of the younger and not so well established designers struggle with a retail environment based on a consignment mode of selling, many sustain and fund their participation in Fashion Weeks by catering to private clients and the Indian wedding and occasion wear segment of the industry. The strategy of turning to the Indian fashion and occasion segment was one that all designers I interviewed had either already pursued or had plans of tapping into. For the ones who identified themselves as Western wear designers, this strategy was employed reluctantly and often accompanied by regret that doing Western wear alone is not a viable business strategy in India 'yet'. Several of the designers I interviewed, who catered to private clients narrated this work as a sometimes highly stressful experience: characterised by a feeling that they had to compromise their design sensibilities and professional fashion identities.

However, the majority of the independent designers also made big profits on private clients and enjoyed designing for them when 'sensibilities matched'. The fact that the Indian wear segment of the industry accounts for more than 70 % of designer wear revenues makes this a valid assumption supported by the experience of designers (Khaire 2011: 356). For small independent designers the shift from small orders on consignment and catering to a few private clients to making it in the centre of the fashion world is a difficult task; one that must be 'cracked with the assistance of the media'. One designer describes a turning point in her career:

> ... the first show I did, I had the most chaotic time. My back end was really wobbly, things had totally crashed, collapsed, everything was crazy. I finished my collection and I sat down and make my headgear. I said, 'hey I need to have something interesting, on the ramp. And this collection was called 'High on Chai', and I got my guys to go and buy me all those little knick-knacks from a chai stall: the big kettles, the smaller ones, the typical glasses in which you drink tea on a roadside chai stall, those racks in which they carry glasses, all those things. And I just came up with these crazy headgears with those things. Just sat 2 days or 1 day before fashion week and I made them by myself. And I still remember, the front page. It said, 'Creativity Outburst, finally'. That is what HT City[23] read, with that show. And it was on the fifth day. First show on the last day or the finale day. I think I got more space than the finale show did.

The way in which this designer used *chai*, a symbolic and ritualised everyday 'Indian' phenomenon, on the catwalk to support a modern Indo-Western collection is a great example of effective 'matter out of place' branding that balances conceptual, cosmopolitan fashion logics and transforms into a highly nationally charged, modern fashion spectacle.

All the designers I talked to were acutely aware that in the highly competitive fashion world being well connected and endorsed by the right people (celebrities, the head of the FDCI, the fashion press, boutique owners, famous fellow designers, and museum curators) opens vital doors for sponsorships and high profile creative collaborations likely to create press and media coverage. In accordance with the resources available to them, most designers attempted to nurture industry networks in different ways: by hosting/actively participating in fashion and art-related events and actively wooing the press and important fashion gatekeepers.

A well-established industry practice is providing the right people with customised pieces. In the month before fashion week, one up-and-coming designer made custom dresses for the fashion editors of prestigious

---

[23] HT City is a section of the Hindustan Times, a daily English language newspaper founded in 1924. The paper has its roots in the independence movement and is the second biggest English daily (after Times of India).

magazines and boutique owners, which they then wore at Fashion week events. In his extremely contemporary and Western collection, he featured metallic fabrics woven by handloom. Another up-and-coming designer — the first to use steel in a hand woven fabric — has set up a design studio with a loom for the development of his fabric. He used this innovative technique in a collection launched at Wills Fashion Week. His use of a handloom for contemporary fashion fabrics earned him a great deal of press and media coverage, as well as the support of the FDCI, who, by giving him a show, also signals their continued allegiance to the values of fashion for development. The use of 'traditional' crafts and handloom textiles is such a well-established strategy for linking fashion to national identity and development that it entered the format of Lakme Fashion Weeks organisational set up in 2012: *'Be there to witness the resurgence of tradition and learn how the pace of the nation is guiding Indian design in a contemporary direction'.* (Lakme Fashion Week. The Daily, 4th March 2012).

The India Textile day is a high profile event with workshops and fashion shows, showing collections made exclusively of Indian textiles. At the Summer/Resort 2013, a designer showed an *All Khadi* collection 'celebrating rural India'. Seventy people, including more than thirty Bollywood stars, walked the ramp. The link between Khadi and nation is still salient and, although many designers before him have used Khadi on the ramp, this dedicated Khadi spectacle reaffirmed the salience of the link. The event allowed the designer to secure press coverage and participants (event organisers and sponsors, designers, celebrities and the media) to signal their simultaneous commitment to the values of a uniquely Indian heritage and of fashion as a category and validate the now attuned to the 'pace of the nation'.

The story of a 'New India' and of Indian fashion interweave categories of identity and difference rooted in the nationalist struggle and post-independence development strategies. In India, fashion discourses and practices are routinely yet creatively spun with a distinct 'national' thread. Indian fashion is anchored in a tale of a unique (marketable) 'unity in diversity' aimed at both domestic and international audiences. 'Indian fashion' and 'dress power' is its tradition and heritage, supported by a confident middle-class who are proud to be Indian and who, through their consumption patterns also connect with the craftsmen, workers and artisans who symbolise the 'old' nation. Fashion designers occupy a difficult position. They must carve out viable and creatively fulfilling business strategies, while contending with their role as mediators, stewards of the old and creators of the new.

# Bibliography

Barley, C. A. 1986. 'The Origins of swadeshi: Cloth and Indian Society, 1700-1930'. In Appadurai A. *The Social Life of Things: Commodities in Cultural Perspective.* Cambridge University Press.

Bean, S. 1989. 'Gandhi and Khadi: The Fabric of Indian Independence'. In A. B. Weiner and J. Schneider (Eds.) *Cloth and Human Experience.* Smithsonian Institution Press.

Breward, C. 2003. *Fashion.* Oxford University Press.

Bourdieu, P. 1993. 'Haute Couture and Houte Culture'. *Sociology in Question.* Sage. London.

Cohn, B. S. 1989. 'Cloth, Clothes, and Colonialism: India in the Nineteenth Century'. In A. B. Weiner and J. Schneider (Eds.) *Cloth and Human Experience.* Smithsonian Institution Press.

Craik, J. 1994. *The Face of Fashion: Cultural Studies in Fashion.* London: Routledge.

Dwyer, C. 2006. 'Fabrications of India: Transnational Fashion Networks'. In *Fashion's World Cities.* Berg Publishers

Gereffi, G. 1999. 'International trade and Industrial upgrading in the apparel commodity chain', *Journal of International Economics,* 48:1.

Jones, C. and Leshkowich A. M. 2003. 'Introduction: The Globalization of Asian Dress: Re-Orienting Fashion or Re-Orientalizing Asia'. In S. Niessen, A. M. Leshkowich and C. Jones (Eds.). *Re-Orienting Fashion: The Globalization of Asian Dress.* Berg Publishers.

Khaire 2011. 'The Indian fashion Industry and Traditional Indian Crafts'. *Business History Review.* 85, 345-366.

Löfgren, O. 2003. 'The New Economy: A cultural History'. *In Global Networks* 3: 3, 239-254.

Löfgren, O. 2005. 'Catwalking and Coolhunting: The Production of Newness'. In O. Löfgren of R. Williams (Eds.) *Magic, Culture and the New Economy.'* Berg.

Mohsini, M. 2011. 'Crafts, Artisans and the Nation State in India', in Clark-Decès, Isabelle (Ed.). *A Companion to the Anthropology of India.* Wiley-Blackwell Publishing.

Nagrath, S. 2003. '(En)countering Orientalism in High Fashion: A Review of India Fashion Week 2002'. *Fashion Theory,* 7: 3-4, 361-376.

Palmar, P. 2006. 'La Mode: Paris and the Development of the French Industry', in: P. Palmar and G.Didier (Eds.) 2006. *Fashion Show: Paris Style,* Hamburg: Ginko Press.

Skov, L. 2002. 'Hong Kong Fashion Designers as Cultural Intermediaries: Out of Global Garment Production, *Cultural Studies,* 16:4.

Skov, L. 2003. ''Fashion-Nation: A Japanese Globalisation experience and a Hong Kong Dilemma, in S. Niessen, A. M. Leshkowich and C. Jones (Eds.) 2003. *Re-Orienting Fashion: The Globalization of Asian Dress.* Berg Publishers.

Skov, L. and Riegels, M. 2011 'Letters from the Editors'. *Fashion Theory,* 15: 2, 133-136.

Srinivasan T. N. 2011. *Growth, Sustainability, and India's Economic Reforms.* Oxford University Press.

Steele, V. 1988. *Oaris Fashion: A cultural History.* Bloomsbury Publishing.

Tarlo, E. 1996. *Clothing Matters: Dress and Identity in India.* Hurst and Co.

Tewari, M. 2006. 'Adjustment in India's textile and Apparel Industry: Reworking Historical Legacies in a Post-MFA world, *Environment and Planning, A.* 38:12, 2325 – 2344.

Tewari, M. 2008. Varieties of Global Integration: Navigating Institutional Legacies and Global Networks in India's Garment Industry. *Competition & Change*, 12: 1, 49-67.

Trivedi, L. 2007. *Clothing Gandhi's Nation: Homespun and Modern India.* Indiana University Press.

Venkatesan. S. 2009. *Craft Matters: Artisans, Development and the Indian Nation.* Orient Blackswan.

Wilson, E. 1987. *Adorned in Dreams: Fashion and Modernity.* Virago Press.

## Suggested Reading

Fernandes, L. 2006. *India's New Middle Class: Democratic Politics in an Era of Economic Reform.* Oxford University Press.

Mathur, S. 2011. *India by Design: Colonial History and Cultural Display.* Orient BlackSwan.

Mazarella, W. 2003. *Shoveling Smoke: Advertising and globalization in Contemporary India.* Duke University Press.

Riello, G. 2009. *How India Clothed the World: The World of South Asian Textiles, 1500-1850.* Brill.

Riello, G. and McNeil, P. (Eds.) 2010. *The Fashion History Reader: Global Perspectives.* Routledge.

Riello, G. 2013. *Cotton: The Fabric that made the Modern World.* Cambridge University Press.

Rocca, F. 2009. (Ed.) *Contemporary Indian Fashion.* Damiani.

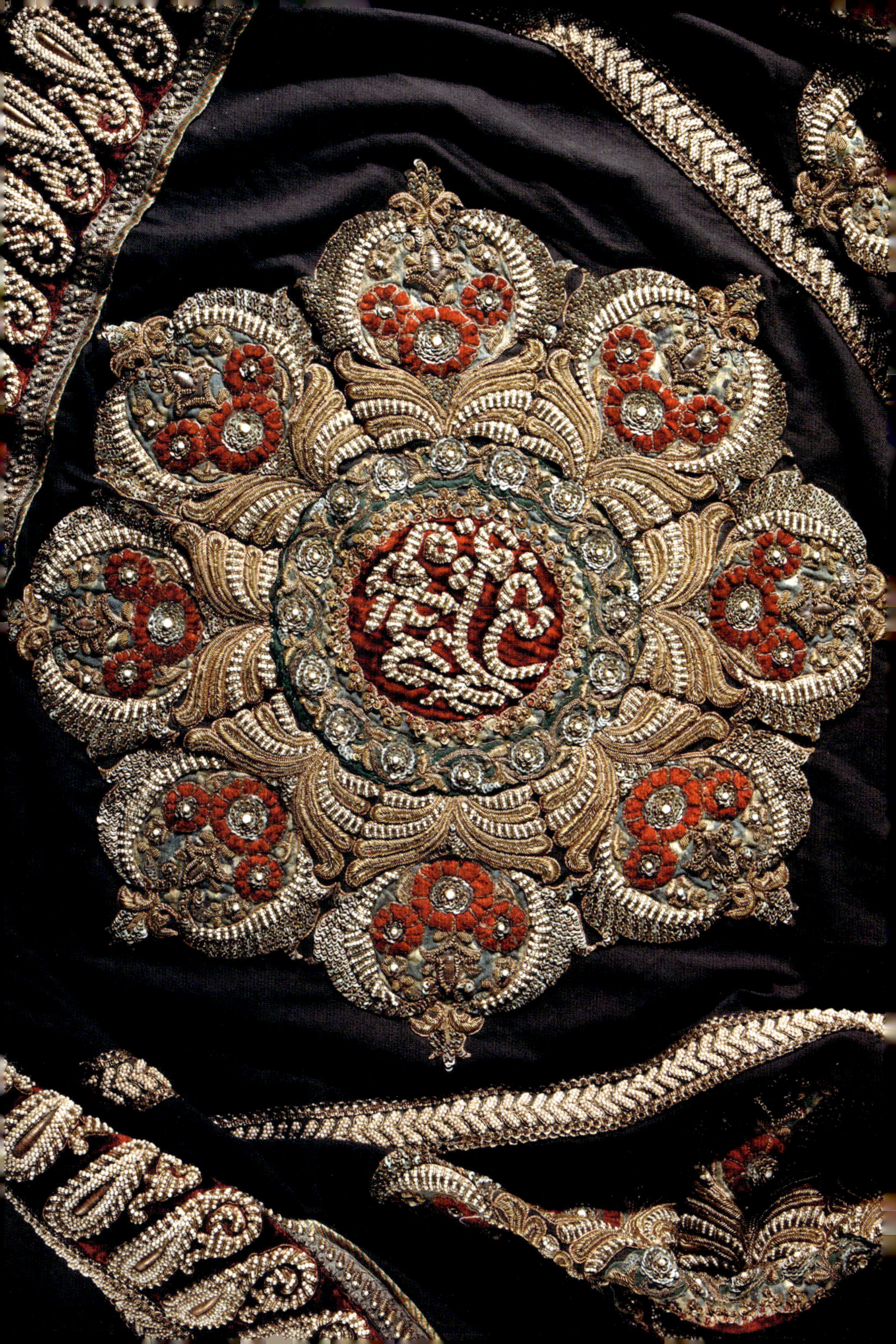

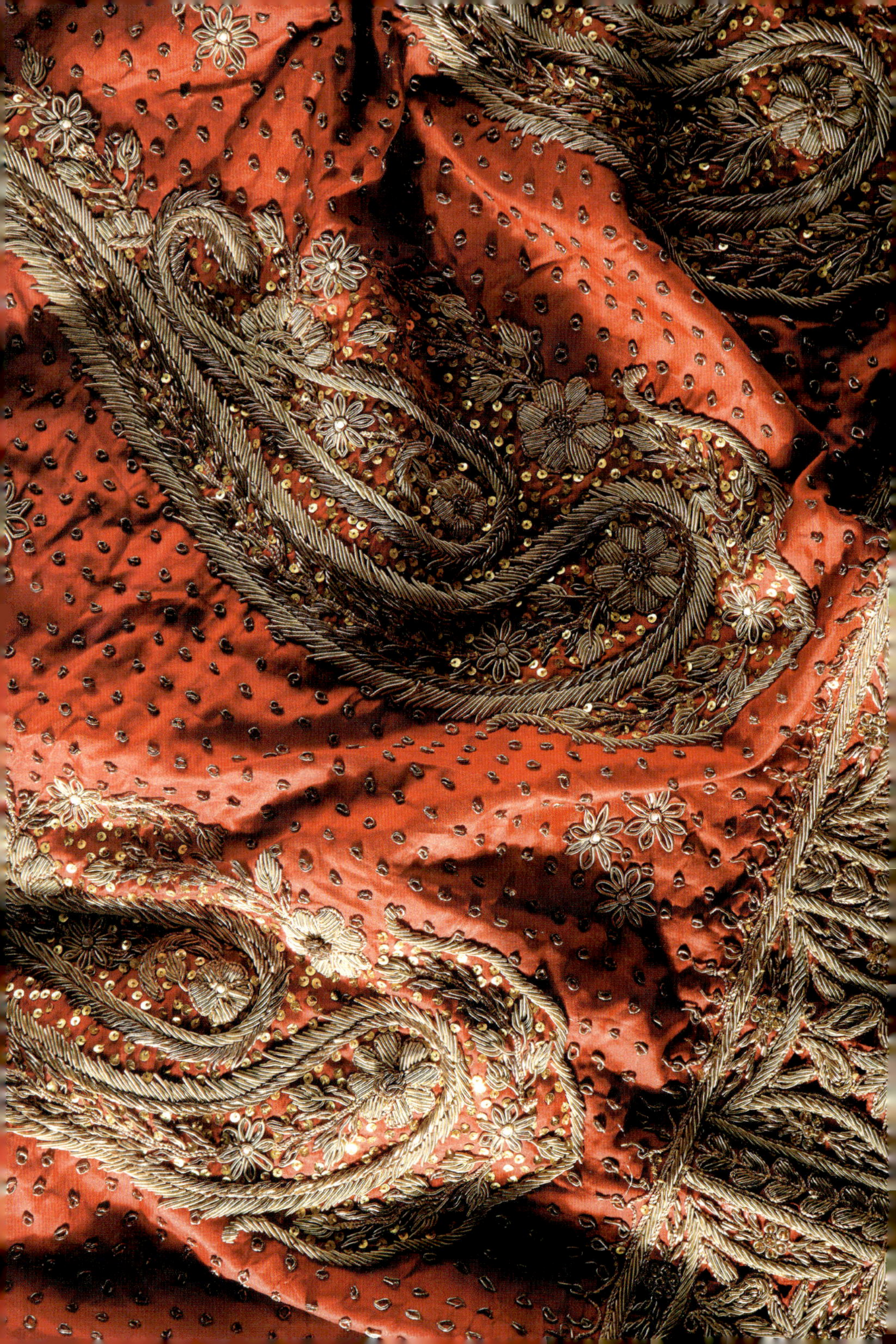

# Memories of Luxury, Aspirations Towards Glamour, and Cultivations of Morality
How south Indian Muslim women craft their style

Caroline Osella

## Introduction

Among Muslims in Calicut[1] (a town in Kerala, South India), neither the strict observance of Islamic reformist dress codes, nor even their binding to the South Indian region's wider sense of modesty and simplicity as a valued marker of distinction (against allegedly 'loose' North Indian public moralities and displays), in any way work to cut women off from a keen interest in beauty, fashion and glamour. In fact, shopkeepers and popular discourse alike characterise Muslim women as distinguished by their exceptionally high spending on personal adornment and by their particularly strong interest in clothes and jewellery. As I settled into this community during long-term fieldwork and learned to adapt my own preferences concerning fabric, colour, degree and style of embellishment – in order to 'fit in' better at Muslim weddings and parties – I also began to discern specificities in aesthetics and to ask about about this[2]. Shopkeepers and non-Muslims alike claimed to recognise a particular Muslim aesthetic: flashy, prone to excess and showy. All of these were thinly euphemised codes for 'vulgar'.

At the same time, non-Muslims also lamented the increased adoption of reformist dress styles. The lower middle-class women and girls I spent my time with were always in 'proper Islamic modest dress' (Osella C & F 2007). This usually means a floor-length loose house-dress indoors, which covers arms down to below the elbow; and an outdoor outfit, which masks body shape and covers all except the hands and face. Outerwear might be the old-style loose dark coat (referred to locally as *pardah*) with *maftah* [headscarf] or the newer Gulf-style *abaya* [fitted black coat] and *shaila* [long soft black scarf][3]. Under this outerwear, older women wear *saris* and younger prefer *salwar kameez*[4] , a long loose tunic worn over loose drawstring trousers. Women are very careful about

---

[1] Calicut and Bombay are older names with colonial lineages, and have been replaced officially by Kozhikode and Mumbai. I choose to follow the usage of research interlocutors, who are holding on to the older names.
[2] Two years' fieldwork was funded by ESRC; the period of writing-up was funded by AHRC. Thanks for comments on drafts go to: A. Moores, E. Tarlo, F. Osella, T. Kuldova.
[3] The *abaya* is the Gulf Arab version of *pardah* dress, a Muslim women's long dark outer garment worn over clothing.

maintaining a *decent* appearance, decent being a layered concept into which colonial Victorian ideals, post-colonial and, specifically, regional ideas about South Indian feminine modesty (Devika 2005), and post-1930s successive waves of Islamic reformism have all set certain clear boundaries and expectations.

One analytic predicament is that, as Tereza Kuldova has argued (n.d.), the Indian fashion business blurs several lines which both academic analysis and often consumers and producers would rather keep clearly separate. High-end fashion and vernacular style engage in mutual borrowings, a process which is intensified by the power of film to pick up and spread trends. In an economy where the 'ready made' mass clothing market still lags behind individually produced pieces, the figure of the tailor – as a humble paid servant – and that of the designer-producer – as a high-status creative – likewise blur into each other.

Another paradox is that adornment has been understood in academia as a preoccupation especially associated with the feminine, a gender style stamped with abjection and marginality to the proper business of life, something then at once trivial and also associated with subaltern subjects, one of the compensatory activities of those who are excluded from real power and activity in the world (Lunning 2001). It has also – contrarily – been understood as world-making practice, as a form of cosmic ordering and an expression of timeless and universal principles (Papapetros 2011). It has recently also been read as part of 'erotic capital', an asset which can be cashed in on employment, marriage and other markets (Hakim 2010). I will sidestep these debates here, to follow here one simple theme: tracing some of the ways in which corporeal materiality and embodiment are expressive and self-making processes (Van Wolputte 2004), which I then understand as bearing the traces of entanglements in other realms, to different scales (following Strathern 2004). To clarify, global histories of trade, regional flows of money and faith-wide waves of revivalism have all left their material trace – even on the small scale of the individual body or a single piece of fabric. Calicut's Muslim women locate themselves simultaneously within worlds of Indian luxury and worlds of Islam – where the latter can draw upon both Islamicate ornateness and opulence and also reformist moralities and simplicity.

---

[4] This dress is now subcontinental-wide, although for formal occasions a *sari* is still required by married women. The *salwar* is the trouser part and the *kameez* is the long loose tunic worn on top. Calicut Muslims observe what they name as decent dress by wearing a long, loose, black overcoat on top of either a *sari* or *salwar-kameez*.

[5] Whether it is inhabited by women or by feminised, same-sex desiring or gender-queer males.

Contemporary desires for opulence, willing attachment to orientalising images of the self and of the historically close relationship with the fantasy Arab Other, together with cinematically driven identifications with stars and their dream-world of leisure and luxury all seep into a habitus already formed through a long history of Indian ocean trade, which brought Calicut's Muslims both fortune and intimate encounters.

## Vernacular Cosmopolitanism, Embodied Histories

Muslim women's practice in Calicut acts as material outpouring of histories that have spilled out onto the bodies of those who now live there. Bourdieu's work on consumption has helped us think about how yesterday's histories are lodged in our bodies in the form of today's preferences and tastes (e.g Bourdieu 1984). Calicut Muslim history is one of business and smuggling, fortunes which have waxed and waned, a profitable entanglement with the Gulf region and with Indian ocean trade which dates back to at least the 10$^{th}$ century, and rescue from post-independence economic doldrums via Gulf migration. The community here is part of the Indian ocean's coastal trading erstwhile elite and widespread culture of vernacular cosmopolitanism, something which we find in locations as widespread as Mombassa through to Zanizibar, Gujerat, Dubai and Malaysia, and all the other places which found themselves connected in a network through trans-oceanic travel and trade (Simpson & Kresse 2007; Vora 2013; see also Werbner 2008). If 'Muslim style' is recognised locally as leaning especially towards fantasies of opulence and extravagant display, this history – of a business community that has lived through some spectacularly prosperous moments – is influential.

With a population of roughly 500 000, Calicut is the third largest town in India's southern state, Kerala, and, even though Muslims do not comprise the majority, it is often called the 'Muslim capital' of Kerala. Calicut prospered due to maritime trade from the 10$^{th}$ to the 15$^{th}$ century, rapidly developing over the 12$^{th}$ and 13$^{th}$ centuries as a commercial hub between West Asia, Southeast Asia and the North-Western shores of South Asia. Upon Vasco da Gama's arrival here in 1492, a long and bloody struggle began to wrench away control of the pepper trade from the 'Moors', merchants from Egypt and the Arabian peninsula. The 17$^{th}$ century saw the wane of Portuguese power; the rise of Dutch companies and, at the turn of the 18$^{th}$ century, the Mysorean conquest of Malabar. During this period, Calicut lost its position as an international hub although remained an export centre for local products and an entry point for goods from West Asia and North India. The eventual defeat of Tippu Sultan and the establishment of British rule exacerbated this shift: Bombay developed as the main international export centre and Calicut trade was reduced predominantly to the movement of goods to, and through, Bombay and Gujarat. Emerging as a major regional rice market, Calicut also saw a resurgence of Arab trade. From the 19th century until the mid 1980s, the colonial and post-colonial economy boosted Calicut's position, the town became a world centre for timber export and, later, a centre for (legal) copra commerce and (illegal) gold-smuggling. By the late 1970s, the timber trade declined and, following the Gulf oil boom, Arab *dhow* ships stopped coming to the city, leading to the eventual closure of all port facilities. As in the rest of Malabar, and Kerala as whole, since the 1980s, Calicut's economy has become dependent upon revenues and remittances from the Gulf. Some entrepreneurs run trans-oceanic or Gulf-based businesses and a large number of migrant workers send cash back home (Osella F & C 2007).

Contemporary Calicut sprawls across several zones: the old commercial district of narrow lanes and beach-front *godowns* [warehouses] in the south-east, along and behind the sea front, gives way in importance to new and more spacious commercial zones further inland; new residential areas grow to the city's north and north-east. In the old district, right next to a densely populated Muslim 'old town', the small bazaar meanders, including the famous S.M. [sweet meats] street, where formerly famous halva was made and sold and where now a plethora of cheap and very fast-moving clothing businesses compete for mainstream trade. Most of Calicut's gold shops, from tiny one-man workshops to prestigious three-storey gold and diamond showrooms, are located off and around this zone. Away from the old town, several new areas are emerging, such as Mavoor Road, where concrete three-storeyed open shopping plazas are located or Cherooty Road, where franchises of prestigious chain brands (all-India shops like Raymond's Park Avenue or global brands like Lee jeans) sit beside costly boutiques offering one-off women's 'designer' saris and *salwar* sets – pieces of better quality fabric, hand-worked to individual designs produced by English-speaking middle-class owners who might have a professional design qualification or some higher level experience in Bangalore or Bombay, marking them off from the smaller local tailors. Unlike S.M. Street bazaar's mostly small, crowded and simple shops, run by one or two men, these post-1990s shops have air conditioning and glass frontage, uniformed assistants, and service professional and business-class clients who live in the more exclusive housing colonies.

Muslim aesthetics mixes strands from past and present flows of cultural influence: Calicut's cosmopolitan past and status as a smuggler's port and space for Arab sailors, traders, ship-owners, visitors, even sometimes lovers and husbands; ghosts of Calicut's past glory as a town of lavish wealth; participation in a rich media culture, woven from 'Bollywood' styles and Kerala movie fashions, from specific local Muslim arts and from attachments to fantasy ideas of specifically Muslim aesthetics (the gauzy veil, the henna decorated hand); and ideas about beauty, lifestyle and glamour which are continually pouring in from the Gulf.

## Muslim Style: Glamorous modesty
There is surely a certain exuberance regarding what is often named as 'Muslim style' and part of my understanding of this style is that it speaks of desire for a powerful presence via personal adornment. It therefore makes sense that Calicut's 'Muslim style' strongly overlaps with what in other locations might be understood as 'low class Hindu' style. Calicut desires for shine, impact, strong colour and eye-catching novelty design can be read – paradoxically – as indices of both richness and of poverty. It speaks to the past that I alluded to above of trade, wealth and social prestige, and to the fast cash of the present Gulf remittance economy, yet at the same time it is also part of an India-wide recognisable subaltern 'flashy' aesthetic, characterised by Srivastava as 'ishtyle' (as opposed to high-class 'fashion' (2007)[6]; which I've written about as being distinctive of low-prestige forms of conspicuous consumption, which are transient, body-centred and personal (Osella & Osella 1999).

In the realms of sexual morality and discussions of desire, South Indians cherish their self-proclaimed superior morality and 'simplicity' over North Indians; and even as Calicut Muslims prize Gulf items, fashions and habits, they adopt them selectively. Both the (imagined) North Indian metropolitan and the Arab woman act as dire figures of abjection or warning, an example of how the desire for glamour can lead one too far and into forms of self-presentation and then to behaviours which are *haram*. In the Arab Gulf states, we sometimes find the 'immodest modest', in the form of flashy *abayas*, body-hugging - albeit body-covering - clothing, and heavy use of cosmetics (Al-Qasimi 2010). By contrast, Kerala Muslims cultivate sets of body practices and conjure up desires and yearnings that gather carefully around only those aspects of adornment that are understood locally as not being *haram*. Therefore, women will not use makeup or nail varnish, but will engage in a frantically fast-moving fashion culture; they have adopted the stylish black *abaya* as outerwear, although not the most heavily embellished forms

---
[6] Kuldova has recently complicated this distinction, pointing out a shared fascination at the top and bottom ends alike of Indian markets with opulence, lavish work and display, epitomised in garments like a prestigious Sabyasachi sari (Kuldova n.d.).

of it. One interesting and specific effect of observing Islamic modesty norms of covering the *awra*[7] is that particular parts of the body can then become objects of attention and elaboration: glamour settles upon the hands and feet, in the form of henna, jewellery and fancy shoes.

## Hands ...

At Calicut Muslim weddings, the *vettilettu* or *mailanchi* night, a party at the bride's house the night before the reception proper, is as grand as the family can afford. Tubes and tubes of henna paste are bought, guests are invited and come richly dressed to stay at the bride's home for the entire evening, to enjoy a feast, to admire each other (in safely segregated space, such that women remove their outerwear (*abaya/pardah*) to show off their party-wear outfits) and in the mood to be entertained: an occasion for music and maybe even dance.

Learning to paint henna is a popular art among young women, and it can – for the skilled – become a respectable source of income later in life, a service offered from home to women and girls who have weddings or functions to attend. Sometimes community organisations offer courses or competitions. Women hone their skill in experimenting with henna powder and oil mixtures to produce different colours and long-lasting effects, offering ranges of designs. The photographs here show the subtle difference in designs offered as 'Indian' style or the increasingly more popular 'Arabic' style, which tends to have bolder and larger blocks of henna, covering the fingertips and nails, and to employ more abstract geometric patterning and cross-hatching, rather than using peacock or flower motifs. This is in line with Islamic injunctions against representational/figurative art, and with reformist desires to purge themselves of Hinduised practice and observe or claim what they perceive as more authentically Muslim forms; it also indexes exposure to 'Gulf style', as a form of sophistication and distinction.

## ... and Feet

Calicut Muslim women are often very shoe conscious and spend more on shoes; own more pairs; and have more elaborate and fancy pairs than their Hindu or Christian neighbours. Little girls are enthusiastic participants in this generalised feminine passion for shoes: they commonly wear high heels – this is sometimes noted with amusement by

---

[7] The part of the body that is, according to most understandings of Islam, to be kept covered. The *awra* is usually understood as the trunk and immediate surround, although often also extending along the limbs. The most common consensus among Calicut's Muslims is that only face, hands and feet can be shown in public.

Fig. 1: 'Araby' style henna

This was an entry in a henna hand painting competition run by an NGO in the Muslim area, and shows what Calicut Muslim women believe to be a more 'Arab' style, in that it uses heavy lines rather than lighter cross-hatching, completely covers the fingertips, and avoids any figurative motifs (flowers, hearts) in favour of strictly geometric patterning.

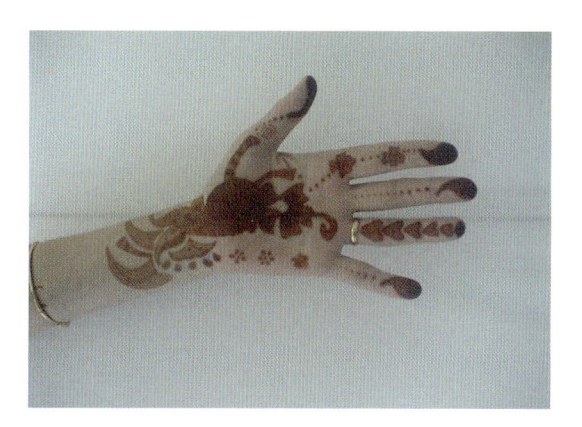

Fig. 2a: Hybrid style henna

In this design, there are some aspects which women claim as 'Arabic style': large blocks form strong contrast with empty space; the fingertips are heavily covered. There are also aspects which women associate more with Hinduised styles of henna: heart and flower motifs; fine cross-hatching.

Fig. 2b: Henna stencils available in stores, coming in from Bombay

In practice, of course, the designs used are a blend of those passed from woman to woman; taught in courses; copied from beauty parlours; seen in magazines and on the TV; carefully reproduced from stencils or pattern books coming from Bombay, along with a good dose of individual creativity and experimentation too (from the most skilled hand-painters). Once again, vernacular cosmopolitanism is at work – a variety of influences flows through and blends into innovative and attractive forms.

community outsiders – and may own three or four pairs of glamorous, glittery or shiny high-heeled shoes. Shoes, of course, like henna and bangles, are a permissible adornment, drawing the eye towards the body's peripheries and away from the modestly concealed central area. High-heeled shoes are especially interesting in that they offer an acoustic announcement of the feminine, an amplification of feminine presence. As work on the anthropology of the senses teaches, the dominance of the visual in the modern western is specific, and other senses may be equally important (Howes 1991). South Indian Hindu women commonly wear anklets, and the jingling they produce is both marked as a highly significant 'sound of femininity' and is also eroticised (as commonly depicted in films and songs). Reformist Muslim women often eschew anklets, but their high heels are essentially fulfilling a similar function.

Fig. 3: 'Women's shoes

While these shoes are 'party wear', even everyday footwear is often highly embellished and glamorous. Women follow fashions here too, as wedges give way to kitten heels, to stilettos, and so on.

Fig. 4: Girls' shoes

Little girls' shoes are often effectively scaled down versions of adult women's shoes.

## Getting a Rush from Gold

According to the World Gold Council, India is globally the largest gold market. Gold is a useful, quickly convertible, investment and durable commodity, perceived as safe and anonymous as currency, but with stronger value. It holds the glow of being an auspicious metal in Hindu traditions: harbinger of prosperity, beauty, good health and good fortune; it is an essential part of a bride's outfit (generally her dowry too) and is a major player in conferring solidity to the fantasies of luxury and opulence that emerge in full power at weddings. A low rate of tax on gold exchange and a competitive market with low, or no, surcharge means that gold in India holds – and lately substantially increases – its value as a near instantly liquid form of wealth, while still allowing women to use it as fashion item, in a fast-moving market of trading and changing jewellery.

Within India's seemingly inexhaustible love for gold, Kerala has 3 % of India's population, but a staggering 25 % of its gold market (The Hindu newspaper, December 6th 2012; see also Kerala page at 'Indian gold Trends' website). It is hardly surprising that in Calicut – a town partly built upon gold smuggling[8] Kerala state's famous and notorious appetite for gold reaches powerful proportions. Many Muslim families here have built their fortunes by way of the gold trade - licit and illicit - and the town is saturated with gold stores, from back lane bazaar artisans to three storeyed a/c showrooms. When I was asking about 'Muslim style', many people mentioned one aspect of it as being an even greater use of gold than other groups, and a preference for heavier-looking, more bulky pieces. The traditional Muslim grandmother's dress and jewellery is well known in films, folk art stage presentations and so on, and does indeed shine out boldly, with multiple helix piercings, many necklaces, and even a precious metal waist belt. In the present reformist moment, when Muslim men (against Kerala-wide trends in masculine adornment) eschew gold and generally use only a watch as decoration – at most a silver semi-precious stone ring – then the burden of carrying and displaying a family's objectified wealth falls more starkly upon its womenfolk.

While the bride at a contemporary wedding is naturally the most bedecked, because she is often wearing a large part of her dowry on her body, women guests too pull out all their gold for the occasion, and also

---

[8] This is common knowledge and even now still widely referred to with pride rather than embarrassment. The perils of gold smuggling and Calicut's part in this achieved literary fame in the novel Arabiponnu, NP Muhammad and MT Vasudevan Nair.

borrow to increase the effect. Those who feel a bit 'gold poor' might risk bulking up with one or two pieces of 22ct covered fake 'one gram gold' (see Varsha website and FIG 5).

Fig. 5: Fake, 22 ct covered 'rolled gold' or 'one gram gold'

A fake 22 ct covered 'rolled gold' or 'one gram gold' necklace, which looks like a classy piece of modern branded jewellery (such as Tanishq). This sort of piece can be used to 'bulk up' the appearance of how much gold is being worn as a wedding guest, and can be worn above the more traditional Kerala style long gold pendant chains or long necklaces.

There are classic pieces like bangles, which all women own at least a couple of.

Fig. 6: Bangles

Bangles vary in thickness and weight, and a bride will wear several sets at once. For everyday use, women often keep just one thin pair or a single thick bangle. A fairly minimal amount of gold to own use for everyday wear would be (in order of degree to which they are felt essential) earrings, a long neck chain with pendant plus bangles. Not to have any one of these three key items is felt as a shame, and even a working class and relatively badly off woman would not attend a wedding without wearing at least those three items.

Earrings are deemed essential and are often very large, albeit beaten thinly, to provide maximum effect at a minimal cost.

Fig 7: Earrings

A 'bridal set' comprises heavy and immensely costly pieces – even weighing up to half a kilogram. Only a bride would wear adornment such as this.

Fig. 8: Bridal 'set'

A 'bridal 'set' is designed to make maximum effect, by using gold hollow-moulded and spread very thinly. Kerala brides famously wear a lot of gold, and to wear five or six necklaces of different lengths – to achieve a 'step' – is absolutely expected. Usually not much heed is paid to whether the necklace styles blend in with each other, but in this set two have been provided which do match.

Novelty items are designed to allow more gold to be worn on the body, and to be talking points and thereby bring prestige.

Fig. 9: Gold fingernail or belt

In the attempt to find ever more novelty talking points and parts of the body to which gold can be attached, we have seen gold fake nails – attached to chains for safety – appear.

Although a wedding proper calls for real gold (or even fake gold), costume jewellery is also often worn to maximise the impact of glitter and colour. Such pieces are typical at pre-wedding henna nights, post-wedding dinners, and even at weddings (as a supplement to real jewellery). Mostly younger women (teenagers and newly-weds) use such fake rhinestone pieces for extra embellishment, typically alongside high style *salwaar kameez* sets, or high fashion embellished saris.

Fig. 10: Cocktail ring

At less formal functions and among younger women who are wearing maximum impact colours and designs of salwaar sets, costume jewellery like this cocktail ring – carefully chosen to match clothing – appear.

## Fashion: Making and Subverting Distinction Hierarchies

Wholesalers and retailers all agreed in interviews that fashion in Calicut – as it is elsewhere in India – is heavily influenced by the movies. A new film introduces a new style, colour and pattern, adopted two to three months after the film's release. Although there are also clear fashion seasons when new styles appear and everyone buys new clothes – the two Eids, summer hot season, rainy season – movie-related fashion trends appear all-year-round and business keeps going throughout the year. Calicut shops can be tied into the local, the Gulf economy or both: strictly local ones say that monsoon is a relatively dead time; by contrast, Gulf-style upmarket shops are at their most busy then, as this is the season when Gulf families return home during the vacation and stock up with new clothes. As Emma Tarlo notes, since economic liberalisation, fashion seems to have accelerated, with new styles continually appearing (1996:337). A distinction we might try to draw here, following Sanjay Srivastava (2007), is that which is between fashion proper – driven by metro city designers and trends, part of branded global styles, available in high end boutiques - and what I am mostly talking about here in Calicut, a more vernacular, popular, ishtyle, driven more by cinema than by global or even metro trends. *Ishtyle* veers towards the extravagant, albeit done on the cheap: bright colours, shiny or two-tone fabrics and strong designs with impact, heavy embellishment and contrast. *Ishtyle* draws the eye and is a heavily externalising aesthetic.

The ready-made market is small, since women prefer carefully measured and fitted *salwar kameez* sets. Some sew their own clothes, although most use tailors; and almost all make use of the ready printed, embellished and embroidered *salwar* sets, which allow the purchaser to choose length, fit, flare, cut and neckline style. Tailors have pattern books of different cuts and the individualisation of a design is a project undertaken with considerable commitment, with women spending a great deal of time, comprehensve measurement and discussion with friends. There is a competitive market among tailors in terms of offering quality stitching and techniques, extra embellishments and singular style points, such as quality buttons or particularly well-cut *salwars*.

Another effect of clothing that blends glamour with modesty is that borders and hems become sites of attention and embellishment, while the parts counted as *awra* and needing - under Islamic injunctions - to be covered are kept plain. One aspect of the Muslim *kameez* is that, unlike Hindus, the neckline is invariably covered; even when women remove their outer dress in women's rooms at functions, they keep the *mafta* headscarf on, covering the neckline. So, while Hindu women often favour *salwar* fabric sets with a little work around the neckline, Muslim women prefer work on the bottom hem of the *kameez*, where it can be admired[9].

*Salwar* fabrics mostly arrive from Gujarat, Bombay, Tamil Nadu and Bangalore. Some of Calicut's small shopkeepers buy from travelling wholesalers, but shops at the cutting edge of style – which is where Muslim women of all social classes like to be – send their staff out on buying trips, to try to be the first out with a new fashion. Upmarket shops stock a few pieces of 'foreign' material – prestigious and costly even though not necessarily better (Chinese, Gulf).

The owner of an up-market Cherooty Road boutique, Nasreen, accompanied her sister on shopping trips to Thailand. Nasreen told me that

---

[9] There are two interesting aspects in which the universal Indian fabric sets, which arrive in Calicut from wholesalers, are not helpful. Firstly, *sari* sets commonly have a matching piece for making a sari blouse, however these pieces are never large enough to make a long sleeved, body-covering loose blouse, which is how Calicut Muslim women prefer to dress; and *salwar* sets often have strong design or embroidery around the neckline, rather than what would be the *kameez* bottom hem. I also note that girls' ready-made party-wear sets arrive sleeveless, with matching short sleeves. Kerala mothers generally sew the short sleeves, but the option of having three-quarter or full sleeves is generally not available. There is a clear market for fabric sets designed specifically with 'decent dress' Muslims in mind.

Fig. 11: Salwar set

Fabric pieces arrive ready to be sewn according to individual specific requirements. Muslim women prefer long, loose, fully lined and long sleeved. This can call for highly creative and skilled tailoring given that the fabric 'sets' are generally produced with the Hindu majority community dress code in mind – short sleeves, and body-fitting.

she can find and buy there, and at cheap prices, which she could then afford to subsequently sell upon her return for just 300–400 rupees per set. Selling to the more sophisticated upper middle classes and a mixed clientele, Nasreen also tries to satisfy the local Muslim demand for both striking display and a more subtle aesthetic. She maintained that Thai manufacturers:

> ... know better than Indians how to match colours and make nice things. The Chinese also. If you go to Dubai and start looking around at fabrics, you will buy Arabian or Chinese, and never want the Indian stuff. If it is blue and yellow, the Chinese will match exactly the right subtle shades of blue and yellow; the Indian one will be too bright, jazzy, too loud. Indians do not understand colour or subtlety.

Nasreen echoes then Kuldova's point that even high-end consumers in India acquire bright fabrics. Nasreen's upper middle-class boutique clientele, the tastes of whom she nudges towards subtlety, stand apart from most locals, who demand the bright colours and strong designs which the S.M. Street small bazaar shops happily stock. I have written in more detail more elsewhere about the insistence upon heavy work (embroidery, stones, beads) and the fondness for bold colours and synthetic fabrics that seem to be part that which what distinguishes 'Muslim style', something which seemed to me to be most apparent among unsophisticated Muslims from rural areas or working class beach-side communties, but which was for sure generalised among Muslims in contrast to Christians and Hindus (Osella 2007). Higher-end shopkeepers sometimes lamented to me that even their middle-class Muslim customers share this subaltern 'flashy' aesthetics:

> They come here, loads of them, in a jeep, look at our pieces, and say 'oh, can't you put a bit more *work* on it?' It is a *designer piece*, it is done to a style, but they have no sense of style at all; they just want to see lots of work, to show the money: it is just dressing to show off. And it does not look nice ... they just want a very heavy work piece – this is *their* idea of what looks nice. They have so much cash that they do not care at all about the price; actually, they *want* to spend more, they want a high price.

Mid and mid-upper market retailers buy from Bombay and Bangalore; bottom-end retailers buy from nearby Tamil Nadu and cheap Gujarat. Calicut's clothing market is highly segmented and there is a price range for everyone, but these hierarchies can also be subverted. Distinction is a difficult game to play in Calicut.

There are many embroidery classes around Calicut, especially in the Muslim stronghold around the bazaar, in which lower-middle class Muslim women learn to decorate fabric themselves in order to cut costs and for the finished product to still appear unique and cutting edge in dress. I joined a class for the six months it took me to learn 'simple machine embroidery'. More advanced students move onto regional Indian styles, such as Kutch work, and the most advanced learn to do the sort of hand-embroidery that the high-end boutiques sell. In this way too, women can enhance a disappointingly low level of *work* on a set hemline, and can customise an individual 'look'.

One middle-class woman who knew about my research asked me, critically, 'We have social functions all the time also, but we don't wear something new every time; yet they [i.e. the lower middle and working-class Muslims] do – how can they do this? How much money are they spending?' What she and other outsiders may not realise is that she was thinking of buying a 'worked' fabric piece from a retailer at Rs 900 (rupees), then paying a further Rs 300 to get it stitched. Yet a woman with menfolk in the trade (which means almost any women living around the bazaar) can get cloth free or at wholesale rate, perhaps Rs 250 for something otherwise sold at Rs 900. If she then sews it up and embellishes the fabric herself, she has the outfit ready at a far lower cost. When we see a woman, we may think she is wearing Rs 500, but it may actually have been done for Rs 150. Women with men in the rag trade can afford lots of clothes, and enjoy making the most of this privilege, an affordable luxury which allows them to maximise their desires for lavish display and making strong fashion statements (Vanessa Maher 1987).

Fig. 12: A party-wear outfit

Women hope to find bold and newly-fashionable shades and colour combinations, heavy embellishment, and patterns along the hem rather than the neckline. Calicut women do not generally care about fabric quality, preferring their cash to be spent on the visible component of the *work*.

As women from a community with a history of trade going back for centuries, these women are also expert shoppers and share knowledge of trends, prices and good retail outlets. As networks are very tightly knit, knowledge is deep. Women enjoy being well turned out and, rather than using their insider knowledge and discounts to cut the cost of dressing, they use it to extend the amount and lavishness of the outfits that they and their children can wear.

## Children's Clothes and the Heights of Ishtyle
Glamour tends to shower upon particular bodies. In this instance, where negative stereotypes, like the excessively free and inappropriately glamorous Arab/North Indian woman warn about the dangers of excessive attractiveness, it is specifically the bodies of pre-teen girls which become safe spaces for fantasies of luxury and beauty. Upon reflection, we realise that the pre-adolescent girl holds a special place: in that she inhabits exactly that cultural space where the feminine is particularly highly marked, but where sexuality has not broken through to public

display and therefore requires regulation and containment. Desires for exuberant display can, and do, reach their peak here.

As we have seen above, it is certainly not the case that older girls and women do not participate in fashion. Having said that, a lot of what appears as Bombay movie high style is clearly simply not modest for an older female, whatever her community. South Indian 'simplicity' and modesty are jealously maintained throughout all religious communities in socially conservative Kerala.

Calicut Muslim families mostly consider sleeveless attire as improper for girls over around the age of five, and there is a gradual shift towards modest (*decent*) dress, using the headscarf consistently by puberty, full covering by the age of 16. So we have an interesting pattern whereby two, three and four year-old girls are allowed to adopt the most cutting edge fashions, ones that are worn by adult women in the movies and by teenagers and younger women in Indian metro cities.

Families commonly spend more on the *party wear* item for their small girl than for the adult women's clothing. A girl's party *salwar* will often be more elaborate in its *work*; more fashionable; a prestigious branded ready-made item from Bombay. At Eid, I have seen men and boys get a new shirt, pants and shoes; mothers get one or two new outfits and a pair of shoes; while small daughters receive four or five new outfits, with several pairs of shoes and matching fashion jewellery: hair-slides, bangles and so on. The total expenditure on girl's clothes is often the greatest Eid expense.

Adults and children give full rein to fantasy dressing when buying *party wear* for their small girls – the fancy outfits to be worn at weddings or functions – such as one of Calicut Muslims' endless round of social dinners.[10] The fun of playing with hyper-femininity, with no risk of sexuality, is what the body of a small girl can offer. When a Bollywood fashion appeared for a one shouldered top, with one half sleeve and one small strap, it was small girls under five who appeared at weddings dressed in shoulder-revealing salwar tops. Another style which came into local children's clothes-shops (again, via Bombay-wholesalers and copied from a hit Hindi movie) consisted of hugely flared trousers, worn with three-quarter length flimsy over-coats, of perhaps semi-transparent

---

[10] Hosting lavish dinners at home for extended family and friends is another singular aspect of the visions of opulence still practiced in this community, despite increasing financial difficulties in maintaining hospitality.

Fig. 13a:
Typical Calicut clothing shop

Calicut´s S.M. Street is full of small shops with fast-moving stock.

Fig. 13b:
Girl's ready-made party wear

In Calicut, this kind of outfit is understood as a kind of ethnicised 'dressing up'; it is named as a frock and is associated by Muslims with Christian community dress styles.

Fig. 13c:
Girl's ready-made party wear

This is a more traditional style, given a fashion twist. The sleevelessness makes it unsuitable for girls over about age 5 or 6.

lurex or shimmering taffeta, worn over a short top with spaghetti straps. Muslim girls up to the age of eight or nine were to be seen going around in this style (they didn't remove the overcoat to completely show their shoulders).

Many women also stitch their own, and their children's, clothes. Mumtaz and her sister showed me *party* outfits that they had recently made. Made for a seven-year old, was a pink crepe long skirt with a one-shoulder top and shawl, finished with bead and sequin work; and a floor-length red chiffon dress, with silver embroidered flowers. Lastly, they showed me a fantastic piece in red velvet, intended for a 6 month-old niece. The outfit consisted of a mini-skirt and strappy top; the mini-skirt had a split at the back and the top was one-shouldered. It was finished with sequin-work, patterns of individual silver sequins, each sewn in with one blue bead in the centre.

## Conclusion

Although the heyday of Calicut's trade wealth has long since passed, memories of the (real and imagined) luxury living in that period blend with an Indian-wide love of heavy embellishment and with a specific subaltern aesthetic, and all compound in a relatively free-spending stance towards personal consumption, which expects plenty of shine and show for its money. Muslim women's preferences in gold jewellery are for large, hollow pieces which look heavy; in shoes, for high-heels and embellishment; and in clothing, the latest and most directional trends, where fabrics shimmer, have bold colours, and are heavily embroidered with *work*.

The tiny girl – in her Bollywood party-wear style, heavy costume jewellery, hair decorations and high heels – is the epitome of 'Muslim style'. On from this matter, I'd rather not see tiny girls' Bollywood high-style as a displaced or vicarious display, in any negative sense, nor as reflecting mother's thwarted desires. As I have shown, mothers themselves engage energetically in glamour and fashion: from lavish hennaed hands to glitzy platform shoes.

A productive tension between Islamic reformist ideals and aspirations of glamour settle into an interesting distinctive style, where a continuous thread of an orientation towards luxury and opulence draws a highly specific community habitus and set of sedimented embodied memories together, with the contemporary fantasies pouring in from all sides. Something worthy of reiteration, as I have argued elsewhere (2007), is that it is not only Muslim girls who have a dress code; all

Kerala women work within social expectations of decency, modesty and appropriate femininity - just as women everywhere tend to do. Islamic dress codes and South Indian modesty norms allow Calicut women to have a more critical relationship to clothing styles than women whose engagement with fashion is channelled only through what is offered by the market, and then broadcast via positive endorsements presented in women's magazines.

Moreover, quite simply, small girls are permitted to go the whole fashion five-miles into fantasy wear under local modesty expectations, and so they do. However, more importantly, it is not simply modesty or Islamic reformism which displaces the highest expression of 'Muslim style' onto small girls. I would argue that we have to see the Bombay movie high-style fantasy fashion as akin to the 'Disney princess' flouncy net and satin long frocks that pre-pubescent girls in the USA and Europe often love to wear. Such extreme fantasy wear may certainly tell us something about specific forms of femininity and glamour in a particular setting. Nevertheless, at the same time, very few adult woman (outside cosplay scenes, Lunning 2011) would choose to wear one of those Disney-style pink flouncy outfits. In just the same way, Bombay fashion – from a Southern stance – appears as exaggerated fantasy wear, which settles more happily on kids than upon adult women.

## References

Al-Qasimi, N. 2010. 'Immodest modesty: Accommodating dissent and the abaya-as-fashion in the Arab Gulf States.' *Journal of Middle East Women's Studies* 6.1, 46-74.

Bourdieu, P. 1984. *Distinction: A social critique of the judgment of taste.* Harvard University Press.

Devika, J. 2005. 'The aesthetic woman: re-forming female bodies and minds in early twentieth-century Keralam.' *Modern Asian Studies* 39.2, 461-487.

Hakim, C. 2010. 'Erotic capital', *European Sociological Review.* 26(5), 499-518.

Howes, D. (ed.). 1991. *The varieties of sensory experience: a sourcebook in the anthropology of the senses.* Toronto: University of Toronto Press.

Kuldova, T. (n.d.) *Designing Elites: Fashion And Prestige In Urban North India.* Thesis submitted for the degree of PhD at anthropology department, University of Oslo, 2013.

Lunning, Frenchy. 'Under the Ruffles: Shōjo and the Morphology of Power.' *Mechademia* 6.1 (2011): 3-19

Miran, J. 2009. *Red Sea citizens: cosmopolitan society and cultural change in Massawa.* Indiana University Press.

N P Mohammed (with M T Vasudevan Nair). 1960. *Arabian Gold*, Trivandrum: D C Books.

Osella, Caroline, and Filippo Osella. 'Food, memory, community: Kerala as both 'Indian Ocean'zone and as agricultural homeland.' *South Asia: Journal of South Asian Studies* 31.1 (2008): 170-198.

Osella, Caroline, and Filippo Osella. 'Muslim Style in South India.' *Fashion Theory: The Journal of Dress, Body & Culture* 11.2-3 (2007): 2-3.

Osella, Filippo, and Caroline Osella. ''I am Gulf': the production of cosmopolitanism in Kozhikode, Kerala, India.' (2007).

Osella, F., & Osella, C. 1999. 'From transience to immanence: consumption, life-cycle and social mobility in Kerala, South India'. *Modern Asian Studies*, 33(4), 989-1020.

Papapetros, Spyros. 'World Ornament.' *Res: Anthropology and Aesthetics*, 57/58: Spring/Autumn 2010 57 (2011): 309

Simpson, E., & Kresse, K. 2007. *Struggling with history: Islam and cosmopolitanism in the Western Indian Ocean*. Hurst and Company.

Srivastava, Sanjay. *Passionate modernity: sexuality, class, and consumption in India*. Routledge, 2012.

Strathern, Marilyn. 'The whole person and its artifacts.' *Annual Review of Anthropology*. 33 (2004): 1-19.

Van Wolputte, Steven. 'Hang on to your self: Of bodies, embodiment, and selves.' *Annual Review of Anthropology* (2004): 251-269.

Vora, N. (2013). *Impossible Citizens: Dubai's Indian Diaspora*. Duke University Press.

Werbner, P. (ed.). 2008. *Anthropology and the new cosmopolitanism: rooted, feminist and vernacular perspectives*. Berg.

# Online Sources

The Hindu, Businessline. December 6th 2012. 'My Gold Plan. Launched in Kerala.

http://www.thehindubusinessline.com/markets/gold/my-gold-plan-launched-in-kerala/article4170971.ece (Accessed July 15th 2013).

Kerala Wedding Jewellery collection, at http://indiangoldtrends.blogspot.co.uk/2012/11/kerala-wedding-jewellery-collection.html. November 2012. (Accessed July 15th 2013).

Varsha one gram gold website. http://www.varshajewellery.com/. (Accessed July 15th 2013).

# Photographs disclaimer

Several contributions to this book present high end fashion and metropolitan style; we should be very clear that this is not what I am discussing here. To this end, the images I am using to illustrate my chapter are produced in an aesthetic modality similar to the clothing discussed. They lack precision, finesse, glamour and quality; they have a distinctly faded, imperfect, cheap or even home-made quality. These are the images from and appropriate to the world of transient and affordable bazaar style.

11.29.2007

# The Quality of a Copy
Constantine V. Nakassis

### Citational Economies, Part 1

In the area of North Chennai where I conducted fieldwork, clothing shops crowd together. Their export-surplus and defect brand-wares spill into the street, interspersed with uncanny brand forms – 'brands' like Poma; Diesel Industries; Chiesal; Columbian – and garments sporting brand names and designs that few have ever seen before, and probably won't ever again: 'brands' like Dex; The QS; Emperor; Style Jeans; and the like. In search of cheap ready-made apparel, wholesalers and retailers from Chennai and neighboring cities, as well as local, (lower-)middle-class shoppers, examine the wares, some going inside to inquire about, and negotiate, prices, others simply passing along to the next shop. Interested in how certain brand fashions circulate and are taken up among lower-middle- and middle-class college youth in urban Tamil Nadu, my research also led me to this area, one of the sites from which the apparel that was so widely worn among the youth with whom I worked originated.

In addition to retailing and wholesaling, textile manufacture also takes place here. Although locally oriented, the designs and design elements of these manufacturers' wares are global. They are poached, borrowed and inspired by the garments that leak out of export-oriented factories. Such factories, many of them located in Tamil Nadu, produce garments for foreign-brand companies like Diesel, Columbia, Nike, Puma and so on (Nakassis 2012a; Norris 2010:38–41). Anxious about being left behind what's 'moving' in local markets, these low-level producers not only copy export-oriented garment manufacture, they also watch what their neighbors are making (which is to say, what they are copying from such factories), compulsively copying what they (re-)make/copy.[1] A design or, more precisely, some of its qualities are borrowed from other sites and other designers, from a global other and a local competitor. Such qualities are unstitched and restitched, worked over, deformed and re-formed, altered and conserved. What is the quality of such a copy? And what quality does it copy?

During my fieldwork from 2007–2009, certain designs multiplied in urban Tamil markets. Proliferating, copied and recopied, their form was rendered increasingly different from what they copied. With each copy,

---

[1] In addition to export surplus, such manufacturers culled their designs from fashion catalogues, advertisements, the Internet, and local high-end malls and boutiques. For many, however, export surplus was the major source for their designs (Nakassis 2012a).

a newness was introduced, the identity that held together such forms stretched thin, the pull that kept the copy in the orbit of its 'original' weakened. At the same time, with each iteration the cachet of the copy/copied decreased, the newness and aura of the design giving way to the pedestrian, the bland, the old-fashioned. In this cycle, there was a close-distance that had to be maintained from the brand, or design, that was copied, as well as from the other copies that circulated in local markets: not too different, but not too similar either. Of course, with the vagaries of the global market for high-end, ready-made brand-wares, new garments were constantly being produced in nearby factories, their surplus serving as new inputs to this churning replication machine. When I left, it was no longer copies of Diesel and Ferrari that captured the imaginations of local producers and youth consumers, but other brands, for example, Puma.

Brands proliferate in such South Indian markets through a particular mode of what we might call *citational copying*, where a 'copy' – though this term has its own ideological and metaphysical implications that render it problematic, as we shall see – 'quotes' some other discourse, sign, or event, selectively replicating, or reanimating, particular qualities of it. The canonical citation, the direct quotation ('He said "This is a fake!"'), for example, reanimates the informational content and phrasing of what is cited (the speech event '"This is a fake!"'), quoting it 'to the word'. Indirect reported speech, by contrast, simply reanimates informational content, shifting the wording, and perspective, of the cited act ('He claimed that her shirt was fake'). The citation is not necessarily a linguistic act, however. Any representable quality may be brought back to life in any number of media: a pleating technique, fabric choice and cut, for example, may be enough, as in the case of John Galliano of House Dior's homage to Mariano Fortuny's Delphos dress (itself, of course, a citational *renvoi* to the chiton style of antiquity).

Citation here refers to acts which re-presence another('s) semiotic act and mark that re-presencing, or iteration, as *not* what is re-presenced, a disavowing and suspending metacommunication about the very act in question. Citations repeat, but with a difference. And insofar as they are citations, they reflexively mark that difference (Nakassis 2013b). In this sense, local surfeit designs in Chennai markets 'cite' various brands, reanimating their logos and names while marking them as *not* what they presence, that is, authorized instances of the brand. Indeed, such wares were not meant to be seen as 'the same' as the brand commodities they were inspired by. They were not made to deceive anyone as to their origins or affiliation, nor did they.

Through such citations, re-presented branded garments diverge from their 'originals', new qualities creeping into their form, qualities which key their non-authorized, and non-authenticated, self-difference: cheap fabrics, misspelled brand names (Lavi's, Diesal, Ferarri, Lottoo, etc.), sometimes paired with other brands' logos and designs (as well as other design elements), novel color combinations, fonts and the like. The photographs below give some examples of some of the surfeit forms that were consumed by the lower-middle- and middle-class young men in urban Tamil Nadu with whom I worked.

Citational shadow economies such as these are common around the world, and anthropologists have become increasingly interested in them.[2] Often, such economies are criminalized, manufacturers labeled as 'counterfeiters', 'pirates' and the like (Thomas 2009, 2013). Such labeling has increased in the twenty-first century as Euro-American intellectual property (IP) regimes have been exported to third-world locations like India. In India, IP law has been modeled on, and pushed by, recent American and British IP law (Gangjee 2008). As is common in

---

[2] For a bibliography of this growing literature see http://nakassis.com/constantine/anth_of_brand_counterfeits/, last accessed 1st July, 2013; or Nakassis 2012a, 2012b, 2013a *passim*.

brand heartlands like the US and Europe (Coombe 1998; Klein 2000),[3] as well as in peripheries like India, China, Indonesia, Guatemala and elsewhere (Pang 2008; Luvaas 2010, 2013; Thomas 2013), IP regimes have been introduced and strengthened to protect, among others, big brand names from 'piracy' and other forms of infringement ('dilution', 'tarnishment') that proliferate in the shadows of the authentic and authorized. The copy, the counterfeit, the pirated – we, like IP law, tend to talk about such forms as exterior to the brand, as derived from 'original' designs, as parasites of designers' ethical, honest practices (Nakassis 2013c). Through copying, the pirate steals what the brand creates, the author writes, the designer designs. To speak of the copy, then, is already, in some sense, to be within this ideological enclosure, located by its normative coordinates. How might we think, and think differently, this quality of the copy?

## Citational Economies, Part 2

Do not the 'original' and its 'copy' share substance even as they maintain a fundamental alterity? Is there not a line drawn between them that conjoins and separates them, a line of authenticity, creativity and priority that makes them foreign to, and yet intimates of, each other? This is, as I suggested, how we tend to understand 'derivative' citational economies like the urban Tamil one discussed above, markets where inauthentic 'fakes', aping 'real' brand 'originals', are made, sold and worn. And yet, what of the brand heartlands with respect to which such peripheries are put in their place? What of those brands, designers, and design houses who are being copied the world over – Ralph Lauren, Tommy Hilfiger, Diesel, Armani and the like?

Fashion writers and scholars of intellectual property law tell us that in certain ways high-fashion designers are not so different from these Chennai 'pirates' (Agins 2000; Schmidt 1983; Hilton et al. 2004; Raustiala and Sprigman 2006). Both are enmeshed in citational economies. Indeed, the Euro-American fashion cycle can be described as the frenzy of copying the latest design (what's 'moving' in the market), modifying it with small citational marks until the design is played out, the quali-

---

[3] The phrase *brand heartlands* refers not to geographic places as such, but ideological imaginaries and regimes of brand authenticity, of which certain places are recruited as metonymic emblems. In this sense, to speak of a brand heartland is, to use Bakhtin's (1982) term, to speak of a 'chronotope' of brand, one which may abut and even overlap spatially, temporally, and sociologically with other commodity chronotopes, such as the chronotope of surfeit described above. To give a concrete example, from New York to Chennai, it is not difficult to find 'pirate' road-side stalls nearby and even in front of authorized brand retailers, each in their own world and yet also contiguous and in dialogue.

ties that unite and fractionate what is cited abandoned under the swell of the next 'trend'. From this point of view, high fashion is itself split in two, a line of authenticity and originality dividing it internally, separating the copier and the copied, originator and imitator (see Kuldova's chapters in this volume on this dynamic in elite Indian fashion). The distinction that separates fashion from piracy, organizes fashion itself. That which defines the exteriority of fashion is inscribed within it. But is that line, by being drawn, not also etched away, anticipating its erasure and putting itself under erasure?

High fashion has long been ambivalent about the status of the copy, an ambivalence that defines the very sociological organization of the field. Seen as the sign of a designer's success or simply the cost of doing business (Kaufman 2005:532), copying others' designs is often condoned by the industry. It is reported that Elsa Schiaparelli, the great Italian designer, considered laws protecting design 'vain and useless. The moment that people stop copying you, it means that you are no longer any good' (cited in Stewart 2005:130). As one group of authors has put it: 'Copying is thus endemic and could be said to be a core activity of the industry' (Hilton et al. 2004:351; also see Schmidt 1983; Agins 2000:24-25; Nurbhai 2002; Barnett 2005; Kaufman 2005).

While tolerated, such copying has also been seen by certain, but not all, parties in the fashion world as a fundamental problem for the industry, as an impediment to growth, innovation and creativity, not to mention being seen as immoral, unjust and unfair (Hagin 1991:342; Scafidi 2006; Marshall 2007). Despite all this, the fashion industry in the United States and elsewhere has shown continuing economic growth and investment, and, by all accounts, rapid innovation and vibrant creativity.[4] Jonathon Barnett (2005) and Kal Raustiala and Chris Sprigman (2006, 2009) have argued that some amount of copying, and counterfeiting even, benefits fashion designers, and, in one way or another, may be encouraged by them (through inaction and nonchalant attitudes, as we saw above). According to such arguments, copying enhances the prestige of the 'original', functions as a mode of publicity, solidifies trends by making them

---

[4] For discussion of this so-called 'piracy paradox' see Barnett 2005; Raustiala and Sprigman 2006, 2009; Scafidi 2006; Marshall 2007; Cox and Jenkins 2008; Stevens 2012. Of course, while Raustiala and Sprigman (2006) suggest that copying is a projection, or an affordance we might say, of the law, the political economy and culture of copying is crucial as well. See, for example, Weikart 1944 on some of the economic and institutional features of the interwar textile industry (a period of much growth in the industry) that promoted rampant copying (among them, growth of mass markets and the decline of tailoring, reactions to WWI austerities and the depression, 'hand-to-mouth' retailing, and the 'jobber' organization of manufacture).

more visible and thus recruits new consumers.

The similarities, and ironies, that lie between the 'pirate' workshop in Chennai and the great fashion houses of New York, Paris and the rest do not simply stop there. Fashion history underscores that it was the US, the contemporary pusher of IP regimes the world over that was one of the principal pirates of high (French) fashion from its late-nineteenth- and early-twentieth-century inception. Haute couture fashions from France were frequently pilfered by American design houses – sometimes with 'permission' and sometimes not – so as to be reproduced for the American parvenus and masses (Stewart 2005; Scafidi 2006:118). Even contemporary American designers like Ralph Lauren and his own doppelganger Tommy Hilfiger have been described by certain writers within the fashion world as design hacks and fashion thieves, pilferers of others and of each other (Agins 2000).

This line that splits and divides fashion – original/copy; real/fake; true/false – is shifty. It alters its scale and meaning across contexts (Gal 2002), typifying and normatively ordering various objects and persons as belonging to one category or another. This lability makes it possible for a stitch, a color scheme, an individual designer and even a whole nation (Pang 2008; Graan 2013) to be typified as innovative or derivative; real or fake; authentic or inauthentic. It allows Ralph Lauren to be both an originator and a hack, a victim and perpetrator at the same time, depending on one's point of view, the designs in question, or the person to whom he is compared. What is important for me here is that this shifting ideological discourse, this moving line of authenticity construes the citational relations that fashion comprises, ordering and organizing them, giving them cultural substance, normative force and economic value.

Fashion may be viewed, then, as a tiered citational economy or, rather, a set of entangled economies related to each other through this shifting line. Haute couture and big-name elite designers cite/copy each other, and this world inspires and is copied by mass-producing 'ready-made' brands. Such mass-market brands also compete with and cite each other and are in turn copied/cited by 'pirates' across the globe (who also, of course, may 'pirate' high-end designers as well). Since the late twentieth century, this also runs in reverse. Fashion designers today freely draw 'inspiration' from, and cite, the so-called 'street', just as post-colonial designers in places like India cite and appropriate 'traditional' (rural) designs (Tarlo 1996; Kuldova 2013; see Kuldova's chapters in this volume; Wettenstein, this volume). Consider the launch party for Japanese artist Takashi Murakami's 2008 '© MURAKAMI' retrospective at the Brooklyn Museum.[5] As part of the spectacle, 'real' Louis Vuitton goods were sold in a citational simulation of 'pirate' platform shops, a cheeky inversion that aimed to capture, and disavow, some of the aura of the 'fake' so as to recoup it into, and thus augment the value of, the 'real'. The blog notcot.com described the event as such:

> Louis Vuitton is really fighting back against counterfeiting these days. . . . How about their little Canal St-eqsue set up outside the Brooklyn Museum of Art for the Murakami exhibit launch party? It is a fake set up of a fake bag seller that sells real bags. . . . It is really quite a hilarious set up – notice the hand written labels below the paintings for $6000?[6]

Citational copying stitches and unstitches fashion designs and qualities, transporting forms within and across these tiers, across time and space and social class. The citation is the semiotic form by which different social parties – elite designers, mass-market designers, local 'pirates', and all their various publics – are entangled with and oriented to each other. These citational entanglements are one way in, and by, which fashion is materialized.

Today, big name designers have internalized these entanglements between tiers. Since the 1980s, designers have increasingly created multiple commodity lines (and 'labels'), each catering to different market segments and 'lifestyles'. Designers, in effect, have fractionated and multiplied themselves into various brand surrogates. They are not simply designers of particular pieces of clothing, but are now brand names (Klein 2000), the very mass-market 'design pirates' who once copied and parasited the high-fashion designer (Agins 2000). Rather than having their couture copied and mass produced by others, today designers like Giorgio Armani feature different, yet hierarchically ordered, sub-brands: from Armani Privé (the haute couture line), Giorgio Armani (high-end ready-to-wear), Armani Collezioni (not as high-end ready-to-wear for professionals), Emporio Armani (similar to Armani Collezioni but for a more youthful demographic), to Armani Jeans (mass-market,

---

[5] As the Brooklyn Museum's website describes the exhibit: The exhibition © MURAKAMI explores the self-reflexive nature of Murakami's oeuvre by focusing on earlier work produced between 1992 and 2000 in which the artist attempts to explore his own reality through an investigation of branding and identity, as well as through self-portraiture created since 2000 (http://www.brooklynmuseum.org/exhibitions/murakami/, last accessed 1st July, 2013).

[6] http://www.notcot.com/archives/2008/04/lvs-war-on-coun.php, last accessed 1st July, 2013. Also see http://www.nytimes.com/slideshow/2008/04/04/fashion/0406-BROOKLYN_index.html, last accessed 1st July, 2013.

sold in department stores) and Armani Exchange (a 'street'-inspired collection). Designers like Armani, now corporatized brand entities, cannibalize, steal and redistribute their own aura *as* designers, an autocitationality that splits the designer into so many mediatized, and mass-marketized, fractions of the 'same' brand. The brand, now, encompasses design and designer.

If brand heartlands are not so different from their surfeit shadows, then what is the difference? What about their similarity? What, and from where, is the line that separates and unites them?

## Taming Citation, Staying Quality

The operative thesis here is not the truism that 'fake' and 'real', 'original' and 'copy' are merely arbitrary cultural or historical categories. Rather, it is that these binaries are a shifting set of indexical, and fractal, relations that entangle different social parties and projects to each other, and by doing so materialize a range of social and aesthetic forms. Think again of Schiapparelli's image of fashion, a world where 'original' and 'copy' designate a set of mutually defining social positions – those who are 'good', who are 'original', who are trendsetters; and those who copy and validate them, and thus, presumably, are not (as) 'good'. Such relations of 'original' and 'copy' ground, and are grounded in, the creation, circulation and consumption of material objects, just as they map out a terrain of aesthetic and economic value. Or think again of the Chennai market, a space of presumed third-world mimics, designated 'pirates' (not 'good'!) and entangled with IP law, global capital and their target market (non-elite young men). Such entanglements materialize non-elite youth fashion in urban Tamil Nadu. They materialize a particular kind of surfeit aesthetic that differs from the logics and ontological commitments of the forms they copy (viz. the brand), as I discuss below (Nakassis 2012a, 2013d).

Important for me here is the way the limit and protective border that surrounds the 'original' and the 'authentic' depends on the continual, haunting presence of its transgression, of its surfeit. There is an excess that is projected out of, but also introjected into, the 'original'. The surfeit is always already interior to the 'original', the copy already anticipated in the very form of what is copied, the parasite already in the heart of the host, beating its heart and breathing its breaths (Nakassis 2013a, 2013c). 'Fake' and 'real' are not simply discursive designations *about* objects ('That is a fake!', 'This is real!'), but, at the same time, and by that very fact, *material* distinctions. The ideological opposition of 'real' and 'fake', of course, is just that, a rationalization, a cultural discourse, a reflexive reanalysis; but it operates over a range of forms, shifting and moving, variously typifying objects and phenomena as one or the other. And by operating as a shifting discourse, this being the point, it performatively congeals in various ways. It is materialized in the (re)design of a logo, in the writing and enforcement of a law (and in the act of its transgression), in the weave of a garment and the like (Nakassis 2013e). While there are multiform ways in which this materialization happens, below I want to focus on the role of intellectual property law, and in particular, trademark law as one institution that materializes the citationality of surfeit and the surfeit of citationality.

The emergence of the modern brand turned on the mid-nineteenth-century need to reliably mark commodities of otherwise uncertain provenance and quality so that they might, virtually at least, point back to their putative origin, their authorizing producer (Coombe 1998; Bently 2008). This was necessary due to the emergence, and increased prevalence, of transnational mass markets. Such markets were implicated by new technologies and organizational forms (viz. the corporation) to mass produce and manage goods, goods that – as a result of such new modes of mass manufacture, distribution and retailing – were increasingly detached from older social networks that worked to guarantee consumer trust and commodity quality. This dispersed, transnational form of market organization was, by that very fact, plagued by fraud and piracy. The trademark, then, was not simply a 'mark of liability', but also the mark of state force backing the authority, and authenticity, of the good. Trademark law necessarily presupposed the surfeit good, the good that exceeded its authority (Nakassis 2013a). Such law implicitly invoked the surfeit and explicitly damned it at the same time.

The productivist, and referentialist, semiotic ideology of trademark law, then, aimed to make the commodity always point to its unique source. Such a referential relation made commodities compete not just on use value or exchange value, but on the name, on the commodity's 'brand identity', we might say. But such competition wasn't simply staked on the name. It was also staked on the spectral image of the producer that stood behind the commodity – her 'reputation' or 'good will', or 'brand image' as we say today.

Here we see a double parasitism and a double inversion. On the one hand, the trademark parasites the commodity (Nakassis 2013c). The trademark enters the law and the market as a supplemental sign that appends itself to the commodity, communicating the good's quality and value through the detour of the producer's good will. Through this parasitism, however, the trademark also comes to be the origin of the commodity, such that now the commodity – on one understanding of it, at least – exists simply to carry the sign of its producer. On the other hand, the brand parasites the trademark. The brand image is the outgrowth of the trademark, the aura and imaginary projected by, and anchored to, it. Through this parasitism, the brand comes to reverse that ordering, becoming the originating source of value and meaning of the trademark. Indeed, today it is increasingly brand image that determines social value and meaning over and above the trademarked commodity form, imbuing commodities and their marks with their exchange values and social meanings (Lury 2004; Arvidsson 2005; see Schechter 1927 for an early realization of this). Such commodities are merely the brand's earthly extension, the trademark its transparent medium. The brand, by contrast, is a more ethereal, essential(ist) entity, more similar to a Platonic Form (Manning 2010). Consider, for example, then-CEO of Nike, Phil Knight's comment on the relation between the product and brand marketing:

> For years we thought of ourselves [Nike] as a production-oriented company, meaning we put all our emphasis on designing and manufacturing the product. But now we understand that the most important thing we do is market the product. We've come around to saying that Nike is a marketing-oriented company, and the product is our most important marketing tool.
> (cited in Klein 2000:22).

The brand, as a function of trademark law, then, has become the commodity's *élan vital*. The brand stands in where the body of the artisan would, even as the hand that produces the commodity is no longer a 'producer' in any clear sense, but a dispersed set of bodies linked by the corporate form (Klein 2000). It is, of course, doubly ironic, then, that the language of brand marketing has resignified the very body of the designer, evaporating and mediatizing the originator and author of fashion into a brand, inscribing that parasite relationship within the designing subject so that she might, in turn, parasite herself, parlaying her cachet as a designer into a chimerical brand portfolio.

Here my interest is how trademark law defines a material field, and a subjectivity that navigates it, how it outlines the limits of the 'copy' by defining it, determining when a citation becomes a 'fake' and when a 'copy' is acceptable, and even defendable. When, indeed, does homage become theft, inspiration piracy? And when is it legally prosecutable? When does a name or design become someone's property? In drawing that line, trademark law creates and stabilizes semiotic monopolies, arbitrating who is allowed to exclusively use a name or logo and who is not.

It is through such little dominions that brands enter the market. This market, however, is always already composed of spaces of non-monopoly, of – as far as intellectual property law is concerned at least – commodity classes that cannot be owned. While you can trademark 'Xerox', you can't trademark signs that designate the class 'copy (xerox) machines'. That is, the brand and commodity must stand apart from each other, even as they are intimately entangled. Brands compete *within*, but never *as*, those 'generic' commodity classes that they must be distinct from, creating the possibilities of brand imaginaries where love (Foster 2007), loyalty (Fournier 1998) and community (Muniz and O'Guinn 2001), among other marketers' fantasies, may play out through, while never being reducible to, material commodities. Not just a technology to police the surfeit, trademark law is a technology to tether the commodity to a brand imaginary and identity and thus to make both possible. Trademark law never lets the commodity get too far away from the brand, never lets it be seen to exclusively stand under another identity, even as it, at the same time, never lets the commodity get too close to the brand, never letting it merge totally with that identity (see below).[7]

If the trademark makes the brand possible, and thus also makes its surfeit necessary, and if it does so by internalizing that exteriority within itself, what is exterior to it? What kinds of copies fall beyond intellectual property, and how might we understand such 'copies'? Further, what does such copying materialize beyond the 'original'?

## 'Low-IP' Environments and the Materialization of the Copy

High fashion design in the United States and local garment 'counterfeiters' in Chennai are part of what Kal Raustiala and Chris Sprigman (2006) have dubbed 'low-IP' environments, which is to say, citational economies where intellectual property laws only obliquely regiment fashion practices, where there is a 'low' amount of IP protection.

As Raustiala and Sprigman, among others, have noted, fashion design in the United States falls between the 'seams' of IP law (Cox and Jenkins 2008). Simply put, a 'look' or design of a garment or set of garments – the cut of a sleeve, the draping of a dress, the width of a collar, the

---

[7] The merger of brand identity (as invoked by the trademark) and the commodity class of the goods that are instances of that identity is sometimes called 'genericide' (Moore 2003), the lapse of the trademark's unique source-indexicality into mere common nominal reference. This is, for example, what threatened to happen to Xerox, and what did happen to Bayer's once-trademarked Aspirin.

arrangement of a garment's components, or the color palette of a collection – cannot be easily copyrighted, trademarked, or patented. While design is perhaps *the* central aesthetic and commoditized element of fashion, US IP law does not protect it in any straightforward way.[8] Nor has fashion design traditionally received much support from American law-makers or courts of law.[9]

Clothing designs, historically, have been definitionally excluded from copyright.[10] Only in the early twentieth century did clothing, along with music, theater, sculpture, photography, film and other creative practices, come to be considered a type of artistic creation, that is, 'applied art' that could be covered by copyright (Nurbhai 2002:498–500; Tu 2010:424–425). Even with this reclassification, however, the use of copyright for fashion design has been difficult. The primary reason for this is that clothing has been considered primarily a functional commodity.[11] It is a 'useful article', which is to say that clothing has 'an intrinsic utilitarian function that is not merely to portray the appearance of the article or to convey information' (17 USC §101). Coded as nonrepresentational commodities, the utility of garments and the inseparability of their design aesthetics from that utility (Mazer v. Stein 1954) mean that clothing often cannot be copyrighted.

---

[8] Fashion isn't the only such field, of course. Indeed, much of economic activity is characterized as low-IP environments. None of the following are easily protectable by IP law: culinary works, fireworks, magic tricks, typefaces, stand-up comedy, music by 'jam bands' or any musical form where 'standards' are standard, perfumes, sports plays, semiconductor chip design (until 1984), building design (until 1990), and boat hull design (until 1998).

[9] As Schmidt (1983), Hagin (1991), Scafidi (2006) have noted, the fashion industry has been consistently neglected by US Congress and legal interpreters of the law who have resisted extending protections to design. Indeed, of the over 70 proposals to add *ad hoc* protections to fashion design, all have, to date, been rejected. While below I note some of the legal reasons why fashion design has not been protected, Susan Scafidi has also suggested cultural reasons linked to the gendering of fashion and its perceived frivolousness (http://www.counterfeitchic.com/2006/02/law_econ_discovers_fashion.php, last accessed 1st July, 2013).

[10] The original 1790 US copyright statue only protected maps, charts, and books. The general history of copyright since has been the gradual extension in scope and temporal length of copyrights (Nurbhai 2002).

[11] From this functionality doctrine it follows that while designs as texts are protectable, their embodiment in actual material objects (i.e., pieces of clothing) generally are not (Raustiala and Sprigman 2006:1699; Tu 2010:428). Insofar as copyright protects a particular expression of an idea, but not the idea itself (a vague, but powerful distinction of species-genus that applies at every level of IP law), actual garments as tokens of a type are unlikely to be protected, even if their sketches or instructions are. While a sketch represents the design idea and puts it into a protectable aesthetic form (which has no 'utility' except to represent), the embodied garment is an object of utility and thus is not protectable (see below).

The issue for courts here is that extending intellectual property to apparel designs would inhibit competition by de facto leading to unfair forms of monopoly (Schmidt 1983:861ff.). If copying some quality or form is the only way to compete within a commodity market (that is, if that quality is integral to the 'generic' product type and its 'function'), then such qualia are unprotectable by copyright. As the courts have argued, when it comes to clothing there are often a limited number of ways to vary its aesthetico-utilitarian qualities, such that to have exclusive rights over such qualia (or any subset of them) would severely curtail the ability of competitors to operate in the market. If someone owned the length or width of a lapel, how could different producers fairly, and freely, compete to sell shirts?

Trademark, like copyright, is also constrained by the notion of functionality. With respect to trademark, courts generally understand functionality to refer both to the essential 'use or purpose of the article' as well as to the question of whether the feature in question 'affects the cost or quality of the article' (Louboutin v. Yves Saint Laurent 2012). By conflating these rather different notions of function, trademark law asks whether the quality or form under question is central to 'non-reputation-related' (i.e., non-brand-related) competition (Qualitex v. Jacobson 1995), and thus whether protection would cause disadvantage to other producers by laying claim to the larger, unprotected commodity class within which brands are supposed to vie.[12] As fashion designers compete on 'looks' that are not simply indexical of their brand identity (that unique and singular indexicality being what justifies the trademark's protection), aesthetic functionality as a legal doctrine precludes trademark protection being conferred on those ('non-functional') qualities upon which competition in fashion markets is staked, that is, design itself (Qualitex v. Jacobson 1995; Knitwaves v. Lollytags 1995; Adidas-Salomon AG v. Target 2002). In effect, trademark law requires that the mark simply be a diacritic, a pure indexical of its producer, that it not designate a 'generic' commodity class (say, 'blouse', 'skirt', 'collar', 'sneakers', etc.) or its aesthetics. The brand and its trademarks should not come too close to its commodities.

The limits of trademark open up a space of quality beyond identity, beyond the brand, but still tethered to the design(er). If designs can't be

---

[12] See Sicilia Di R. Biebow & Co. v. Cox (1984): 'a design is legally functional, and thus unprotectable if it is one of a limited number [of] equally efficient options available to competitors and free competition would be unduly hindered by [giving] the design trademark protection' (cited in Bharathi 1996:1693; also see Abercrombie & Fitch v. American Eagle 2002:643).

copyrighted, trademarked, or patented[13], they can be liberally copied without legal recrimination. This limit allows for forms of fashion citation – 'referencing', 'inspiration', 'homage', 'dedication', 'borrowing', 're-interpretation', 'updating' and the like being the terms of fashion-speak's citational register. It allows fractions of the commodity to disperse and disseminate in a myriad of ways. It creates a space of surfeit beyond the 'counterfeit'. This is the space of fashion itself, and is, as Schiapparelli noted, the very fabric of fashion's sociology, of its hierarchies of status and aesthetics, and of its vitality in innovation and its normativity in copying.

In the penumbra of the 'original', then, the surfeit materializes as a particular kind of temporality and spatiality: that of the fashion cycle and its 'trends', the multiplication of a quality – the cut of a hemline, a particular kind of fabric, a particular color or color palette – across a number of material instantiations. Such multiplication takes place within a particular temporal envelope, an unfolding synchrony subject to faddish ephemerality, as well as to fashion's characteristically rapid (re)cycling and involuted citational *renvoi* (so-called 'retro') (see Mukherjee, this volume).

Compare this with that fashion design element that *is* protectable by intellectual property – the trademark. The identifying function of the trademark requires some degree of constancy of form and referent across time and space. The citation of trademarks is so tightly regulated that trademarks are, relative to other design elements, static in form. The trademark is seemingly not subject to the same kinds of circulation and dissemination as other design elements, not subject to fashion's temporality in the same way. In fact, by definition, all authorized iterations of a brand's trademarks are, in some sense, (functionally) 'identical', even if distinct. Consider, for example, Louis Vuitton's classic and unchanged 'Toile Monogram' trademark, created in 1896 and registered in France

---

[13] While patents, and design patents in particular, would seem to be applicable to fashion design, they rarely fit the criteria of non-trivial novelty and non-obviousness (Schmidt 1983:867–868; Hagin 1991:354–356; Tsai 2005:455–458; Scafidi 2006:122–123; Jenkins and Cox 2008). Fashion innovations are oftentimes small alterations to an existing design, and hence don't fulfill the necessary criterion for novelty to receive a patent. Moreover, given the rapidity of the fashion cycle (3–6 months) relative to the time to receive a patent (a minimum of 6 months given the requirement to search for novelty) patents are not feasible for much fashion design. Further, given their relative expense (and the high number of designs produced for each fashion season), they are often not economically viable options to protect design. Design patents (unlike utility patents) also have a non-functionality requirement (i.e., that the good's function be purely ornamental) which makes their use in fashion design difficult.

in 1905. In 2002, as part of the revitalization of the brand, Louis Vuitton unveiled its first co-branding venture with Takashi Murakami (see above), the result of which was the 'Louis Vuitton Toile Monogram Murakami Trademarks'. While identical in form and arrangement, the two marks do differ in certain qualia. In the Murukami version, as decorating Louis Vuitton's popular Multicolore handbags, the mark is rendered in multiple colors (33 to be exact) rather than the Toile's classic gold. It is precisely in this difference of quality that the possibility of an exteriority, and citational menace, to the trademark was opened. Shortly after the launch of this trademark the lower-market designer brand, Dooney & Bourke proceeded to create their own multicolored monogram handbag, not with Louis Vuitton's trademark but with its 'look'. Dooney & Bourke's 'It Bag' had DB's trademarked monogram splayed across the bag in multiple colors in a way that was reminiscent of, and in fact shown to be directly inspired by, Vuitton's Multicolore monogrammed bags. Louis Vuitton sued for infringement (Louis Vuitton v. Dooney & Bourke 2008). They ultimately lost, however, which is to say that the courts reiterated that the look is not the trademark. Every trademark has its own aesthetic that exceeds the trademark's status as a trademark. There is a surfeit to the trademark. It itself has its own 'look', one that partially falls outside of its identity, and thus cannot be legally protected. While Louis Vuitton uses the aesthetics of its trademarks to leverage itself in consumer markets – the look of its goods is its trademarks multiplied all over the commodity – this has its own limit. The look of a trademark can, after all, be cited. Its qualia can be copied. Here, then, we see the gap between trademark and fashion, between ownership and copying, identity and aesthetics.

Compare this materialization to the surfeits in Chennai that I discussed above. Here as well we have come to a limit of the trademark, but of a rather different sort. Such economies, as I noted, are seemingly defined by their relationship to the brand heartlands to which they are peripheral. In places like India, surfeit garments exist because of demand for the 'real' thing elsewhere. They are locally desired, presumably, because of that very existence and demand. From the perspective of the brand, such surfeits are 'copies' of an 'original', attempts to capture the aura and steal the profits from that elsewhere. Of course, the irony is that conceptions of intellectual property and aesthetics, and even the very ontology of what a brand 'is', are – for certain people at least – radically different in South India (Nakassis 2012a, 2012b, 2013d), as elsewhere around the globe (Vann 2006; Luvaas 2013; Thomas 2013).

Indeed, the local producers and consumers with whom I worked were rather indifferent to the brand: 'no one cares about brands' was a common refrain. Rather, such garments have a 'look' – they're 'stylish', 'different' and visually interesting. Most producers and their youth consumers didn't know much about, or (communicate their) care to know much about, the brands they so eagerly re-produced and consumed. Rather, they were interested in clothing that looked like it was branded – that is, that had that 'look', as they put it – even as they were indifferent to actual brands and questions of brand authenticity more generally. In any case, for these non-elites, everyone knew that such goods weren't the 'real' thing. In fact, in the peer groups of the lower-middle- and middle-class young men with whom I worked, authentic, authorized brands – with their hefty price tags and presumptions to social status – were likely to provoke undesirable envy and censure from peers. They often elicited claims of arrogance and offensive ostentation, teasing and gossip that one was presuming to be better than others when one was not. Such youth, instead, safely enjoyed surfeits of the brand. Such brand-esque forms, *as* surfeits, kept at an arm's length the problems raised by the authentic brand even as they alluded to its social value and prestige. As a result, these young men were less attentive to the authorized identity and provenance of the commodity than to the commodity's aesthetics as such, with its ability to align its user with a cosmopolitan imaginary of fashion (which they called 'style') while not presuming to be a credentialized member of it (Nakassis 2013d).

From the perspective of the design and manufacture of such surfeits, one principle that disconnects the trademark in these contexts from its legal regimentation is, ironically enough, the law itself, or rather, local producers' understanding of it (Nakassis 2012a). There was an anxiety among local producers about being prosecuted for trademark infringement. When I was doing my fieldwork, some producers, I was told, had been made examples of by big brand companies, brought up on charges and levied heavy fines for 'piracy'. As a result, the producers that I spoke with made sure to alter the trademarks that they reanimated. They didn't, they insisted, make exact replicas of brand garments or of their trademarks. To their mind, any quantum of difference in how they rendered a trademark or design was enough to make their works legal, from a slightly altered curvature to a different spelling or a changed font. They were operating with the understanding that a trademark was not just a diacritic of origin, but part of the garment's 'look'. It was part of fashion. In their hands, then, the trademarks of a brand were design elements, aesthetic forms that could be played with and redeployed. As with their youth consumers, for these producers it wasn't brand identity, image, provenance or authenticity that was important for their practice (Vann 2006), but an *aesthetics of brandedness* (Nakassis 2012a). And indeed, these local producers didn't only copy trademarks, but also whole modalities of presenting brand commodities: they used branded and brand-esque labels, price tags and even packaging to give the commodity a so-called 'royal' look, to look *like* an authentic, authorized good even if it was, obviously, not.

These surfeit producers and designers, and their consumers, exist in the orbit of the trademark but also beyond it, in the possibility of its qualia. They cite the brand, or rather the idea of it. And in doing so, they generate a whole range of garments and aesthetic forms. Interestingly, such forms *were* connected to trends in brand heartlands. Indeed, what they copied, as I noted above, came from export surplus, the detritus of goods produced in India for consumption abroad. One Chennai producer that I spoke with, for example, got his hands on a large surplus of Columbia brand price tags that were produced in the state for export abroad. With his new tags, he began producing Columbian shorts, embroidering his 'new' brand name – only differing from Columbia's by the 'n' appended at its end – along with Columbia's logo onto fabrics culled from other surplus garments and defect goods (Nakassis 2012a).

Note, then, how the 'demand' for a brand in 'foreign' brand heartlands guides what was copied locally even if there was no 'demand' for such brands among local, non-elite consumers.[14] How could there be 'demand' for such brands if these local producers and consumers didn't reckon the signs of the brand as of the brand at all, but as simply 'stylish' aesthetic elements? The surfeit at one end of the world materializes, through citational relay, a surfeit on the other. From high fashion to mass-market brands to 'piracy' in South India, certain qualities of brand forms are transported, repeated, altered, cited.

This aesthetics of brandedness materializes in a locally particular way. Copying, here, is untethered from the brand and its trademarks. Indeed, if no one cares to care about brands, and if the brand is displayed and worn not as a brand but as something else (i.e., as 'style'), then there is no anchor to tether the brand in this citational economy. A brand can be cited into non-existence, into unrecognizability, deformed until its identity is lost along the way, its origin erased. Hence the wide range of

---

[14] It is important to keep in mind the class specificity here. Upper-middle-class and elite consumers, in distinction to non-elite youth, were often fastidious about brands and their authenticity.

brand-esque and fictive brand forms that one finds across South India and similar places. Something remains, of course, just not the identity of the brand. Only the mere idea of it lingers, its aesthetics, its qualities. A brand is decomposed into a set of reanimatable fractions, design elements to be used later and elsewhere to make a different-enough look.

To highlight how this citational economy differently materializes its surfeit, compare this aesthetics of brandedness with 'knock-offs' found in situations where the authenticity and authority of the brand *qua* brand 'original' is highly consequential and performative of status, aesthetics and value: high-end handbags in brand heartlands. Such handbags, especially those from brands like Louis Vuitton and Hermés are widely counterfeited and copied, as we saw above. The surfeits of such bags are also heavily policed and prosecuted through the law. In distinction to Dooney and Bourke's fashion citations, however, knock-offs of high-end handbags are valued for their ability to 'pass' as, or at least figurate passing as, their brand originals. Such surfeits are simulacra, aiming to *be* that which they are not. Rather than marking themselves *as* surfeits, which is to say, as citations, their reflexive signs of difference are downplayed and hidden. Such difference should not be recoverable at all, in fact. The knock-off should be identical in every way (with the exception, of course, of price). Indeed, the very citationality of such surfeits can often only be recovered through specialty knowledge ('taste' or 'connoisseurship' as it is often operationalized) and sleuthing which, luckily for the fashion tyro, the Internet provides in spades. A Google search for 'how to tell if a Louis Vuitton is real' generates pages upon pages of sites pedagogically dedicated to telling the difference between 'real' and 'fake' Vuitton products.

It is in such contexts – where the authenticity and provenance of the brand is paramount for reckoning the commodity's value, aesthetics, meaning and identity – that the distinction between 'copy' and 'original' becomes most ideologically salient, when it can be said to exist. And yet curiously, it is in such contexts that the very material forms typified as 'originals' and 'copies' also become near indistinguishable. While we all know that we *should* know the difference between the 'real' and the 'fake' Hermés bag, telling them apart can be near impossible. As authenticity becomes more and more important, the material differences between 'original' and surfeit become less and less perceptible, more and more minute. They also become further and further removed from the space of the trademark itself. It is the qualia that accompany the trademark (the stitching, the shape, font, etc.), the whole commodity aesthetic and the engineering of the commodity that become the site for the authentication and authority of brand identity. Hence, consider the bagbible.com blog's section for 'how to spot a fake' (last accessed 1st July 2013): here one gets tips on how to compare the contour, the shape, the lock design, the stitching patterns and the 'stamp' of logos on 'real' and 'fake' bags. Comparatively speaking, the material gap between surfeit and 'original' decreases in inverse proportion to the policing of that gap.

By contrast, the materiality of surfeit in the South Indian case becomes more and more detached from what it cites with every copy, the 'original' more and more suspended and deformed. The surfeit floats off, the forms become more and more patently 'fake'. And yet, curiously, this materialized difference, this ever-widening and visible gap, is also seemingly erased and unseen, invisible to these goods' brand-indifferent producers and consumers. Indifference to authenticity opens up a space beyond the brand, and hence allows for the play of material alteration across iterations. Here the materialization of difference proceeds in direct proportion to producers' and consumers' indifference. This epistemology of surfeit, we might say, materializes a different ontology. Brands are not the issue, for they don't quite exist anymore. Suspended by indifference and inscribed in material difference, they are cited out of being.

## Quality Beyond the Copy

At the edge of authorization, identity is perilous. Intellectual property law enables forms of copying that conserve the identity of that which is cited, and yet such copies always threaten to lose their origin, to cease being copies altogether. Trademark, from this point of view, is a regime of authorization, a semiotic and economic anchor to never let the commodity get too far from the brand (but also not too close). Trademark law polices a fine line between surfeits and 'originals'. It aims to protect the identity of the 'original', to stabilize it by projecting, and introjecting, its surfeit. But what of the forms of unanchoring and decentering that occur when the trademark's authority is ignored, when its importance is met with indifference, when the very distinction between 'original' and 'copy' is itself put into question? Perhaps it is this possibility that most troubles the brand (to say nothing of other regimes of originality). The brand, as the center of this regime of authenticity and authorization, attempts to catch both itself and its surfeits in its web, to make itself always and everywhere the coordinates of commodity intelligibility, a Jupiter around which all its surfeit satellites rotate. This is a tenuous achievement indeed, one that attempts to stay the never-ending quivering of quality, the unbridling of possibility latent in every act of citation.

This is why it is not enough to show how 'real' and 'fake' are cultural categories, mere epistemologies over a messy 'reality' that abides, unto itself, no such distinctions. These issues of citation and quality, the quality of a copy, and the status of a copy as copy, are ontological questions. They are questions of materiality and materialization. What does it mean for something to be 'a copy'? What is the materiality of a surfeit when it stands under or outside of a regime of authenticity, when it is typified as a 'copy' or not? How does it open up a social field of relations and performative force? How does it temporalize itself, how does it spatialize itself, how does it map out a social terrain? Only by asking these questions can we come to understand what makes high fashion in New York and surfeit fashion in South India so different and so similar, what makes a 'low-IP' environment, and what it makes.

Citations act on, and activate, the quality of things. They materialize and create possibilities out of them. And in doing so, they open up other imaginaries and forms of social relation. It is these spaces, their materiality, their sociality and their performativity that must be the grounds upon which any analysis of 'real' and 'fake' must operate, which any analysis of 'original' and 'copy' must occupy, for it is this space which is constantly on the move, shifting beneath this metaphysics and its institutional manifestations. The exteriority opened by the citation is not simply on the margins, but at the very center of the (brand) universe. Or to put it another way, the quality of the copy is that it is also always *not* a copy, but something else still. And it is *that* quality which allows it to be a copy, to whatever extent it is. In repetition, something is elicited and created, something that cannot be reduced back to the identity of the thing copied. Beyond 'real' and 'fake' and beyond repetition we might ask what are the horizons that are opened, what qualities and possibilities exist? Is not fashion itself one of them?

# References

**Legal Cases**

Abercrombie & Fitch Stores, Inc. v. American Eagle Outfitters, Inc., 6th Circuit, US Court of Appeals, 2002.

Adidas-Salomon AG v. Target Corp., US District Court, Oregon, 2002.

Knitwaves, Inc. v. Lollytags, Ltd. (Inc.), 2d Circuit, US Court of Appeals, 1995.

Louboutin v. Yves Saint Laurent, 2d Circuit, US Court of Appeals, 2012.

Louis Vuitton Malletier v. Dooney & Bourke, Inc., US District Court, SDNY, 2008.

Mazer et al. v. Stein et al., US Supreme Court, 1954.

Qualitex Co. v. Jacobson Products Co., US Supreme Court, 1995.

## Academic Citations

Agins, Terri. 2000. *The End of Fashion: How Marketing Changed the Clothing Business Forever.* New York: Quill.

Arvidsson, Adam. 2005. *Brands: Meaning and Value in Media Culture.* London: Routledge.

Bakhtin, Mikhail. 1982. *The Dialogic Imagination.* Austin: University of Texas Press.

Barnett, Jonathon. 2005. 'Shopping for Gucci on Canal Street: Reflections on Status Consumption, Intellectual Property, and the Incentive Thesis'. *Virginia Law Review* 91, 1381–1423.

Bharati, S. Priya. 1996. 'There Is More Than One Way to Skin a Copycat: The Emergency of Trade Dress to Combat Design Piracy of Fashion Works'. *Texas Tech Law Review* 27, 1667–1695.

Bently, Lionel. 2008. 'The Making of Modern Trade Mark Law: The Construction of the Legal Concept of Trade Mark (1860–1880)'. In L. Bently, J. Davis, and J. Ginsburg (Eds.) *Trademarks and Brands.* New York: Cambridge University Press.

Coombe, Rosemary. 1998. *The Cultural Life of Intellectual Property.* Durham, NC: Duke University Press.

Cox, Christine and Jennifer Jenkins. 2008. 'Between the Seams, a Fertile Commons: An Overview of the Relationship between Fashion and Intellectual Property'. *Ready to Share: Fashion and the Ownership of Creativity,* Norman Lear Center Conference, USC Annenberg School of Communication, 28 January, 2005. http://learcenter.org/pdf/RTSJenkinsCox.pdf

Foster, Robert. 2007. 'The Work of the New Economy: Consumers, Brands, and Value Creation'. *Cultural Anthropology* 22:4, 707–731.

Fournier, Susan. 1998. 'Consumers and Their Brands: Developing Relationship Theory in Consumer Research'. *Journal of Consumer Research* 24:4, 343–373.

Gal, Susan. 2002. 'A Semiotics of the Public/Private Distinction'. *differences* 13:1, 77–95.

Gangjee, Dev. 2008. 'The Polymorphism of Trademark Dilution in India'. *Transnational Law and Contemporary Problems* 17:3, 611–630.

Graan, Andrew. 2013. 'Counterfeiting the Nation? Skopje 2014 and the Politics of Nation Branding in Macedonia'. *Cultural Anthropology* 28:1, 161–179.

Hagin, Leslie. 1991. 'A Comparative Analysis of Copyright Laws Applied to Fashion Works'. *Texas International Law Journal* 26, 341–388.

Hilton, Brian, Chong Ju Choi, and Stephen Chen. 2004. 'The Ethics of Counterfeiting in the Fashion Industry'. *Journal of Business Ethics* 55:345–354.

Kaufman, Sarah J. 2005. 'Trend Forecast: Imitation is a Legal Form of Flattery—Louis Vuitton Malletier v. Dooney and Bourke, Inc'. *Cardozo Arts and Entertainment Law Journal* 23, 531–566.

Klein, Naomi. 2000. *No Logo.* New York: Picador.

Kuldova, Tereza. 2013. *Designing Elites: Fashion and Prestige in Urban North India.* PhD thesis, University of Oslo.

Lury, Celia. 2004. *Brands: The Logos of the Global Economy.* London: Routledge.

Luvaas, Brent. 2010. 'Designer Vandalism: Indonesian Indie Fashion and the Cultural Practice of Cut 'n' Paste'. *Visual Anthropology Review* 26:1, 1–16.

‐‐‐‐‐‐‐‐‐. 2013. 'Material Interventions: Indonesian DIY Fashion and the Regime of the Global Brand'. *Cultural Anthropology* 28:1, 127-143.

Manning, Paul. 2010. 'The Semiotics of Brand'. *Annual Review of Anthropology* 39, 33-49.

Marshall, Laura C. 2007. 'Catwalk Copycats: Why Congress Should Adopt a Modified Version of the Design Piracy Prohibition Act'. *Journal of Intellectual Property Law* 14, 305-331.

Moore, Robert. 2003. 'From Genericide to Viral Marketing: On 'Brand''. *Language and Communication* 23, 331-357.

Muniz, Albert and Thomas O'Guinn. 2001. 'Brand Community'. *Journal of Consumer Research*.27:4, 412-432.

Nakassis, Constantine. 2012a. 'Counterfeiting What? Aesthetics of Brandedness and BRAND in Tamil Nadu, India'. *Anthropological Quarterly* 85:3, 701-722.
‐‐‐‐‐‐‐‐. 2012b. 'Brand, Citationality, Performativity'. *American Anthropologist* 114:4, 624-638.
‐‐‐‐‐‐‐‐. 2013a. 'Brands and Their Surfeits'. *Cultural Anthropology* 28:1, 111-126.
‐‐‐‐‐‐‐‐. 2013b. 'Citation and Citationality'. *Signs and Society* 1:1, 51-78.
‐‐‐‐‐‐‐‐. 2013c. 'The Para-s/cite'. *Semiotic Review* (May). http://semioticreview.com.
‐‐‐‐‐‐‐‐. 2013d. 'Youth Masculinity, 'Style', and the Peer Group in Tamil Nadu, India'. *Contributions to Indian Sociology* 47:2, 245-269.
‐‐‐‐‐‐‐‐. 2013e. 'Materiality, Materialization. A Comment on Hull, Matthew. 2012. *Government of Paper*. Berkeley: University of California Press.' *HAU: Journal of Ethnographic Theory* 3:3.

Norris, Lucy. 2010. Recycling Indian Clothing. Bloomington: Indiana University Press.

Nurbhai, Safia. 2002. 'Style Piracy Revisited'. *Journal of Law and Policy* 10, 489-537.

Pang, Laikwan. 2008. ''China Who Makes and Fakes': A Semiotics of the Counterfeit'. *Theory, Culture, and Society* 25:6, 117-140.

Raustiala, Kal and Christopher Sprigman. 2006. 'The Piracy Paradox: Innovation and Intellectual Property in Fashion Design'. *Virginia Law Review* 92:8, 1687-1777.
‐‐‐‐‐‐‐‐. 2009. 'The Piracy Paradox Revisited'. *Stanford Law Review* 61:5, 1201-1225.

Scafidi, Susan. 2006. 'Intellectual Property and Fashion Design'. In Peter K. Yu (Ed.) *Intellectual Property and Information Wealth*, volume 1. Praeger.

Schechter, Frank I. 1927. 'The Rational Basis of Trademark Protection'. *Harvard Law Review* 40:6, 813-833.

Schmidt, Rocky. 1983. 'Designer Law: Fashioning a Remedy for Design Piracy'. *UCLA Law Review* 30, 861-880.

Stevens, Alexis. 2012. 'Not Designed to Fit: Why the Innovative Design Protection and Piracy Prevention Act Should Not Be Made into Law'. *Pace Law Review* 32:3, 856-894.

Stewart, Mary Lynn. 2005. 'Copying and Copyrighting Haute Couture: Democratizing Fashion, 1900-1930s'. *French Historical Studies* 28:1, 103-130.

Tarlo, Emma. 1996. *Clothing Matters*. Chicago: University of Chicago Press.

Thomas, Kedron. 2009. 'Structural Adjustment, Spatial Imaginaries, and "Piracy" in Guatemala's Apparel Industry'. *Anthropology of Work Review* 30:1, 1-10.
‐‐‐‐‐‐‐‐. 2013. 'Brand "Piracy" and Postwar Statecraft in Guatemala'. *Cultural Anthropology* 28:1, 144-160.

Tsai, Julie. 2005. 'Fashioning Protection: A Note on the Protection of Fashion Designs in the United States'. *Lewis and Clark Law Review* 9:2, 447-468.

Tu, Kevin. 2010. 'Counterfeit Fashion: The Interplay between Copyright and Trademark Law in Original Fashion Designs and Designer Knockoffs'. *Texas Intellectual Property Law Journal* 18:3, 419-449.

Vann, Elizabeth. 2006. 'The Limits of Authenticity in Vietnamese Consumer Markets'. *American Anthropologist* 108:2, 286-296.

Weikart, Maurice A. 1944. 'Design Piracy'. *Indiana Law Journal* 19, 235-257.

Wilkins, Mira. 1992. 'The Neglected Intangible Asset: The Influence of the Trade Mark on the Rise of the Modern Corporation'. *Business History* 34:1, 66-99.

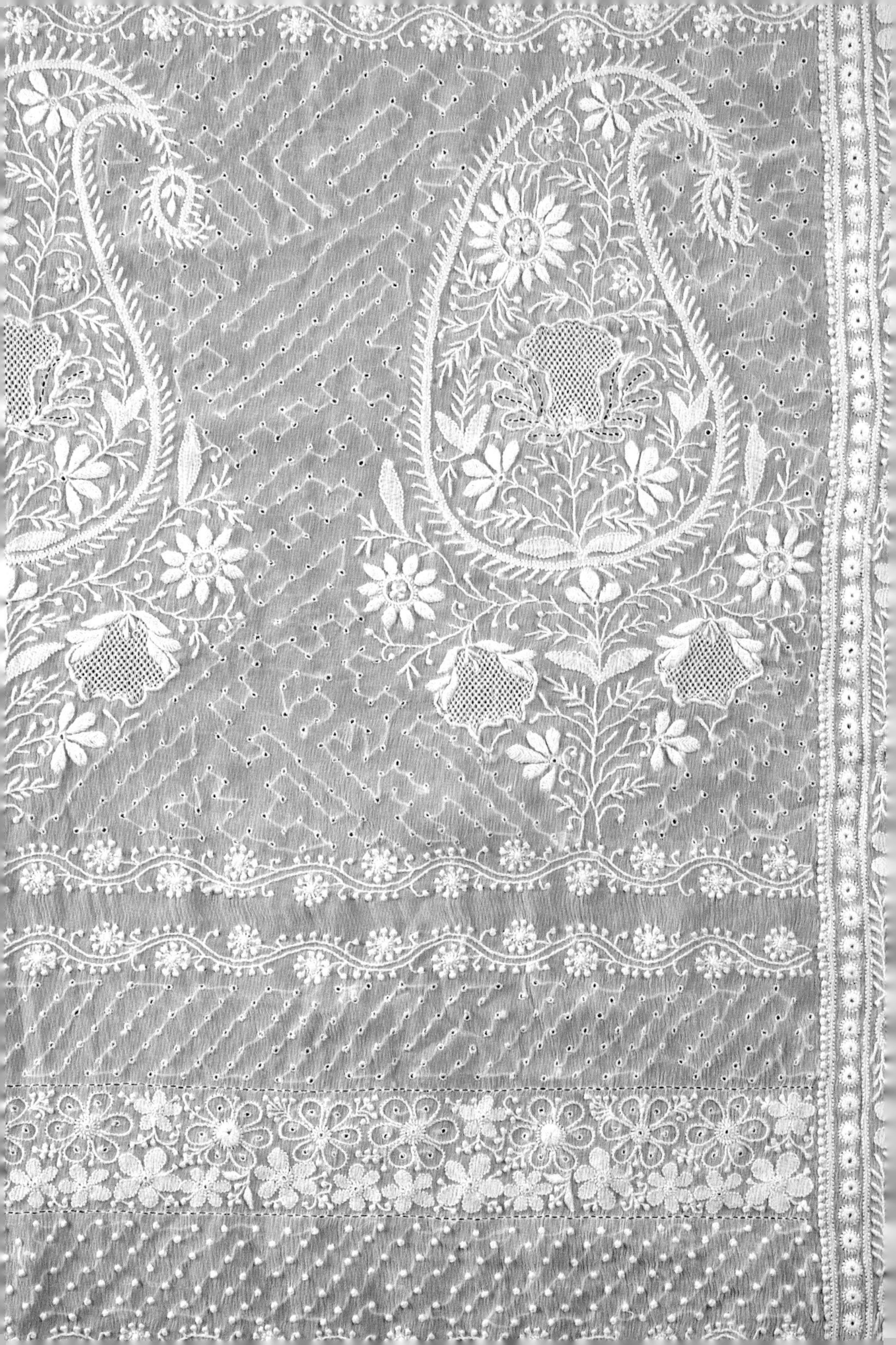

# Laughing at Luxury
## Mocking Fashion Designers
Tereza Kuldova

> *We laugh at them, they have everything but still they are miserable. They think that we are poor, that we don't have anything. But we have everything we need. Look at the village, everything is here, fresh air, water, fields, food, and look at the city, it is just dirt and people miserable and fighting, and they come to teach us how to live?*[1]

Indian high-end fashion design and the heritage luxury segment depend on the work of thousands of artisans and craftsmen around the country. These artisans imbue the products with the 'spirit of India', with the 'Indian touch', as the rhetoric goes. Indian handicrafts are without doubt the *unique selling point* (USP) of the vast majority of Indian fashion designers. Therefore, fashion designers are forced to work and directly cooperate with craftsmen, as the aesthetics of their own products depends on the negotiations with, and creative potentials of, the *individual* artisans. Accordingly, the fashion garments force the urban elite and rural poor into networks of mutual dependency: a dependency that often goes unacknowledged yet still lurks behind, and haunts the designers, even when they are on the relatively safe grounds of the city. Let us now look at the world of production, concretely the production of chikan embroidery, traditional embroidery from Lucknow. Let us enter a world that is largely kept invisible and hidden, set apart from the designers' theatrical displays, and look at the ways in which the designers are kept at a distance by village *chikan* embroiderers.

*Chikan* embroidery, traditional embroidery produced in Lucknow, Uttar Pradesh, North India. The embroidery is produced in a multi-stage process, where the fabrics are first printed with the desired design using carved wooden blocks dipped in indigo colour by a *chikan* printer, then embroidered by skilled female embroiderers, finally the colour is washed away by washer-men specialising in *chikan*.
© Tereza Kuldova, 2011

---

[1] Reconstructed from field-notes, 22/8/2011.

*Chikan* blockmaker carving a wooden block for the printing of *chikan* design.
© Tereza Kuldova, 2012

An exclusive carved wooden block in the shape of an elephant containing eighteen female figures within, from the collection of Muhammad Ali, a famous Lucknow printer.
© Tereza Kuldova, 2012

*Chikan* signature printing block, custom-made for Tarun Tahiliani, one of India's leading fashion designers.
© Tereza Kuldova, 2011

Muhammad Ali, a Lucknow-based printer, with his collection of old wooden blocks.
© Arash Taheri, 2012

*Chikan* printing block with the logo of the luxury chain of Oberoi Hotels, custom made for the Mumbai branch. The logo was then embroidered on the bed sheets for the deluxe suits.
© Tereza Kuldova, 2011

## Ironic Encounters and the Production of Distance

India at times appears as though it consists of parallel worlds that meet daily while at the same time not meeting. We can see how luxury depends on poverty – how the lotus always grows from the mud – yet this appearance of separation also needs to be discursively, aesthetically and materially reproduced on everyday basis (see Kuldova, p. 51-70). We will now examine how the city depends on the village; how the designer depends on the artisans; and how the powerless execute their power over the powerful, while haunting them with their ironic self-reflexivity. The idea of two parallel universes within India relates to the notion of parallel economies (Sarkar 2010) and the split between the formal (organised) and informal (unorganised) sector, a split that mirrors the dichotomies between neo-liberal capitalist economy and vernacular economy (Jain 2007). Thus the Indian world often appears as if it is bifurcated along the lines of the formal and the informal, the neo-liberal and the vernacular, the legal and the black market.

Within this logic, the fashion designer would represent the formal economy, the neo-liberal capitalist logic and the legal market, while craftswomen, on the other hand, would be represent the informal vernacular economy, stretched to the margins of legality (Mahmud 2010), indeed this, to a large degree, *becomes* true. I would argue, however, that this should not be taken as a starting point, but should rather be questioned. The ironic actions of the embroiderers bear the potential of revealing this strict bifurcation to be a well-crafted illusion. This appearance of disjunct worlds that are in reality performatively connected has to be continually produced through everyday practices of distantiation that keep each other *mutually* 'in place' and as such is therefore far from given. This appearance is dependent on everyday mutual production of distance. Practices of distantiation are often considered a privilege of those in power (gated communities, restricted access to social arenas etc.). I wish to argue for a reverse look at these practices, whereby those who we might often believe want to do something to minimise the gap in fact actively partake in its creation.

The mutual dependence of designers and craftswomen suggests a relationship of mutual constitutiveness, while at the same time existing contemporaneously across 'epistemologically parallel economies' (Jain 2007: 365). This ethnographic excursus will reveal how the craftswomen mock the designers, along with their neo-liberal approach to life predicated upon the Western cosmology of needs and suffering (Sahlins 1996) in which consumption becomes a path to worldly salvation (Appelbaum 1998), happiness and well-being. Mocking the concerns of

Village-based *chikan* embroiderers laughing while embroidering. © Tereza Kuldova, 2011

the designer, laughing at the luxury embroideries they produce, and intentionally frustrating the designer and causing them to suffer, may be perceived as manifestations of the ways in which 'postcolonial subjects function across *epistemologically disjunct yet performatively networked worlds*: the worlds of bourgeois-liberal and neoliberal modernism on the one hand and those of 'vernacular' discourses and practices on the other' (Jain 2007: 14).

While designers often try to position themselves as patrons, rescuers, innovators, creative heads, guides, experts, caretakers of the 'poor' and 'illiterate' by virtue of supplying them with work, providing extra income and no less than giving them 'self-respect' and 'dignity', the craftswomen more often than not laugh these agendas off as silly and as of no use, employing the notorious '*humko kyaa faidaa hogaa?*', which loosely translates as 'what is in it for us?'.

This ironic distantiation provides them with a space for self-reflection and security in their own lifeworlds, in their own truths and values. The neoliberal market, together with its commodification and glamorisation of the work of craftsmen, is, through this ironic distantiation, revealed as a *particular regime*, a contingent regime. The ironic distantiation of the craftswomen haunts the world of the designers, shaking up the taken for granted ontology of their world and replacing it instead with hauntology (Derrida 1994) that reveals a multitude of possible realities. The ironic remarks of the village based chikan embroiderers also revealed how in order for elites to be able to fashion themselves in nationalism, retro-futuristic courtly splendour and transnational elitism, the *craftsmen need to be kept where they are*, producing the material stuff of the mythologies of the nation, producing commodities that would most suitably brand the locality for the global markets.

In the direct encounters with the designers the chikan craftswomen, especially the older ones, often challenged the role of the designer as a patron, as a taste connoisseur and as a knowledgeable authority, emphasising the designer's dependence on their specialised knowledge as much as mocking the designer's ability to perform the function of a patron in a proper manner, constantly threatening by leaving the work, not finishing the work and so on, emphasising their power over the designer and his dependence on them. Only those designers who 'behaved' could been, if lucky, rewarded by having stable embroiderers. Those designers who did not behave and became known for delayed payments or irregular work, established over time a reputation that travelled through the women's craft and family networks and often resulted in great difficulties for the designer to establish his own craft centres in the villages. And so while the designer is fully immersed in the neoliberal economy, dependent on money to satisfy most of his needs, the rural embroiderers claim their relative independence from this economy due to what they themselves call the simplicity of their lives.

## The Regimes of the Village and the City
The rural women work on the embroidery for couple of hours a day and are, strictly-speaking, not dependent on the income derived from this for survival, as they often have not only fields but also male relatives (such as fathers, brothers, husbands) who all combine their income from diverse activities. This is in addition to other supportive extended kin networks, coupled with considerably low expenditure. With good enough reason, many would surely stop working for a designer who does not live up to the role of a reliable patron, that is, fails to provide regular work; payment; increases in times of need (such as weddings, deaths, violent encounters and so on). Some have chosen to stop working, privileging 'peace of mind' over 'hassle' with designers. Peace of mind often appeared to be the priority. Provided the work could be done on their own terms and at their own pace the women would

*Chikan* embroiderers in a workshop in the city, while the designer is absent.
© Arash Taheri, 2012

accept it, should the pressure for deliveries increase however, many would prefer to either switch to another designer or businessman or perhaps leave the work temporary.

The fact that many women would opt to leave the work if dissatisfied with the work provider was perceived by the designers, NGOs and middle-class urban intelligentsia as a 'great loss', a 'sad fact', a 'problem', something that needed to be fixed. This was, again, grounded in the argument that should this issue not be resolved then these women would forever remain impoverished. Such thinking, however, only makes sense within the logic of craft preservation, that is, conservation of the idealised nation, something not necessarily within the logic of the craftswomen.

There is a striking difference between the rural and urban embroiderers that must be accounted for here. The rural embroiderers, as opposed to the urban embroiderers in Lucknow, are in a position from which they can challenge the notions of elite dominance in a much more straightforward fashion than urban embroiderers can, who become drawn into the economy of the city: working full days; depending on their income for survival; and, eventually, becoming less and less likely to challenge, oppose or 'misbehave'. Compared to the rural *chikan* embroiderers, the urban embroiderers appeared much easier to control to the designer. Therefore, more and more designers are insisting on shifting the women from villages to urban centres into workshop-like spaces, where they would be controlled, under supervision and working effectively. In the case of *chikan* embroidery, still predominantly rural-based, even though the number of urban embroiderers is increasing, such a step is still difficult. For one, most women do not wish to leave the village, for the second they may be restrained by the observation of *purdah*. Establishing centres within villages is often the best designers can do, and even that was initially problematic as it tended to be threatening to the village patriarchy – women gathering and chatting each afternoon and discussing local issues certainly meant that their local power would increase, as they would share local news and gossip. (The empowerment of women through embroidery might thus paradoxically lie in their daily gathering in one space rather than in the extra income, which often ends up in the hands of their fathers or husbands anyway).

The support of village crafts thus often merges with the business need of the designers to produce faster and more effectively. Therefore, under the development logic of female empowerment, women migrate from villages to cities and this often transpires to be not as great a trade-off as promised – ironic realisations of this follow. The *chikan* embroidery finds itself in between the village and the city and thus offers us unique insight into the differences, possibilities and limitations of rural and urban craftswomen and of their possibilities for subversion.

The arguments of the designers, NGOs and so forth regarding the necessity of such supervised workshops always tends to be predicated upon the neoliberal logic of effectivity; higher payment and a clean environment; fixed schedules and routine; and maximisation of profit, combined with the corporate ethical logic intended to avoid any critique amongst the upper segment and foreign buyers – on the *formal* paper the workers are treated well, according to the ethical code. However, this produces 'a form of governance that seeks to maintain strict control over production regimes and workers' movements' (De Neve 2012: 7). The *chikan* embroiderers in the villages mocked the urban settings of production and the designer's 'mind-set', often actively seeking to avoid these neoliberal labour regimes. The *chikan* embroiderers critiqued the neoliberal labour regimes, precisely because of the discrepancy between what they are assumed to, or should be, valuing according to the capitalist and what they actually value. The women preferred to retain control over their lives and, therefore, also their independence and dignity over strict regimes of time discipline and clean environment with a 'fair wage'. The labour regimes that the designers and traders-cum-designers, as much as NGOs attempt to instigate often, under the rhetoric of ethics, empowerment, development and improved conditions of work, turn out to be often 'divorced from the actual needs and aspirations of the workers on which they are imposed (...); these largely Western projects of imposition do not go unchallenged when viewed from a worker's perspective' (De Neve 2012: 21).

## Irony and the Curse of Money

The ironic attitude stems from a discrepancy experienced between words and actions of the designers and other 'development helpers', combined with a feeling that money is cursed. While lacking money can make life hard, suddenly having more money can make life even harder, leading to unanticipated troubles, family fights and lack of, rather than the increase of, freedom and so on. The increase in money implies erasure of 'leisure', the most sought after quality, particularly so in Lucknow and its surroundings, where leisure has a quite specific meaning. Here it is connected to the era of the Nawabs of Lucknow, who are still remembered as elites living in leisure, lying around all day long, being served the best food and indulging in luxuries from all over the world. It is said in Lucknow that, no matter how poor, everyone behaves like a nawab, always lazing around and having plenty of time. While some embroiderers imagined that given more money they would have more time for leisure, the opposite turned out to be the case – yet another reason for the ironic attitude. For one of the Lucknow-based designers that I have worked with, the desire for leisure was the main obstacle when it came to dealing with 'her workers'. As she said:

> ... they always have enough time, they are never in a hurry, in fact they have no concept of time, they just want to lie around; they don't understand one cannot live life like that. It is so hard to come by anyone hardworking, they all just want to relax, that is the Lucknow *tehzeeb* [culture].

Like all the other designers, she juxtaposed her hectic working tempo, with no space left for relaxation, with the slow-paced leisurely life of the craftswomen:

> They don't understand that I have to run around whole day, manage all orders, manage designers in Delhi and Mumbai, distribute work, design my own pieces, sample pieces for abroad, you have to market it, you have to network and all. They don't understand that I have to do all that in order to be even able to pay them.[2]

---

[2] Reconstructed from field-notes, 10/9/2010.

*Chhota Imambara*, the famous monument in Lucknow built by Muhammad Ali Shah, the third Nawab of Lucknow in 1838. Lucknow is associated with the lavish and luxurious lifestyle of the Nawabs (governors appointed by the Mughal emperor, in practice independent rulers of their respective territories) of Awadh and the syncretic composite Indo-Muslim culture that they nurtured in the city. During their reign, the city became the cultural hub of India, renowned for its poetry and arts as much as fashion. Chikan is largely associated with this pre-British glorious period of Lucknow's past.
© Arash Taheri, 2012

From the perspective of the craftswomen, the designers are always stressed, always running after something, always giving orders, always hectic, as they say *'yeh log aaraam aur shaanti kabhi nahi milte hai'* [these people never relax and get peace]. They often connect this to their own stories, recounting their experiences with the *effect* of money. These stories are marked by the ambiguity of the necessity of having (enough) money on the one hand and of having too much money as a bad thing, on the other. One of the embroiderers, after a great deal of encouragement from one of the Delhi-based designers began working particularly intensely; she learned new stitches and worked more hours (increasing from previously four hours to around nine). She believed that she would then be more independent and have more power, as the designer had promised. The other girls laughed at her sitting up late, arguing that it wouldn't make any difference. Once she began earning more, her husband realised that there was therefore no need for him to work and so left his jobs and began to quite literally laze around. In the end, she even had to borrow money from the designer to reconstruct the simple house they were living in, she assumed all the responsibility in the household, paid her children's school fees and so on, reversing the traditional husband-wife roles, while her husband was simply hanging around and sleeping throughout the day.

A number of women, who came from the village but whose husbands began working in the city in various low paying jobs, and had since relocated to work in the city themselves, mourned the times that they were in the village. In the city, they now had to work six or even seven days a week from morning to evening, the only thing they felt they were good for was earning money. 'Money snatched away my life from me', as one said. The only thing they wanted was to go back to life in the village, but the situation was now altered, their relatives were eager for the money earned in the city, their living expenses were also far higher and so they felt trapped in the city. Men related with similar stories. One of them used to be a *zardoz*[3] in Lucknow but took up driving and relocated to Delhi with his wife and children and, over the course of several years, drove a taxi, which provided him with significantly more money. Nevertheless he lamented this money at every occasion. Primarily, he knew that he was nothing if he did not have money in the city and so he had to keep taking more and more shifts, working long nights, lacking sleep; secondly, he blamed money for all his troubles with his wife.

> The moment she saw I can earn, she became obsessed with it, she would argue about anything I wanted to send to my parents, she wanted it all for herself, now she stopped working too and only keeps roaming in the markets. The first three years of our marriage were great, we did not have much money, and we had a simple home, but we had each other. When the money came it destroyed everything. I am ruined because of having money! I used to laugh at the designers and business people who used to come to my home to give me work, I saw how they were worried all the time. Now I am helpless too, I work night and day and when I get home we fight about money. Now I am slave of money, without it I am nothing. When I used to be a *zardoz* I was poor, but life was easier, I would work at home, my kids were around and my wife too and we had good time. There were quarrels and local fights in village, but still we lived *aaraam se* [relaxed].

The ironic attitude thus emerges at an intersection of several dominant experiential backdrops. Firstly, the curse of money and conspicuous consumption, where increase in money and spending tends to decrease experienced levels of well-being. Secondly, the discrepancy between the designer's claims to creativity and the reality of the production process that directly depends on the creativity, knowledge and individual skill

---

[3] Embroiderer of *zardozi*, traditional metal thread and beads embroidery.

A village embroiderer with her son, exemplifying the freedom of the village space, as opposed to the controlled setting of the city-based workshops, where children would not be allowed.
© Tereza Kuldova, 2011

of the craftsmen, which nevertheless goes unrecognised. The craftsman is valuable only as an abstracted sign, and, as such, needs to be *kept in place, at a distance*. The ironic attitude thus resides in the experience of the neoliberal pollution, of which the dirt of the city and its notoriously stressed designers, are the most visible manifestation for the village women – combined with the personal experiences of the detrimental effects of too much money and the resulting conspicuous consumption, competition and desires.

The *chikan* craftswomen recognised that craft *products* are necessary in order to complement and *Indianise* modernity (Hancock 2002) for the middle-classes and elites, and that they often remain a mere abstraction, through which their real bodies are pushed into invisibility. The fact that Indianness emerges only at special, social and imaginative distance from those who are among its most pronounced abstracted symbols lends itself easily to irony in the craftswomen's interactions with designers. Being treated as an idealisation is directly offensive to real people. The craftswomen that are turned into ghost-like creatures, existing only as a fantasy, a dream, a non-present present, then reveal in their irony the hollow character of contemporary ideals of neoliberalism, progress and capital accumulation (Nietzsche et al. 2001). Their irony, which represents a clear conflict of perspectives, works to discredit this ideal and thus reveal it as a mere fantasy.

## Mocking Designers

Once, when I was visiting a village with a Delhi-based designer, who went in person to check on some of his special orders (for a couple of saris for a wedding trousseau of one of the Delhi millionaire daughters about to be wed), something else rather typical happened. The designer was unhappy with the quality of the embroidery, having expected something more delicate and intricate from the girls and he instantly became frustrated, thinking of the problems ahead concerning the delivery. Such embroidery takes time: a sari like this can take six girls up to three months to make. He began to shout at the women, blaming them for being irresponsible and lazy, threatening to cut their wage or give the work to someone else. The women sat still, staring at him, until then one of them began laughing, threw the sari at his head and shouted:

> Then take it, we don't care for your money, we don't need people like you here shouting, get lost, and remember, we don't need to do this work, we do it because there is nothing else to do in the day; you come here and give us work and what you think you are? You designers come and go; one piece here, one piece there and think you are saving us. You are the irresponsible people here, not us. We don't care for your work, take it! You come here and you want embroidery, we don't run after your work. You are the one who is dependent on us. Without us you are nobody, you can't do anything. Now stop shouting and making a fool of yourself and either get lost or let us continue working.[4]

The other girls started nodding and laughing,

> She is right, we have seen those like you before, big people, you only keep thinking how big you are, in truth you are nothing without us, absolutely nothing.

---

[4] Reconstructed from field-notes, 7/6/2011.

A *chikan* embroiderer laughing at the customer's desire and obsession with *chikan*, while being interviewed.
© Arash Taheri, 2012

The designer was angry and frustrated on the way back, complaining that these women are very hard to deal with; he also alluded to the distinction between embroiderers based in the city and those in the village:

> Those who are in the city are much easier to handle, they do what you say and keep their mouth shut, they are dependent on the work you give them, and that makes them thankful and obedient, these women here think so much of themselves. They make my life hell. I have to establish some proper workshop in the city, or just drag some of the good ones to Delhi to work for me, but it is so hard to get good ones, they are all bound by tradition. [...] The moment you step in the village, you are stepping on their territory, no matter how poor they are, they let you know that you don't belong there, when the same girls are in the city, you can make them do anything, they know who is the boss.

The two cosmological grounds, one of the middle and upper-class city and one of the village; with their related logic, aesthetic sense, ideologies and tastes were actively performatively produced and kept at a distance. Even when the cosmologies of the city expand and threaten to swallow the villages into the logic of money, profit and conspicuous consumption, it still does not seem to be that easy or straightforward: the city is imagined by the village women as a space of neoliberal

Washing *chikan* embroidery on the banks of the Gomti river. Washing is traditionally carried out by *dhobis* [Hindu occupational caste of washermen]. © Tereza Kuldova, 2010

pollution, a space clearly juxtaposed to the village. On the one hand, the designers may believe that they are giving these women a favour, that without them they would not be able to survive; on the other, the craftswomen enjoy pointing out that it is the designer who is the dependent one, thereby reversing the dependency and, with it, the hierarchy. They show their power through purposefully mocking the designer, frustrating him, laughing at the ugliness of what they are making, pointing out that 'nation' and 'tradition' – the words the designers tend to use when educating these girls about the virtues and value of their products – are simply mere words that mean very little to them, indeed, that that which is meant to comprise them is actually missing.

## On and Off Camera: Haunted by Irony

We have seen, throughout this exposition, that 'irony arises in practice and excites the moral imagination by its identification of a gap, contradiction, inconsistency or incongruity' (Fernandez and Huber 2001: 262-3). However, this moral imagination and self-reflexivity is not ignited solely on behalf of the craftswomen, indeed that is why the designers feel uncomfortable when dealing with the village women (and comfort-

*Chikan* embroidery being dyed in a professional establishment in Aminabad market, Lucknow.
© Tereza Kuldova, 2011

The final product, dyed according to the shade desired by the customer.
© Arash Taheri, 2012

able when dealing with city based embroiderers) – the mockery and irony (when recognised) triggers reflexivity around one's actions and position. The trouble with irony, and thus also with its potential subversive power, is that, in order to be effective it would have to be acknowledged, but irony does not have to be acknowledged (in our case, by the designer). Nevertheless, in private, in the secure space of their living rooms, with nobody else around, many of the designers would admit to being haunted by the words, giggles, actions, and ironic performative reproductions of their own discourse, a discourse that defines the very core of who they are, imagine to be and project to be to their surroundings.

This discrepancy between public confidence in the discourse, its value and meaning, and the private tension and insecurity about its real potential, became most obviously visible to me when I was shooting some footage on camera with one of the Lucknow-based small-scale niche designers who supplies a rather famous Delhi designer with *chikan* pieces and who has been in the business for the last 18 years. Being an academic at the same time, she likes to be perceived as committed to the upliftment of the *chikan* workers. On camera, she talked about the history of *chikan*, the patronage of the Nawabs, the exquisite pieces of the past; she talked of SEWA (Self-Employed Women's Association) Lucknow. According to her, they gave the workers a proper, clean environment to work in, a better wage, organised the employment, standardised working hours, trained the girls and thus increased the quality and promoted chikan in India and abroad. When questioned about the collaborative nature of the creative process of production she recounted in a typical fashion the authoritative narrative, naming the various production stages and workers involved while justifying the designer's work as follows:

> The designer is conscious of quality, he makes a qualitative difference, then he brings freshness of input into it. He moves away from the traditional patterns and brings in his own personality, his own interest, his own creativity, so he then works on the layout, on the stitches, on the designing of the garment that is where the designer comes in.

In line with other designers, she suggested, on camera, that the only solution for the *chikan* workers, the only thing that would elevate them from poverty is inclusion in the organised sector:

> The *chikan* workforce is really large and fragmented. But for them it is a matter of survival. Let's face it. They cannot decide. What I feel is, the government should intervene and if possible give them at least basic wages. And *chikankaar* should move from the unorganised sector into the organised sector. I don't know when and if that is possible. But only then can the *chikankaar* be paid proper wages. And if that happens the quality of *chikan* will definitely improve.[5]

She then continued with the argument that a better working environment is needed in the city: a workshop-like setting and better working hours. Such discourse is based on the assumption that the village is dirty (note that, for most village-based women, the city is the space par excellence of pollution) and that the village women are working more hours than the city women (which is very rarely the case). Nor do village women depend on chikan for their survival, on the contrary they become dependent the moment they move into the city and lose a significant proportion of their networks of support. She then continued to argue that they deserve 'fair wage for the beauty they produce'. I pointed out, only in order to provoke her, that if they really were paid on equal terms as, for instance, a middle-class bureaucrat – if we really claim that we value their skill and knowledge so much – then, most probably, the embroidery, as with the embroideries of Europe, would disappear, and, simply, nobody would be able to buy it as the price of the actual work would stagger enormously. To that she replied,

---

[5] Video in the author's archive, 20/4/2012.

> That won't happen for two reasons. See, these are unskilled workers, when I say unskilled, they are unlettered, illiterate. One. And secondly, what they lack is, their work is not market driven, if it were market driven they could be really paid very well, unfortunately it does not happen that way. So they are economically dependent on other people. [...] They have to become part of the organised sector, get better working environment, better wages.

The skill that deserves better wage and which is praised and celebrated in one moment only to be degraded within seconds is due to presumed illiteracy of the women. Such illiteracy applies largely to the older women, who are a minority nowadays: the majority of girls in villages study while doing embroidery – indeed some are even local school-teachers. However, the discourse of empowerment would not work without this assumption of *dependency* for survival, of victimisation, inability to act (note above, 'they cannot decide') and an assumption regarding their desire for a good middle-class life as the ultimate goal.

Although a number of women have televisions in their households, the majority do not, most even lack the desire to have television. They prefer to roam around [*ghumne*], visit neighbours and relatives, talk, cook and work. Even those who were studying, all pointed out that they do not wish to relocate to the city; they wanted to live in the village. Zakiya, now 17 years old, wanted to study medicine, or at least the basics, to then return to the village and work in the local medical centre, yet she did not want to change her lifestyle. She neither had a television at home or electricity, but was deeply content with her life. She frequently repeated that 'village is nice, here there is everything, you don't need anything more'. This attitude to life proved near impossible for our designer to grasp, she could not accept it as valid, instead projecting her own middle-class desires upon these women (where owning a TV was perceived as a basic human right, for example).

Even the embroiderers who had an old television at home were more proud showing me their cows and fields: the number and size of which is the real marker of local distinction. Furthermore, saying that *chikan* is not market-driven directly contradicts the reality of *chikan*, which is hugely popular both in Lucknow and even more so in Delhi, Mumbai, Chandigarh, Calcutta and no less China, the US, UK and Dubai. (China began even imitating it, producing cheaper copies, trying to sell them both inland and on the Indian market.) Again, this peculiar rejection feeds into the legitimisation of the role of the designer, who 'had to create the market almost *ex nihilo*'; while the history of *chikan* at the same time clearly shows us how the craft has constantly adapted itself to the market and to its demands and is in no way static.

I tried to challenge her views and to point to discrepancies within the logic, which, on the one hand, speaks of empowerment, while, on the other, immediately denounces its possibility. This results in a mere reproduction of situation, indeed keeping the craftswomen where they are; which ultimately only benefits the businessmen and the designer. She told me to switch the camera off and suddenly appeared to no longer be as convinced as she had been about her views. She retaliated that she felt that they never understood her view: she always had to convince them that this is the right way.

> They do not understand what is good for them. They always laugh at me. They tell me, 'why would I need all that?' But I feel they too deserve that, they should have that. They should have better life. But then I think, maybe they are happy the way they are, but then that must be wrong too. Once I came to the village and tried to educate them about *chikan*. They don't even know the value of their own craft. Then one of them stood up and said, appearing serious: '... *acchaa beheno, ab to samajh lijiye ki voh sahi baat bolti hai, ham yeh sab karte hai hamaari desh ke liye, hamaare Bhaarat mahaan ke liye, hamaari izzat ki savaal hai yeh, ham hi to hai parampara, voh log jo dur rahte hai hamko bahut izzat karte hai, hamaari kaam Aishwariya*[6] *bhi pehenti hai, yeh samajh lijiye.*' [... now sisters, understand that what she is saying is right, we are doing all of this for our nation, for our Great India, it is a question of our honour, we are tradition, those that live far away respect us a lot, even Aishwariya is wearing our work, understand that! (translated by the author)] Upon hearing this, all of them began laughing, something I did not understand. Then one of the others said, '*kyaa bhagwaas hai, vah vah vah*' [what nonsense/rubbish], (*vah vah* is a traditional way of praising poets). I then understood that they were making fun of me. I still don't know what to make out of it, you can't help those who do not want to be helped. I told them *they should not talk like that*. But I still cannot forget the incident. I don't go to that village anymore.[7]

Another female designer, with whom I visited several villages around Lucknow, once admitted (from the comfort of her luxury farm-house close to Chattarpur, Delhi) that she sometimes feels guilty when she meets the craftspeople.

> You know, everybody praises me for my work, I take all the credit. But to be honest I would be nothing without the craftsmen. I studied fashion design at NIFT, but what did we learn? Western cuts, stitches, marketing, we only got to know little about different crafts. But then if you are into fashion in India, you have to do embroidery, else you won't survive a day in the elite market. So I had to go to the craftsmen and learn from them. I learned from them more than from NIFT. Sometimes I feel without them I would be nothing. I mean, what do I really do? (...) They know I am more dependent on them than they are on me. These people will always manage one way or the other, but me, without them I cannot do anything. But you cannot tell you learned from craftsmen, everyone looks down upon them.

---

[6] Aishwariya Rai Bachchan, famous Bollywood actress and former Miss World.
[7] Reconstructed based on field-notes.

On another occasion, she remembered a Bollywood comedy from 2005, *Garam Masala* [Hot Spice], a crazy ride of two boys, fooling around with a number of air hostesses at the same time, which begins with Sam (John Abraham) and Mac (Akshay Kumar) working as photographers yet doing a miserable job. One day, Sam goes to a *bazaar* shop to meet an old photographer, claiming that he is one of his biggest fans; he manages to get hold of his recent negatives. The next day, upon arriving at the office, he is welcomed with flowers and applause and is told that his photograph won an international press photography award and that, out of an award of ten million rupees, one million is at his disposal, as well as a free one-month trip to America.

Nobody seems to really question the award, with the sole exception of Mac, Mac goes to his boss stating that Sam is a fraud, a cheat (and even that he holds camera as though he were holding a coconut), yet his boss just laughs, saying that he knows none of them can take photos, and exactly from which shop Sam stole the photos, he has still made their magazine famous and that is what matters. Mac reacts and says that he will fight, upon which the boss becomes angry screaming 'Shut up! Calm down! Idiot!', throwing him out of the office. The issue is never brought up again in the movie; the character of the old photographer is forgotten, as is the injustice. Yet the scene left an impression on the designer and she recalled the village women and the craftsmen in her workshop in Shahpur Jat and felt guilty for a moment, saying that 'this is exactly the same thing, we do same thing and you just don't talk about that.'

The scene in the movie is thus symptomatic of the distance produced between the parallel economic realms: be it the village or craft workshop and the designer showroom, or the bazaar and the elite magazine. It also captures the way in which the designers are themselves caught in-between, haunted by the voices, ironies and mockery of crafts-people, while having to suppress them so that they can performatively reproduce the authoritative narrative: one that further perpetuates the distance and establishes it as an unshakeable fact of life. In doing so, they guard the boundary between the speakable and the unspeakable, which is so clearly visible in the scene where it becomes obvious that certain things cannot be said out loud in order to protect one's world as much as profit.

Only in a safe space can the unspeakable be uttered and the irony acknowledged. This observation certainly mirrors Escobar's critique of the development discourse. Escobar has argued that 'development' is a historically and culturally specific project that 'created a space in which only certain things could be said and even imagined" (Escobar 2011: 39) and a discourse in which only certain things are visible and expressible and in which certain things are conceived of as a problem, in our case it would be 'women', 'illiteracy', 'backwardness' and even 'craft sector', a discourse through which global relations of inequality not only intensifies, but becomes taken for granted.

We must not forget at this point that, since the financial crisis of 2008, there has been a growing realisation among the Indian business elite, economists and political commentators that brutal American capitalism will fail and that India would rather be suited for capitalism with a more human face, something that led to a proliferation of companies with strong statements of 'corporate responsibility', developmental programs and the notion of ethical business which has been widely established over the past four years. The idea of 'business for social good' has been propagated, for instance, by the magazine *Forbes India* and its annual Philanthropy Awards, which is awarded to leading businessmen[8]. Most designers operate within this current business paradigm, selling their 'ethical' products together with good conscience. Within this context, the ironic voices of the craftswomen not only haunt the designers, but also the whole 'business for good' implicated in the majority of Indian fashion design labels catering to business-class consumers, thus revealing it as a historically, socially, spatially contingent discourse among many possible others.

## Conclusion: Laughing Designers into Place and Distance

Mocking and irony can thus be understood as ways of retaining meaningfulness of the village women's daily lives, while planting doubts in the minds of the designers. Keeping an ironic relationship to the designers thus seems to be a viable strategy that keeps the two worlds at a safe distance, confirming the validity of one's own value systems and, in fact exposing the reversed dependency. Joking relations have been studied by anthropologist before (Mann and Spradley 1975, Radcliffe-Brown 1961, Douglas 1968). Some claim that the function of jokes is to symbolically attack established order without subverting it (Yoshida 2001), to challenge a dominant structure and belittle it (Douglas 1968), or, in fact, to establish and maintain social equilibrium and order (Radcliffe-Brown 1961), while at the same time keeping excessive order at bay (Radcliffe-Brown 1961, Willerslev and Pedersen 2011). In light of the ethnography, there seems to be some truth in all of these views,

---

[8] 'Forbes India Awards Philanthropy Leaders', see http://forbesindia.com/blog/giving/forbes-india-awards-the-countrys-philanthropy-leaders/, accessed 23/11/2012.

and yet the ironic and mocking attitudes of the craftswomen towards the designers points rather to a dynamics of insubordination. The irony transposes the visible and the invisible; it exposes the complex nature of the creative process, stripping it from the dominance of the *individual* designer; it reveals the dependence of the designers on the craftsmen as much as the dependence of the imagined nation on people who dominate its population but at the same time are excluded from the new economic superpower, while at the same time embroidering the attires of the new business leaders of the nation. The village embroiderers show that 'by laughing at power, we expose its contingency, we realise that what appeared to be fixed and oppressive is in fact emperor's new clothes, and just the sort of thing that should be mocked and ridiculed.' (Critchley 2002: 11).

# References

Appelbaum, K. 1998. 'The Sweetness of Salvation: Consumer Marketing and the Liberal-Bourgeois Theory of Needs.' *Current Anthropology*, 39:3, 323-50.

Critchley, S. 2002. *On Humour*. London: Routledge.

De Neve, G. 2012. 'Fordism, flexible specialisation and CSR: How Indian garment workers critique neoliberal labour regimes.' *Ethnography*:November 22, 1-24.

Derrida, J. 1994. *Specters of Marx: The State of the Debt, the Work of Mourning, and the New International*. London: Routledge.

Douglas, M. 1968. 'The Social Control of Cognition: Some Factors in Joke Perception.' *Man*, 3:3, 361-76.

Escobar, A. 2011. *Encountering Development: The Making and Unmaking of the Third World*. Princeton, NJ: Princeton University Press.

Fernandez, J. & Huber, M. T. 2001. 'Irony, Practice and the Moral Imagination.' *Irony in Action: Anthropology, Practice and the Moral Imagination*. Chicago: Chicago University Press.

Hancock, M. 2002. 'Subjects of Heritage in Urban Southern India.' *Environment and Planning D: Society and Space*, 20, 693-717.

Jain, K. 2007. *Gods in the Bazaar: The Economies of Indian Calender Art*. Durham: Duke University Press.

Mahmud, T. 2010. ''Surplus Humanity' and Margin of Legality: Slums, Slumdogs, and Accumulation by Dispossession.' *Chapman Law Journal*, 14.

Mann, B. J. & Spradley, J. P. 1975. *The Cocktail Waitress: Woman's Work in a Man's World*. New York: John Wiley & Sons, Inc.

Nietzsche, F., Williams, B., Nauckhoff, J. & Caro, A. D. 2001. *Nietzsche: The Gay Science: With a Prelude in German Rhymes and an Appendix of Songs*. Cambridge: Cambridge University Press.

Radcliffe-Brown, A. R. 1961. *Structure and Function in Primitive Society: Essays and Addresses*. London: Cohen & West.

Sahlins, M. 1996. 'The sadness of sweetness: The native anthropology of Western cosmology.' *Current Anthropology*, 37, 395-428.

Sarkar, S. 2010. 'The Parallel Economy in India: Causes, Impacts and Governmental Initiatives.' *Economic Journal of Develoment Issues*, 11&12:1-2, 124-34.

Willerslev, R. & Pedersen, M. A. 2011. 'Proportional Holism: Joking the Cosmos into the Right Shape in North Asia ' In T. Otto & N. Bubandt (Eds.) *Experiments in Holism:*

*Theory and Practice in Contemporary Anthropology.* New York: John Wiley & Sons.

Yoshida, M. 2001. 'Joking, Gender, Power, and Professionalism among Japanese Inn Workers.' *Ethnology*, 40:4, 361-69.

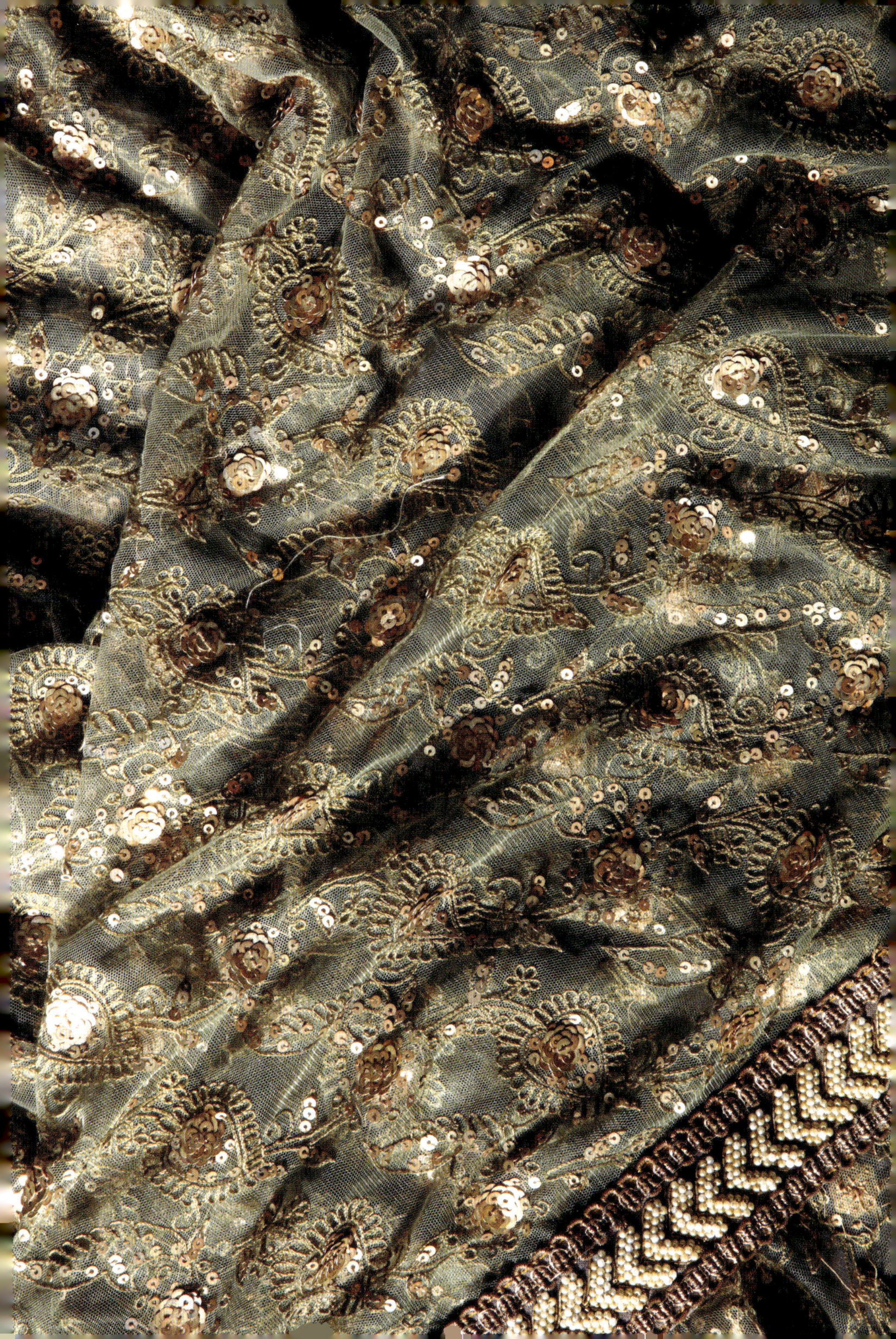

39
LIGHT CUT
HAND SHOE TACKS
SIZE
8
450 GRAMS NET
MADE IN INDIA

# Walking with Kolhapuri Artisans
## On the art of designing and wearing shoes
Catherine Willems and Kristiaan D'Août

Footwear tells us a great deal about ourselves, as well as about the world around us. Different environments and climates lead to different footwear (which, in turn, might influence gait). Local skills, traditions and their meaning find their way into different shoe designs. Shoes are more complex than one might imagine: many requirements have a bearing upon their design. Are these requirements usually compatible or do they pose conflicting demands? Looking at high-street fashion footwear, one might think that there is a trade-off, whereby the most elegant footwear is, by necessity, never the most comfortable, and vice versa. In this chapter, we will attempt to answer this question by exploring the requirements of different footwear types, focusing on indigenous and contemporary footwear.

We distinguish two main groups of requirements, which reflect different types of functions for the footwear in focus. The first function is *cultural*, by which we mean all aspects of the shoe that are predominantly linked to form and are determined by learned skills, social relations, aesthetics and the meaning in their context. The second function is *biomechanical*, by which we mean all aspects that are predominantly linked to use and that should allow a shoe to be used as a "practical tool" for walking in an injury-free, comfortable way – including providing isolation in cold climates – irrespective of 'look'. In reality, these two functions are rarely completely disparate, although it is easy to see how, for instance, stilettos and walking boots are situated at opposing ends of the spectrum.

Here, we will first present examples of indigenous footwear that primarily have a cultural function. Then, we assess indigenous footwear that may provide a balance and potentially a very good compromise between cultural and biomechanical functions. We will discuss how insights from ancient and modern footwear can help us design better luxury footwear. Can the role of the 'ancient' amount to more than just a form-related inspiration in the design of new footwear? Looking at the skills of making and the ways of wearing footwear in its context helps to denaturalise and make strange what we have learned and mastered. Finally, we question the impact of the action research for the artisans in the community in question.

Example of a Paduka. © Museum of Cultural History

## Two Extreme Examples

We first look at two examples of footwear that have a predominantly cultural purpose. The first example dates back more or less a millennium and is found in the *Chinese lotus shoes*. First worn by upper-class women in China, at the beginning of the 17th century the lotus shoe was subsequently adopted by women of all classes in order to imitate the elite. Small feet were considered beautiful and attractive and the ideal length of the shoe was no more than 6 cm. The shoes are cone or sheath-shaped – intended to resemble a lotus bud – and are made of decorated cotton and silk. From the age of four years on, the toes of girls were necessarily broken (with the exception of the big toe) and bound daily, or every couple of days, with cloth to reshape the feet and prevent further growth. Although this type of footwear meant that the girls had to suffer, it also displayed their privileged position in terms of belonging to a higher class. These women were exempt from work and had servants to take care of them. A second cultural example is the Paduka. Paduka is the name of India's oldest, most typical footwear. In fact, it is little more than a sole with a toe-knob, positioned between the big and the second toe. The Paduka exists in a variety of forms and materials throughout India. They can either be designed in the shape of actual feet or of fish and are made of wood, ivory and even silver. They are

Kolhapuri sandals. © Kristiaan D'Août

sometimes elaborately decorated. The more elaborate shoes can be part of a bride's trousseau, although they could also be proffered as religious offerings or indeed be the object of veneration themselves. Although simple wooden Padukas could be worn by common people, Padukas of fine teak, ebony and sandalwood, inlaid with ivory or wire, were a mark of the wearer's high status. Today, these toe-knob sandals are usually associated with the Indian *sadhus* and *sadhvis*, the ascetic holy men and women who wander from village to village. They are worn to protect the feet from the hot and dirty surfaces the wearer is subject to. The two narrow, curved stilts reflect the principle of non-violence practised by Hindu Brahmins, certain other castes and Jains, to minimise the risk of accidentally trampling insects and vegetation. The ideal of 'ahimsa' or non-killing also forbids such individuals from wearing leather footwear.

Although the Lotus shoe and the Paduka are two rather extreme examples, they can be extended to contemporary shoes, such as designs by Alexander McQueen, Christian Louboutin or Jimmy Choo. Such shoes are not designed to stimulate natural gait – in some cases quite the opposite – but they do have a strong cultural function. Within this cultural function, the boundaries between meaning and aesthetics are not

Right: Biomechanical assessment of, in this example, walking barefoot on a natural substrate. Note the hip-mounted data logger connected to a 3-D accelerometer (mounted on the heel), a 2-D goniometer (mounted on the ankle) and surface electromyographic (sEMG) electrodes on the M. gastrocnemius medialis and M. tibialis anterior (the latter are not visible on this photograph).
© Kristiaan D'Août

always easy to trace. From simple foot-coverings to high-heeled shoes, footwear reflects different cultures, fashions and behaviours and does not always serve a practical purpose. Put another way, as Louboutin said in an interview: "I have no problem with the idea of comfort but it is not an important thing aesthetically." How we wrap our feet, how we walk and what we consider as luxury depends on the period and the context.

## Kolhapuri Footwear: The Journey

The Paduka might be the most typical footwear, but it is not the most common footwear. Even in ancient times in India, the most common footwear was a strapped sandal of the type that Mahatma Gandhi developed 2000 years later. These sandals consist of one leather strap across the instep and another leather lace connecting the instep with the sole at the front, between the first and the second toe. Although the trend of high-heeled shoes and wedges is followed in India, this flat leather sandal is still widely used and is better known under the name of 'Kolhapuri footwear'. Kolhapuris are a favourite with every generation and appeal to people from all walks of life. How are form and use balanced/united in the design of Kolhapuri's? Do they perform well in both cultural and biomechanical terms? We worked with the *Kolhapuri artisans of Toehold*: a non-profit organisation in Athani, Karnataka, promoting the empowerment of rural women with an emphasis on social accountability[1]. The artisans in the research participated on a voluntary basis. Since we aim for a multidisciplinary insight into Kolhapuri footwear, we employed both qualitative and quantitative analyses, incorporating input from design sciences, biomechanics and anthropology. To investigate the cultural component of the footwear, we have used methods ranging from interviews with the artisans and other members of the community, action research among the artisans, to apprenticeship with the artisans. We have used such qualitative methods to gain insight into the skills of making footwear and the community's relation to the environment. When it comes to the biomechanical analyses, we employed quantitative methods, comparing gait patterns and distinguishing between four conditions:

---

[1] The project investigates two cases on indigenous footwear, one in South India on Kolhapuri footwear and one in Northern Europe on Saami boots. The two cases deliver the necessary data to develop a framework for the efficient creation of footwear

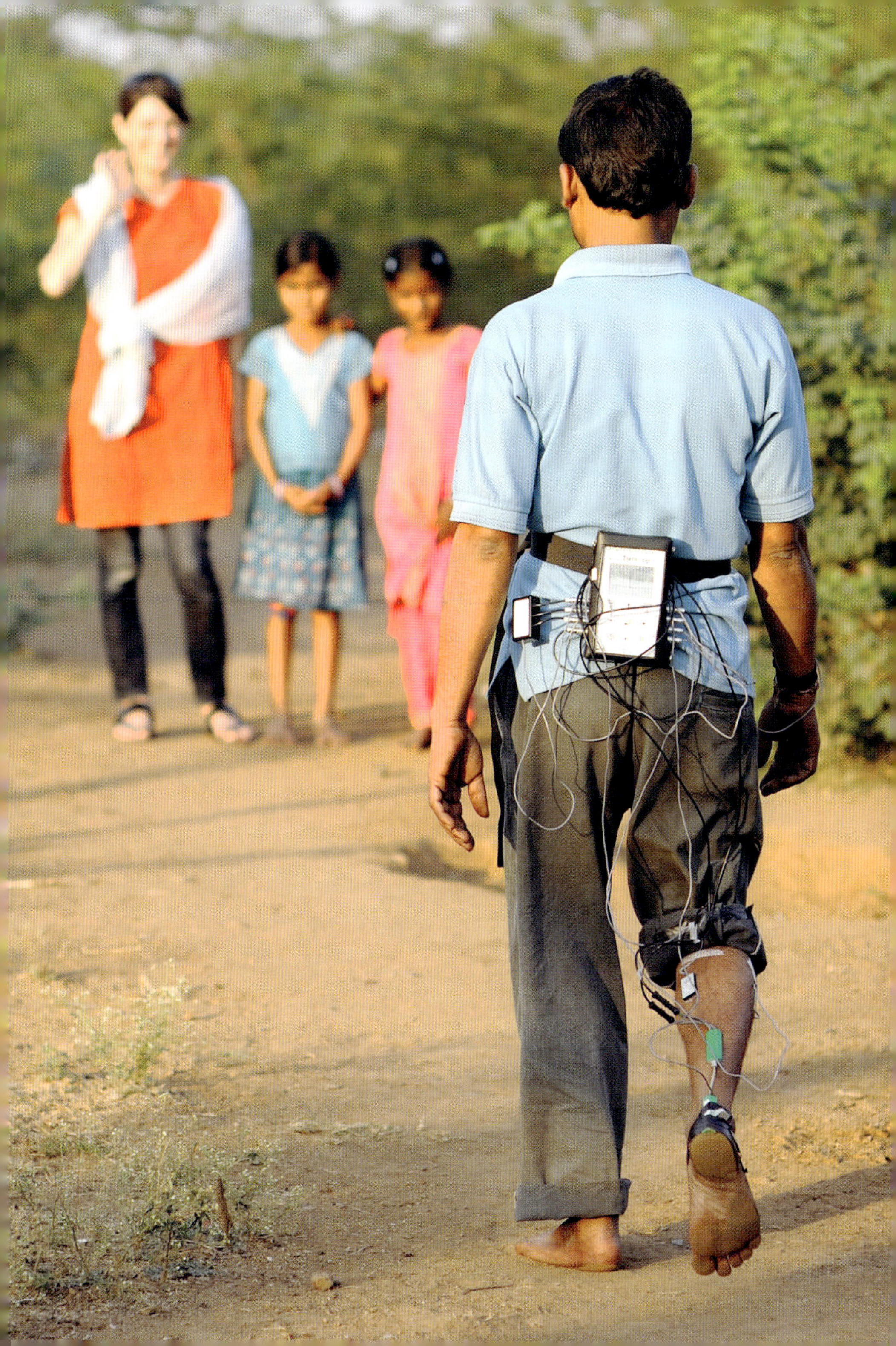

(1) barefoot on a natural substrate;
(2) shod on a natural substrate;
(3) barefoot on a hard substrate;
(4) shod on a hard substrate.

Techniques resembled those of a typical human gait lab. Such a setup enabled us to assess the effect of substrate and of indigenous footwear (and the combination thereof) upon gait. Let us now describe the indigenous Kolhapuri footwear, its material and the production process in specific detail.

## Kolhapuri Footwear: The Material

The Kolhapuri footwear is made from buffalo hides by the traditional cobbler caste, known locally as *chamar*. Water buffaloes, used for dairy production throughout India and other parts of Asia, provide tough and effective hides. In such communities, the buffaloes are not slaughtered for meat consumption, only when a buffalo dies of natural causes is its leather used for footwear and other products yielded. Tanning of the hides is traditionally carried out by the tanner community, they are situated in the same neighbourhood as the cobblers and are interdependent. The tanners and cobblers belong to the Hindu religion. Both professions are carried out by some of the lowest castes of labourers – the dhor and the chamar – who are part of the untouchable communities, or dalits, now classified as scheduled castes under modern India's system of positive discrimination.

To render the hides ready for use, the tanners employ a procedure known as bag tanning. Once the raw hides are cleaned of blood and dirt, they are immersed in a bath of lime solution. This treatment of the hides causes them to become plump and swollen, and after ten days they are ready for depilation with a knife. The stock then becomes ready for vegetable tanning, which involves colouring and suspension. The colouring of both flesh and skin sides is done in a bath – consisting of babul bark, myrobalan nut and water – both sides are coloured and the central part of the skin is left untanned. When it comes to tanning the middle part, the hide is stitched with strong sisal fibre into a cylindrical bag with a narrow opening at the neck. The bag is filled with a mixture of babul bark and crushed myrobalan nuts and suspended over wooden logs. The tanning liquor is poured into the bag at frequent intervals. Depending on the amount of tanning material used and the percentage of babul bark and myrobalan nuts, the leather is softened: leather produced using a higher proportions of babul bark is more firm and durable, although it is also harsher and more darkly coloured. The whole production of the

Depilation and removal of the flesh side of the hide. © Kristiaan D'Août

raw hide to tanning takes about 35 days. The tanning does not use any synthetic industrial materials and is eco-friendly. The waste generated in the tanning process is used as compost in agriculture.

Buffalo hide is far from a static entity with fixed attributes. The tanning process does not make the hides equal in thickness. Depending upon the age of the buffalo, any illnesses, its diet and so forth, the thickness of the hide of the buffalo will vary. Even when derived from the same animal, no two hides will be the same. Once human intervention ceases the hide continues to grow and undergoes changes according to the weather and light conditions, as well as through being worn or not (Willems, 2013).

## The Making of Kolhapuri Footwear
Bag tanned leather is the main material used to make the Kolhapuri footwear. From around the age of six years, the artisans of the community wear their own footwear on a daily basis (before this age they usually walk barefoot). They claim that there is no better footwear than their own: suited to their specific environment. In Athani, a sandal made from bag tanned leather is by far the best option available to withstand the heat and the humidity of the climate. The summer months in this region are extremely hot, with temperatures reaching up to 40 degrees Celsius.

Bag tanning: hides stitched together into a cylindrical bag. © Kristiaan D'Août

Detail of the cylindrical bag. © Kristiaan D'Août

Dry hides for sale at the local market in Athani. © Kristiaan D'Août

Kolhapuri footwear or Kolhapuri *chappal* is a sandal that is open at the back. The name refers to a city, although the geographical area of production is wider and also encompasses Athani. The *chappal* features a leather sole, two side flaps (*kanwali*), an instep band and a toe strap. The outer sole, insole, upper section, toe ring and heel are sewn using leather threads from the tail of the buffalo. Most artisans work in family-based establishments, transferring skills and knowledge from one generation to the next. The men master the skill for the soles while the women are in charge of the uppers and hand-stitching the different pieces. The bag tanned leather is first wetted for easy cutting. The leather is perfectly cut using a crescent knife. The ability to improvise according to the uneven thickness of the hides and use the knives with skill comes from years of experience. The artisans know the potential of the material and how to collaborate with it. We follow Ingold who sees production as a process of correspondence rather than the imposition of a preconceived form on raw substance. The material is not simply formed it is also formative. In this view, making is thought of as a process of growth (Ingold, 2013). While still damp, the leather is hammered heavily and repeatedly to make it even, flat and pressed. The soles are then polished by rubbing them with buffalo horn (for a full report, refer to Willems, 2013).

What can science tell us? What about biomechanical analyses of the case studied? Characteristic of the Kolhapuri *chappal* is the initial stiffness of the outsole. Only the parts of the outsole where the feet, the outsole and the surface touch each other soften and become less stiff. The other parts retain their stiffness and ensure protection of the foot on the clayish rocky terrain. During the process of wearing the *chappal*, the sole and the feet thus adapt to each other. Preliminary biomechanical data strongly suggest that Kolhapuri footwear has little influence on the overall characteristics of walking. The differences that do exist between barefoot and shod walking may well only be in the same order of magnitude than the difference between walking on substrates of slightly different compliance. We suggest that Kolhapuri footwear enables natural gait and probably enhances proprioception, meaning that you can still feel the ground you walk on with a maximum of protection in order not to get hurt.

From a biomechanical point of view, good contact between the surface and the feet is needed as input for the body to adjust to different positions and surfaces and to control its balance and stability. In the broader context which we examine – looking at the cultural and biomechanical functions of footwear – we consider the footwear to be part of an

Wetting the outsoles for easy treatment. © Kristiaan D'Août

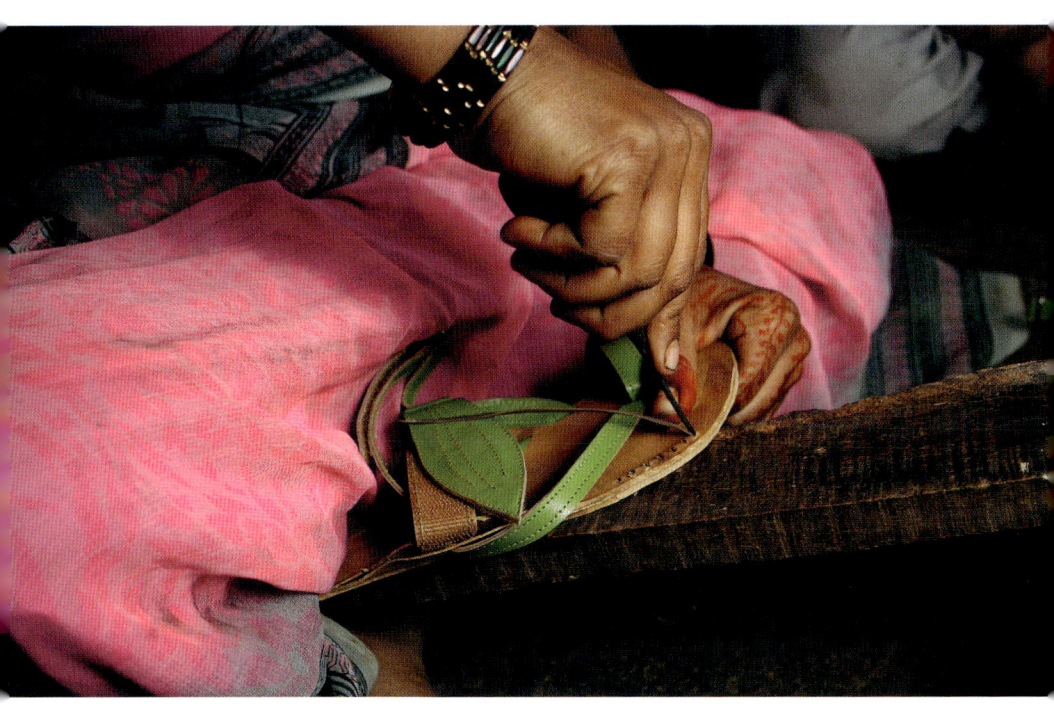

A female artisan is hand-stitching the soles. The heel, the sole and the insole are stitched together at the edges using fine strips of leather from buffalo tail. © Shiva Kumar

un-broken proprioceptive loop that runs from the brain of the person wearing the footwear, through the feet and into the surface walked upon; then to run back again, allowing the individual to monitor and adapt the pattern of their gait.

## Action Research: A Design Experiment

With all the information on Kolhapuri footwear, we created variations on the footwear in collaboration with the artisans, using the bag tanned leather for the outsoles and their specific skills. The aim is to integrate the artisans into the design process, both as viewers and as makers. We want to create footwear for another environment: in this case, for a city environment, in India and abroad, providing an alternative to plastic and synthetic chappals and footwear. Making new models is a means with which to engage with the artisans and to rethink designs. During the action research, we created several wearable products and selected different products for limited editions. The editions spanning 2009-2010 focused on the outsoles and feature different uppers: from coloured buffalo hides to shiny goat-skins. These collections were on sale in high-end fashion shops in Europe. The latest collection, launched in 2013 under the name '100 % bag tanned', is made entirely from bag tanned leather. '100 % bag tanned' focuses on maximum use of the raw material and the application of the skills observed.

What is the impact of the experiment for the artisan designers and for the community? We have already mentioned that the artisans prefer their own footwear in their daily context. Yet how do they value their own work and skills?

Different organisations and companies are interested in preserving skills for different reasons. The main aim of these developmental interventions is to ensure that the footwear continues to be *made*. It is considered to be important for the shoemakers who would otherwise lose their livelihood and also in terms of the preservation of a valuable element of their material and cultural heritage. In addition the Leather Council of India is interested in preserving the skill and in skill-mapping, as handmade products are considered more and more luxury items that confer economic benefits. However, the artisans do not value their profession highly, despite the fact that this household industry allows for a certain degree of freedom, For the artisans, becoming a shoemaker is not really a matter of choice, rather it stems from a lack of choice. Almost all artisans of these communities practise their profession simply to make a living; yet they want a different future for their children. Acquiring, utilising, or depending upon, a skill positions individuals or groups in

Bokhara in collaboration with Toehold. Summer 2009: vegetable-tanned buffalo hide for the soles and perlati goat-skin for the upper. © David Willems

Eastern pearl in collaboration with Toehold. Summer 2009: vegetable-tanned buffalo hide for the soles and coloured goat-skin for the upper. © David Willems

particular ways, not necessarily of their choosing.

## What is True Luxury?
The focus of this study is not on preserving a particular set of skills, but on what it means to make things, including many contexts and practices. Should there be openings in other jobs or in higher education the artisans would not hesitate to switch their careers. Our appreciation of the craft as such is probably greater than that of the artisans themselves. Nevertheless the way this footwear is made offers a different perspective of design and we consider this footwear a luxury accessory *'avant la lettre'* for four reasons. Firstly, we saw that the material is treated in a respectful way; secondly, neither the tanning nor the production exert undue pressure on the environment; thirdly, the products also have subsequent value (an afterlife, if you will) as fertiliser; and a fourth and final aspect refers to the biomechanics: the footwear respects human anatomy. Material-soil-climate-feet are all in balance. The role of the researcher as a designing anthropologist is to foster creativity, ownership and empowerment, rather than appearing as a final authority on creativity. It is through the contextualisation of the skills that we avoid partial engagement with the community. Design can be a practice of anthropology in so far that it is more than an-after-the-fact description of what is observed.

How people design and use their footwear and what people consider as luxury is very much connected to the environment and the context. We first examined two extreme examples of footwear, neglecting the comfort of the user, despite having a considerable cultural impact. We then looked at Kolhapuri footwear, as an example of a more balanced design between the biomechanical and the cultural function. Looking at the different stages of the making process and at the use of the buffalo hide, we notice that different parts of the animal are used for different purposes: the tail is used as thread for hand-stitching and the horns are used for polishing the leather. The leftovers are used in-between the layers of the heel parts, while the smaller pieces are sold to the farmers to fertilise the ground. The footwear is hand-made without the use of harmful adhesives and mass production is not possible. The footwear exploits maximum use of the material; even waste (leftovers) is also recycled. The process is environmentally conscious and the material is considered comfortable for the feet. We demonstrate how indigenous knowledge can be studied in a thorough manner, and, at the same time, can be recognised as genuine and relevant knowledge. We want people to think not only in terms of artefacts, but also in terms of the ground they walk upon and the materials used to make the footwear.

# Acknowledgements

We wish to express our sincere gratitude to the artisans and the management of Toehold Artisans Cooperative for their enthusiastic participation and extensive support throughout this project. A special thanks to Ms. Madhura Chatrapathy, Mr. K. Raghu and Mr. Muthalik of Toehold for facilitating all logistics and communications between us and the artisan communities. We also would like to express our deep gratitude to Mr. B.N. Das of CLRI for his support and sharing his technical expertise.

# References

D'Aout, K. et al. 2009. The effects of habitual footwear use: foot shape and function in native barefoot walkers. *Footwear Science* 1 (2): 81-94.

D'Août K and C. Willems. 2011. Mobility and function of the human foot during shod and barefoot walking. *American Journal of Physical Anthropology* 144 (s52), 121.

Ingold, T. 2013. *Making: Anthropology, Archaeology, Art and Architecture*. Abingdon: Routledge.

Jain-Neubauer, J. ed. 2000. *Feet and Footwear in Indian Culture*. Toronto: The Bata Shoe Museum Foundation.

Willems, C. et al. 2012. Beyond ethnic footwear: Action research generating new educational insights on design processes. In *Design Education for Future Wellbeing. The Design Society*. 231-236.

Willems, C. 2013 (in press). 100 % bag tanned: action research generating new insights on design processes. In *Critical Arts*, October 2013.

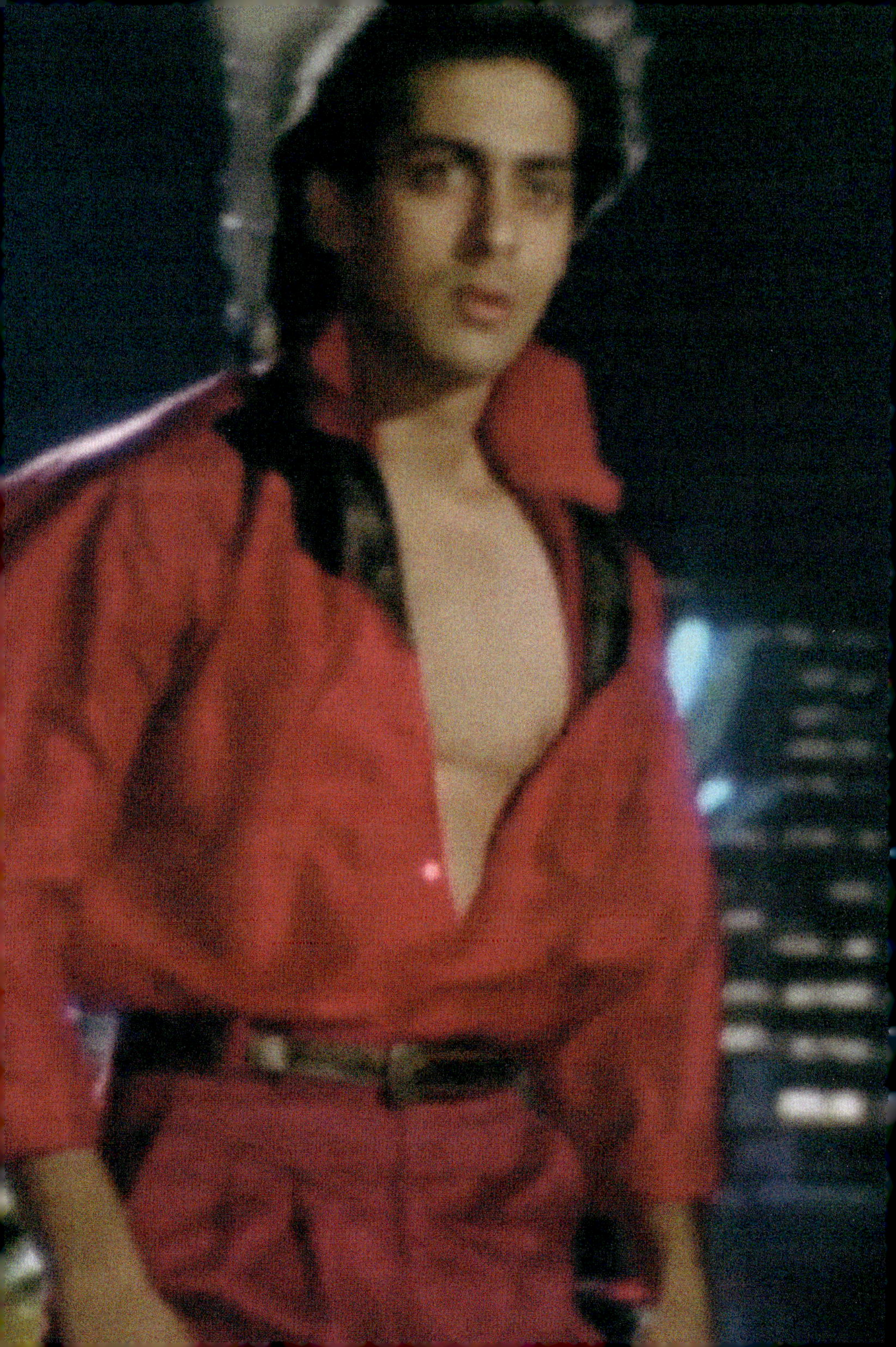

# Hindi cinema[1] and masculinities
## From Salman Khan to John Abraham
Némésis Srour

> Virility is historic as it is, necessarily, anthropological[2]
> (Corbin et al. 2011: 8)

While feminist studies are abundant, masculinity remains a less interrogated subject in the social sciences, even more so when it comes to non-Western masculinities. The theories and key concepts developed in gender and feminist studies are mostly grounded in Western empirical material, while South Asia, in particular, remains an under-covered field in terms of theorising the male and the masculine[3]. While masculinity is no longer a muted field in gender studies (Chopra et al. 2004: 1), men's Studies is still an emerging field in India (Kulkarni 2007: 207). I will indeed draw in this essay on the works of gender studies, while remaining rooted in a historical approach combined with an anthropological method, in line with Corbin, Courtine and Vigarello's work (2011)[4]. I will focus here on the changing embodiments of masculinity in Hindi popular cinema linked to the general context of the time. The anthropology of the male body while providing an understanding of a gendered way of being in the world is also a means to apprehend today's Indian society with its complexities. The body and its gestures act as cultural embodiment. The question is: how do social and historical interactions shape the male body, and what can an investigation of cinematic masculinities reveal about contemporary India?

From Independence till today, the idealised male body has undergone many changes, yet the hegemony of the muscular body in contemporary Hindi cinema finds its origin at a crossroads of contexts that emerges in the nineties: Hindu nationalism, awareness of the importance of the diaspora, liberalism and intensified access to global visual imagery. The

---

[1] By Hindi cinema, the author defines the commercial films made by the industry of Mumbai, of which Hindi is the main language.
[2] The author translates from French: '*La virilité est historique comme elle est, inévitablement, anthropologique*'.
[3] On this point, one can refer to the Introduction to *South Asian Masculinities, context of change, sites of continuity* (Chopra et al. 2004), which carries out an impressive survey of the existing literature on the subject.
[4] Yet, Corbin, Courtine and Vigarello made a 'history of virility', distancing themselves from the vocabulary of gender studies, without clearly defining the terms of masculinity and virility. See, on this point, the review of the book (Roynette 2012).

history of masculinity defining virility with muscles is actually the history of how a subsidiary quality came to epitomise virility itself. If the building of a muscular body, apt to fighting, could find its philosophical and physical roots not only in Indian wrestling but also in the growing ideology of Hindu nationalism, its transformation into an object of desire and consumption is also the result of a leisure and consumption society, developing since the economic liberalisation of India.

Focusing on three paradigmatical shifts in the representation of male bodies on screen from the nineties until today, with the emblematic actors Salman Khan, Shah Rukh Khan and John Abraham, I will see how the male body has gradually transformed into an erotic device, challenging at the same time gender codes of representations and Indianess' definition.

## I. 1989 – Masculinity as gym-trained body
### The muscular hero - Salman Khan

From Salman Khan[5] and so on, muscles have begun to be the dominant incarnation of virility on screen. It marks a difference from the influential decade of Amitabh Bachchan. The fighting scenes in the seventies, rhetorical as well as physical, are an essential attribute of a masculinity defined by 'virtuous anger' (Rajamani 2012). Masculinity was symbolised through a body shaped by hard-work conditions and a rightful revolt against social injustice, expressing the particular social context of India in the seventies. Amitabh Bachchan's long and thin body was nothing but the embodiment of the working class body, where strength and muscles cannot develop as much as the wrestler's because the latter does not concentrate on his labour (Alter 1992). The actor of the nineties focus on his training, as much as the media become obsessed with actors' diets and training programs. Having a muscular body has now become a central requirement in the industry.

Since 1989 and Salman Khan's first commercial hit, *Maine Pyar Kiya* (Barjatya 1989), the actor has led the trend of showing off his muscular body. He never objects to take his shirt off – making now the audience eagerly wait for the unavoidable 'take-off shirt' sequence in each of his films. In this movie, the American model is omnipresent, from the posters of Michael Jackson, Sylvester Stallone and Marilyn Monroe in the male hero's room to his clothing fashion (the T-shirt, the black leather cap

---

[5] Salman Khan follows the line of Sanjay Dutt, a popular actor of the eighties and already a muscle-man. One could trace this back to the films of Dara Singh or even Dharmendra, yet it is with Salman Khan that muscles have become a real trend in cinema.

and jacket, the jeans), and the use of objects as symbolic referents, such as the boxing gloves hanging in the room. Used symbolically to demonstrate the fighting skills of the hero, even though there are no actual fighting scenes in the films. We also have shifted from the British model to the American. It is expressed in the plot choices: the hero returns from America, and not from London as it was the case in the post-Independence movie *Andaz* (Khan 1949); thus highlighting the growing importance of Hollywood influence. The dominance of the muscular hero on screen in the Indian context comes to existence at the crossroad of the multiple threads mentioned above.

Historically, the expression of virility through muscles can find its roots, in the Venice Beach movement – also known as 'Muscle Beach' – which began in the thirties. It consolidates in the fifties, when Venice Beach meets Hollywood, providing all its peplums with strong and muscular soldiers and thus introducing popular culture with muscular bodies. In the seventies, this movement enters a second Golden Age, and its members suddenly become ambassadors for an oversized virility, with Arnold Schwarzenegger as their most famous symbol. As Mauss had foreseen early when talking of cinema's ability to influence body language[6], the story of virility and muscles has rapidly ceased to be an American one and has now become universal (Courtine 2011), with Salman Khan as its Indian pioneer. If in his first movies he has a hairy torso, it will transform into a clean shaven chest afterwards, fitting into the beauty norms of the Muscle Beach men whose clean, shaven, oily and tanned skin were the beauty norms. Yet, the Venice Beach movement begins in Los Angeles in a time of crisis: *Muscle Beach* opens its doors at the heart of the economic recession of the thirties, giving a distraction, close to work and labour, to a masculine population hit by unemployment.

---

[6] Marcel Mauss is a French thinker, generally considered as the 'father' of French anthropology. In an anecdote, he demonstrates the efficiency of cinema on the modelling of body gesture: while he was at the hospital in New York, he realised that the nurses walked the same way Hollywood actresses did and he could make the same observation in Paris. Thus, 'American walking fashions had begun to arrive over here, thanks to the cinema.' (Mauss 1966).

In Hindi cinema however, building up a muscular body relies on two things: a philosophy and ethics close to the wrestling tradition which find a point of mutual interest in Hindu nationalism, and the development of a leisure society. On the social level, being muscular means more than having a healthy and fit body, it tells that you can afford to go to the gym and that you have enough time to spend there, along with a kind of life that leads you to consider your body in its aesthetic dimension (going to the beach as part of a leisure activity, or working in the fashion or cinema milieu). Thus, being able to afford a life made of leisure times excludes the worker's kind of life, as was the case in the Bachchan era. From the hero of the masses, we go to a hero that literarily embodies the values of leisure and consumption of the growing urban middle-class in India.

On the other hand, the philosophy of wrestling which consists of 'an elaborate way of involving general prescription of physical culture, diet, health, ethics and morality' (Alter 1992) is echoed in the way actors and the press magazines talk about the male physique, as a long-term endeavour and a form of ascetism. This philosophy still finds some bonds with Hindu nationalism as, being an ideological construct, the notion of a fit and healthy body is a fairly common theme in discourses of nationalism and power (Alter 1992). As such, the *Bharatya Janata Party* (BJP, a right-wing party linked to a militant group known as the Hindu Rashtriya Swayamsevak Sangh) plays an important role in the appreciation and virilisation of the Indian male body. A change in the religious iconography is symptomatic of this undertaking (D'Azevedo 2013): during the 1992 Ayodhya riots[7] popular images on calendars and matchboxes show Rama as a warrior, with firm and well-drawn muscles, ready to fight and named *ugra Rama* (upset, aggressive). On screen, the muscular body is indeed used in impressive fights or as the embodiment of the perfect solider of the nation, as Hrithik Roshan in *Lakshiya* (2004) for instance.

Concomitantly to the specifically American influences expressed in *Maine Pyar Kiya*, the particular context of the nineties borne out of the rise of nationalism leads to the collateral infusion of what is defined by the BJP as the 'traditional Indian values'. It echoes in films, in the return of the 'romantic hero' and a 'resurging' tradition in the archetypical male character played by Shah Rukh Khan.

---

[7] On 6th December 1992, Hindu nationalists set about destroying the Babri Masjid, a mosque supposedly erected on God Rama birthplace. This led to violent inter-communal riots, causing 2,000 deaths.

## II. 1995[8] – Masculinity as 'resurgent India'[9]
### The romantic lover - Shah Rukh Khan

The Bollywood movies of the nineties, especially Yash & Aditya Chopra, and Karan Johar's productions, were very much in tune with the Indian context of the time – Indian movies being an efficient way of entering Indian society, its aspirations, desires and how it perceives itself (Dwyer 2010). The antagonistic forces of liberalisation and the *Hindutva* movement shaped a 'neotraditional' body, meaning 'tradition with a "modern" face' (Virdi 2003: 192). The increasing awareness of a significant Indian diaspora since the late eighties and the early nineties, which, moreover, is in demand of films from India to educate and transmit its values to its children born on a foreign land (Gillespie 1995) is also a factor that shapes this 'resurgent' body, interfacing with the West, understood as the space of modernity, and India, as the embodiment of a pure tradition.

Whereas, in his era, Amitabh Bachchan eclipsed all the other male actors as the exclusive super star of the seventies, in the nineties, two apparently contradictory tendencies coexist, embodied by both Shah Rukh Khan and Salman Khan. These two heroes were born on screen in the ambivalent context of the nineties, made of the economic liberal reforms and the increasing power of the nationalist Hindu movement. This ambiguous context, valorising liberalism as well as the 'traditional' Indian values, gives way to two kinds of masculinities. The muscular hero, seen above, is then a subaltern, emerging, trend with the figure of Salman Khan, whereas the dominant male actor of this period, Shah Rukh Khan, is the incarnation of the Non-Resident Indian (NRI) from the diaspora, still faithful however to the Indian 'traditional' values.

The Indian 'traditional' values defined by the importance of upholding the traditions through the establishment of an Indian family, find their expression in most Hindi films of this period – Aditya Chopra's *Dilwale Dulhania Le Jayenge (DDLJ)* (Chopra 1995) being the most famous emblem of its time. In this film, Shah Rukh Khan plays a young boy, Raj, who falls in love with the young girl Simran (Kajol). Both are born and raised in England, but Simran's father does not think Shah Rukh Khan is the right person for his daughter as he wants to marry her in India.

---

[8] 1995 is a landmark in the history of Hindi cinema as it is the release year of one of the most important blockbusters: *Dilwale Dulhania Le Jayenge*, and it embodies the particular style and atmosphere of the nineties' movies where nationalism, diaspora and liberalism meet.

[9] This expression comes from Jean-Luc Racine, as he has elaborated it in his article: '*L'Inde et l'ordre du monde*' (Racine 2003).

Yet, Raj, who appears spoilt by having lived abroad, finally reveals that he is more 'Indian' and has more respect to 'traditional Indian' values than Simran's Indian husband-to-be. Setting the trend of the NRI hero, this romantic lover personified by Shah Rukh Khan is also embodying a 'neotraditional' self, at the intersection of the Western and the Indian world, as symbolised by the travels between India and London in the film. In each world, the character adopts its codes, as well as body gesture and clothing. Modern reincarnation of the romantic hero of the fifties played by Dilip Kumar, also known as the 'king of tragedy', Shah Rukh Khan is the embodiment of the 'good' hero, who will fight for his love, yet respect his elders and their teachings.

From this tradition of the romantic hero of the fifties, Shah Rukh Khan's character diverges on three points. First, he is born and lives abroad: he thus embodies the second generation of Indian from the diaspora, established outside the country. The interest of cinema in representing the NRIs is the result of the homeland politics: after Nehru's turn away from the Indian diaspora, the nineties have seen a growing interest in the Indian living abroad for the resources it can provide to the country. It is also the increasing awareness in the Bollywood industry of the importance of this overseas market. Secondly, unlike a film like *Andaz* where the Western costume is the norm for the young hero (the father wears the Indian outfit by contrast), in *DDLJ* the hero wears an updated Indian outfit during the wedding song sequence, a sign of this 'resurgent' India. Thirdly, on the cinematographic level, the filmmaker plays obviously on Indian cinematographic references, denoting affiliation with the Bollywood codes and signifying the appropriation of Western influence, rather than insisting on Western imports, as could be the case in a film like *Maine Pyar Kiya*. The leather jacket and the motorcycle is a direct reference to Amitabh Bachchan's character; the piano scene in the cabaret song sequence in Paris refers to Raj Kapoor's movies of the fifties, and another song sequence in the hay is a reference to *Maine Pyar Kiya*. The visual rhetoric is thus staging the atmosphere of a 'resurgent' India.

Moreover, Shah Rukh Khan as an actor used to be a proponent for 'no kissing on screen', arguing that he did not need to kiss to represent love or desire. This ethics of the romantic lover, also built on the idea that he could control his desires, places masculinity in the ethereal world of morality and loyalty to Indian values. Masculinity here as 'resurgent' India is linked to the fact that the ideology of the film lies in the NRI's fidelity to India and its traditions, making *Bharat* (India in Hindi) the essential homeland. Yet, it is the first step towards the elaboration of masculinity in the much wider space than that of the nation-state, where

*Bharat* will be extended to *desh* (meaning country in Hindi, but referring to all South Asia).

## III. 2008 - Masculinity as transnational *desi*[10] body
### The item boy – John Abraham
Since 2000, the muscular male body, after having embodied the 'romantic hero', as was the trend in the previous decade, now asserts itself at the same time as the action male character perfect body and as an aesthetic and sexual device. Salman Khan has gradually embodied the typical action hero, as in *Dabangg*, as did Hrithik Roshan in the urban

---
[10] In Hindi, *desi* means from the country, as opposed to *videshi* [stranger]. In the diasporic context, it holds a specific meaning, as it encompasses all South Asia and refers to a particular culture and the values associated with it, as we will see in the last part of this paper.

young film *Dhoom*, and even Aamir Khan in *Fanaa*. The muscular body as an object of desire becomes an increasingly important trend, especially in the transnational movies aimed at the diaspora and the urban middle-class in India. This development brings change into the visual construction of the male body itself by transposing the female body visual imagery and aesthetic over to the male body.

Salman Khan works as a landmark for the contemporary audience and has become a model for a whole youth that asserts its virility by gaining more and more muscles; and masculinity has been closely defined by a muscularly-shaped body in Hindi movies' visual imagery[11]. A whole new generation of actors, some of them who come from the fashion world, have entered the cinema world, contributing to the increasing importance of body appearances and the infusion of the Western beauty norms in Indian popular culture through films. Even Shah Rukh Khan, whose sex-appeal was not based on a muscular body, has given into this trend for the particular song sequence of *Om Shanti Om* (Khan 2007). This muscular virility has had an important consequence: that of changing the norms for visual representation of the male body, in films at least. Next to the muscular, fit and healthy hero who embodies a national ethic and morality close to the wrestlers' ideology, comes the *item* boy. His body *mise en scène* following the visual grammar of the female body, contributes to a change in the norms of gender representations.

The *item* number usually invites, like a guest star, an actress (or a dancer, a model) from outside the movie plot to perform a special dance sequence intended to arouse desire and thus interest in the film to the audience. It has even become a commercial technique as the video-songs are broadcasted before the release of the film as PR. For example, the song 'Sheila ki Jawaani' performed by Katrina Kaif for the movie *Tees Maar Khan* (Khan 2010), is sold as 'the most awaited, sizzling, sexiest, seductive item song of the year'. Putting into practice the *item* number by muscular men for male actors as well strongly modifies gender perception and thus the codes of representation of characters on screen.

In the films of the nineties, one can identify recurring sequences, going hand in hand and working together as *topos*: introduction of the male and female characters, the romantic encounter, the seduction dances, and finally, the wedding. Each of these *topos* followed visual rules, which can be found from film to film, and particularly, the introduction of the

---

[11] The overwhelming presence of muscles in visual imagery in India exceeds the world of films, as it expands not only to religious iconography but also to comics, and to the male population, as attested by the expansion of gyms all over India.

characters followed a strict visual grammar, depending on whether it was a male or a female character on screen. Men were always depicted doing sports or in (spectacular) action, surrounded by objects that symbolise modernity, strength, or speed. In the emblematic *DDLJ*, Shah Rukh Khan is variously depicted playing rugby, going for a kart ride, running after a plane and driving a motorcycle, while the female lead character, played by Kajol, is shown dancing in her room wearing a towel. Playing with these codes of representation, Sanjay Leela Bhansali reverses them in his film *Saawariya* (Bhansali 2007) by staging Ranbir Kapoor also dancing in a towel, employing the typical feminine gestures that were enacted by Kajol, yet far more suggestive in his play with nudity.

With the particular muscular body embodied by John Abraham and the influence of the fashion milieu, a new way of looking at virility and of depicting it has emerged which titillates and evokes desire. On this point, Tarun Mansukhani's film *Dostana* (Mansukhani 2008) marks a shifting point as, situated in the Chopra-Johar filiation[12] which has established the visual grammar of body *topos* in the nineties, he paves a new way. The introduction of the muscular male character, John Abraham, follows the same pattern of women's introduction on screen: the body appears on screen slice by slice, with an emphasis placed on the chest and bottom, as in female bodies. When filming the lead actress, there is an established visual rhetoric: the camera begins at the feet and

---

[12] The Chopra-Johar filiation refers to the influential cinema of Yash Chopra and his son Aditya Chopra, in the wake of which Karan Johar places himself and then Tarun Mansukhani, by a system of nods and winks in the movies style.

then slowly pans up to the face, detailing on the way the ankle chains, the thighs, the bangles, her belly, chest, lips and finally her kohl black eyes. In a conversation with Tarun Mansukhani (February 2011), he said that the idea of the introduction of John Abraham was to arise desire in the spectator's eyes. He wanted to make of the male body an object of desire and consumption, as much as the female body is. This way of depicting men's bodies disengages them from the action sphere and makes them enter the passive sphere of the contemplative gaze, to become the object of consumerism, as is the case with women's bodies.

John Abraham is an emblematic actor of the transnational section of Bollywood films. He made his cinematographic *début* in *Jism* (Saxena 2003), an erotic thriller. The movie title, which means 'body' symbolises at the same time the importance of the body in John Abraham's career: mainly, his body is his principal advantage and the importance that the body as an object of consumption has gained in Indian society. He is one of many examples of item boys or of actors who performs item numbers that one can see now in Bollywood, such as Hrithik Roshan, Ranbir Kapoor, Shahid Kapoor[13]. One interesting feature is that at the same time he reaches the status of an iconic desi boy.

In Hindi, *desi* is an adjective that derives from the word *desh* – country – which has, in the Indian context, the meaning of something local and not necessarily modern, with a slightly pejorative connotation. In the diasporic context, being *desi* means more than just coming from a specific geographical space – being *desi* refers to a whole culture that has its own codes. It refers to a trendy, urban, modern culture shared by South Asians – including Pakistan, Nepal, Bangladesh and Sri Lanka. As Sunaina Maira puts it, 'first, it's about living in a big city, about parties and fashion' (Maira 2009). The use of Hinglish (Deprez 2010) – a mix of Hindi and English – echoes this insertion of Bollywood in the global market, aiming at the Indian diaspora, the NRIs and constructing now a *desi* culture. From *Jism*, John Abraham moves to *Desi Boyz* (Dhawan 2011). Set during the financial crisis in London, the film relates the story of two friends who are trying hard to overcome their financial difficulties, and who become gigolos to maintain their way of life. For each of them, their body definitively becomes their mean of subsistence, permeating deeply into the consumer society (Baudrillard 1974). The *desi* boy thus embodies a transnational culture from the diaspora point of view as, through Bollywood, India comes to symbolise all South Asia. Resting on an actual transnational space yet contributing to its definition and elab-

---

[13] Yet, one must underscore that these actors embody at the same time the muscular action hero as well as, from time to time, the item boy.

oration, national boundaries between India and its diaspora are shattered by these films.

## Conclusion

Today, if an actor wants to play the main protagonist, a muscular body is an unavoidable norm. Having an un-muscularly shaped body will be seen as more fitting for comic roles. While in the fifties it was the skinny Johnny Walker in opposition to the plump and wealthy hero who was playing the funny part; since the nineties, the plump and unfit character is seen as more comic, as one of the elements of comedy lies in the contrasting features of two characters. Even though the history of muscles is going global, leaving only scarce space in popular visual imagery for non-muscular men, Indian cinema however created its own visual grammar for depicting the muscular male body. Inverting gender codes of representation, the muscular body is actually challenging the traditional definition of both male and female identities. It is also opening the space for female desire and allows for the concept of male homosexuality to emerge clearly.

Assuming the male body as an erotic device is seen by some filmmakers as a means to enable the expression of women's desire. With the opening to the global market and the importation of American magazines such as Vanity Fair, the question of sexuality and the right of women to assert their sexual desire has emerged in the public field and discourse. For a long time, women on screen have been depicted as the upholders of traditions. Their modernity and freedom was severely condemned, being it with Nargis in *Andaz*, or in the figure of the vamp embodied by Helen or Parveen Babi, who smokes, drinks and wears sexy outfits. The only possible dreams for her were that of the *pativrata*: being a humble and devoted wife for her husband and an accomplished mother. The muscular male bodies, firstly meant as a sign of power, but then used as an erotic device, have thus opened a space for women to express their sexual desire. Despite all the superficial appeal that one can associate with muscular male bodies, they have, paradoxically enough, paved the way for an important social change in contemporary India.

## Filmography

Barjatya, S. R. 1989. *Maine Pyar Kiya*.

Bhansali S. L. 2007. *Saawariya*.

Chopra, A. 1995. *Dilwale Dulhania Le Jayenge*.

Dhawan, R. 2011. *Desi Boyz*.

Khan F. 2007. *Om Shanti Om*.

------ 2010. *Tees Maar Khan*.

Khan, M. 1949. *Andaz*.

Saxena, A. 2003. *Jism*.

# Bibliography

Alter, J. S. 1992. *The Wrestler's Body: Identity and Ideology in North India.* Berkeley: University of California Press (available on-line: *http://ark.cdlib.org/ark:/13030/ ft6n39p104/*, accessed 16 June 2013).

Baudrillard J. 1974. *La Société de consommation: ses mythes, ses structures...* (Collection Idées 316). Paris: Gallimard.

Chopra, R., C. Osella & F. Osella 2004. *South Asian masculinities: context of change, sites of continuity.* New Delhi: Women Unlimited an associate of Kali for Women.

Corbin A., J.-J. Courtine & G. Vigarello 2011. *Histoire de la virilité.* (L'univers historique). Paris: Éd. du Seuil.

Courtine, J.-J. 2011. Balaise dans la civilisation : mythe viril et puissance musculaire. In *Histoire de la virilité : la virilité en crise? XXe - XXIe siècle.* (L'univers historique). Paris: Éd. du Seuil.

D'Azevedo, A. 2013. Cinéma et virilité, mutations du corps masculin à Bollywood. L'Harmattan (available on-line: *http://www.larevuedelinde.com/sommaire6.htm*, accessed 16 June 2013).

Deprez, C. 2010. *Bollywood: cinéma et mondialisation.* (Arts du spectacle). Villeneuve d'Ascq: Presses universitaires du Septentrion.

Dwyer, R. 2010. Bollywood's India: Hindi Cinema as a Guide to Modern India. *Asian affairs : journal of the Royal Society for Asian Affairs.* - London : Royal Soc., ISSN 0306-8374, ZDB-ID 2192433. - Vol. 41.2010, 3, p. 381-399.

Gillespie, M. 1995. *Television, ethnicity and cultural change.* (Comedia). London New York: Routledge.

Kulkarni, M. 2007. Indian Masculinities: A Million Mutations Now? In *Interpreting Indian Masculinities. Breaking the Moulds: Indian Men Look at Patriarchy Looking at Men.* New Delhi: Books for Change (available on-line: *http://www.academia.edu/747702/ Indian_Masculinities_A_Million_Mutations_Now*, accessed 16 June 2013).

Maira, S. 2009. Desi Land: Teen Culture, Class, and Success in Silicon Valley. *Contemporary Sociology: A Journal of Reviews* 38, 406-407.

Mauss, M. 1966. *Sociologie et anthropologie.* (3e édition). Paris: Presses universitaires de France.

Rajamani, I. 2012. Pictures, Emotions, Conceptual Change: Anger in Popular Hindi Cinema. *Contributions to the History of Concepts* 7, 52-77.

Roynette, O. 2012. Comptes rendus. Genre. *Annales. Histoire, Sciences Sociales* **67e année**, 755-821.

Virdi, J. 2003. *The cinematic imagiNation [sic]: Indian popular films as social history.* New Brunswick, N. J. London: Rutgers university press.

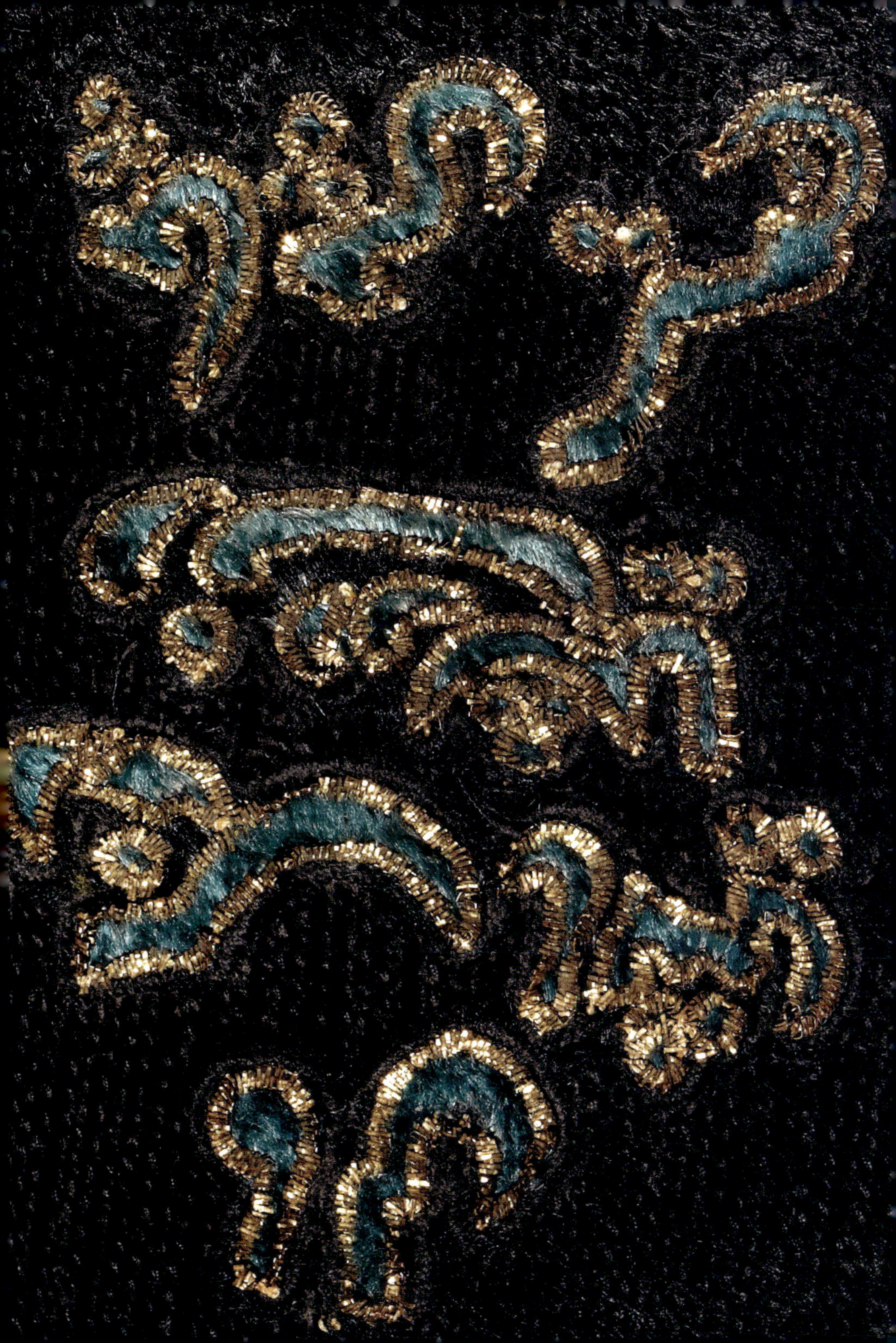

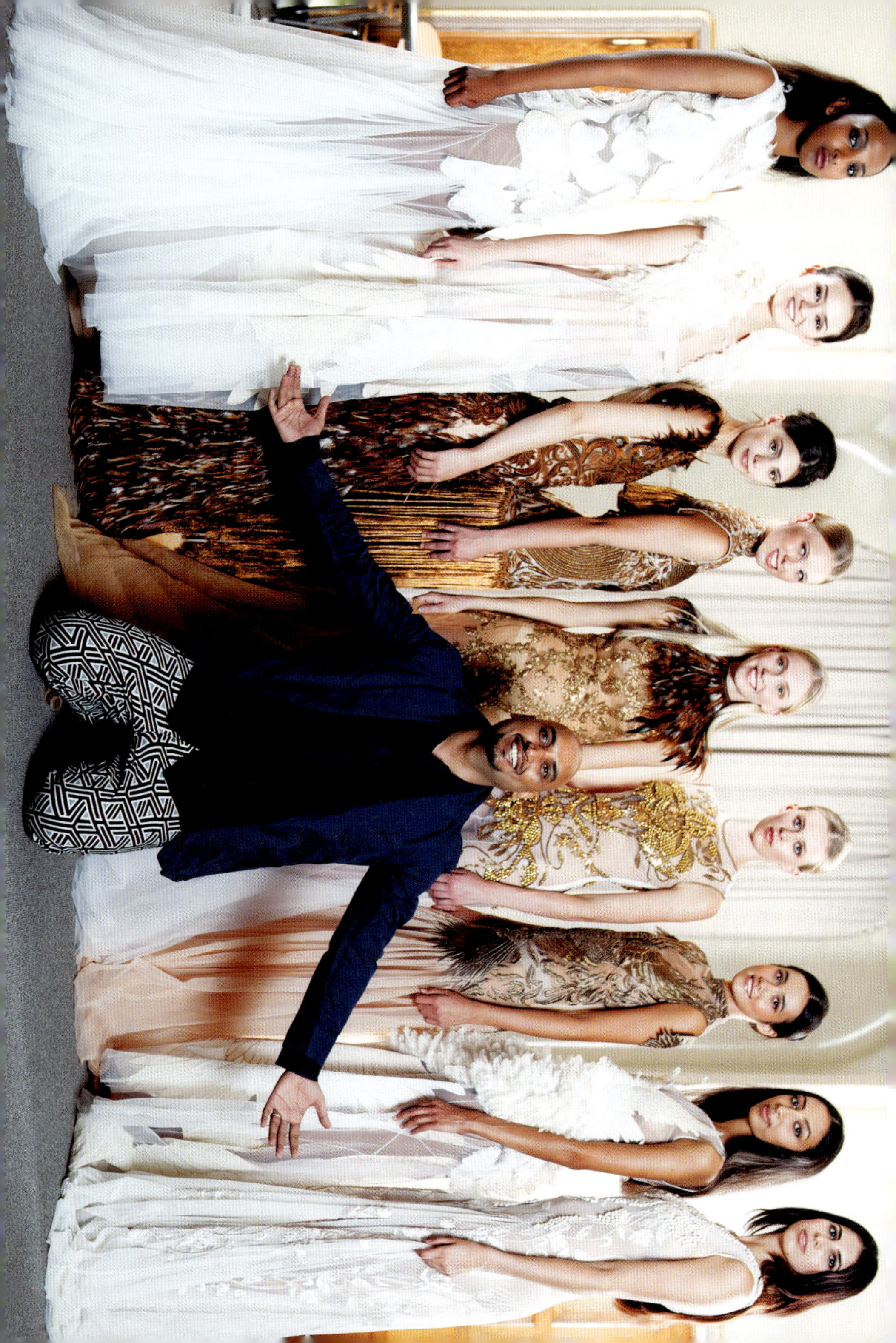

# Epilogue
## Thomas Hylland Eriksen

This delightful and enlightening book interrogates the multiple tensions arising between aesthetics and power, between the globally standardised and that which is locally embedded and unique, between hierarchy and individualism and between craft and industry. With contributions from both Western and Indian scholars, it is emphatically not about 'the encounter between the East and the West', but rather about a specific moment in Indian history, which has always been a history of flows and intersections, new impulses creating unique blends by meeting old traditions.

The book is woven around questions concerning cultural authenticity as something perceived to exist in opposition to a standardised modernity; a perennial topic in the ongoing public debate about Indian identity. Questions relating to cultural property rights, the production of symbolic capital and the real versus the fake crop up throughout this material, which almost spans the entire subcontinent, from the remote north-east to Kerala in the south-west. These questions deserve to be taken for a brief comparative spin, as they are being raised throughout the world, although – naturally – with a local twist everywhere.

Commercialisation of traditional cultural products entails a form of reification and 'musealisation' of cultural production which is historically connected to nation-building, and which currently feeds directly into debates about culture and identity. Stable national identities have presupposed the standardisation of cultural expression, and it is no accident that Benedict Anderson, in the second edition of his seminal study of nationalism, *Imagined Communities* (1991) added material on museums, maps and censuses. Routinely associated with the Romantic movement in 19th century Europe and North America, the folk and national museums have later proven to be important elements of postcolonial nation-building worldwide. Moreover, the same concerns that gave the initial impetus to developing national museums in European countries are today at the core of a variety of projects across the world aiming at

---

Left and after the epilogue:

These images were taken at the opening of the exhibition 'Fashion India: Spectacular Capitalism' at the Historical Museum in Oslo, on the 13th of September 2013. Samant Chauhan, a well-known fashion designer from New Delhi, inaugurated the exhibition with a fashion show, presenting his Spring/Summer 2014 collection at the museum. These are some of the dresses that were on show.

profiting politically or commercially from a collective sense of cultural identity. It is in this sense that studies of the Indian fashion industry and its varying claims of historical rootedness become relevant for theory about modern identities.

The topic of cultural property rights has emerged partly as a consequence of an increased global traffic in signs and goods, partly due to an increased reification of culture and concomitant recognition of its potential as a resource. Culture has become a widespread idiom for discourse about politics in the wide sense, tourism, the arts, dress and so on. For many years, it has been a staple of what we may label an ironic anthropology to deconstruct and critically interrogate 'native' reifications of and manipulations with their own presumed cultural productions. Following in the footsteps of historians like Hugh Trevor-Roper (1983), whose research on the Scottish highland tradition revealed it to be a recent creation, numerous anthropologists have explored 'native essentialisms' and showed them to be inscribed into political and sometimes commercial discourses.

Reacting to this ironic turn in anthropology, Marshall Sahlins complained years ago that too many 'anthropologists say that the so-called traditions the peoples are flaunting are not much more than serviceable humbuggery' (Sahlins 1999: 402). He then went on to argue that the 'afterological' strategies so typical of contemporary intellectual life fail to take seriously the meaningful structures that make up people's lifeworlds, which continue to vary in discontinuous ways and not least, in ways which are crucial to the actors involved.

In an earlier, similar argument against radical constructivism in research on nationalism, A. D. Smith (1991) pointed out that although the reified symbols of nations may be recent constructions or even fabrications, that does not mean that the members of a nation do not have anything substantial in common. Being paranoid is no guarantee that nobody is after you. Smith, unlike Sahlins, distinguished between shared culture as embedded in popular experience and shared culture as political tools. The point is well taken – the majority of people who live in a given country may have a lot of untheorised, unmarked and unpoliticised culture in common, in spite of the fact that the official national symbolism is recently and perhaps even cunningly constructed. Diverging from Smith's view, Sahlins (1999) suggests that it is not always possible, or even interesting, to distinguish between 'fabricated' and 'real' culture.

Is the distinction between 'real and 'fabricated' culture relevant or spurious? To be sure, the distinction is often blurred in practice. Yet there are several strong arguments in favour of exploring commercialised or politicised expressions of culture as contestable acts of symbolic invention; we just need to make it clear that such analyses do not offer the whole story. Firstly, the politics of tradition in societies studied by anthropologists now entails the appropriation of a vaguely anthropological (or perhaps nationalist) concept of culture: Anthropologists are no longer needed to identify other people's culture, since the latter are perfectly capable of doing it themselves. It is clearly a matter of interest how a particular local culture is being trimmed and shaped to meet immediate political needs. Secondly, research on 'ethnic art' shows that both form and content of symbolic production associated with particular cultures undergoes dramatic transformations when the products are incorporated into a wider system of exchange, such as the global arts market – a process well documented in this book with its focus on the Indian fashion market. Thirdly, it must be said that whenever a particular use of symbols associated with a group are contested, asking the question *cui bono*? – who benefits? – is less an act of cynicism or ironic anthropology than an earnest wish to find out what is going on. Fourthly and finally, it is sometimes both relevant and enlightening to distinguish between culture seen as the shared understandings of a particular collectivity of people and culture seen as a commodity or political resource. If it is true, as rumour has it, that Irish theme pubs are becoming so popular these days that they are even appearing in Dublin, then no anthropologist worthy of his grant money would describe them without making a distinction between the generic, globalised Irish franchise pubs and the ancient local on the corner.

The argument of this book is not that culture is reducible to its expression as commodity or political resource, or that it is meaningful to make an absolute distinction between 'artificially created' and 'organically created' culture, but rather that a complex relationship exists between lived culture and reified or commercialised culture, and – most importantly – that the aesthetic cannot be separated from the political. As Kuldova puts it, the white lotus, so reminiscent of many Indian fashion pieces, grows out of mud which is nevertheless concealed from sight and rarely spoken about by the people who praise the beauty of the lotus.

# References

Anderson, Benedict. 1991. *Imagined Communities. Reflections on the Origins and Spread of Nationalism*, 2nd edition. London: Verso.

Sahlins, Marshall D. 1999. Two or three things that I know about culture. *Journal of the Royal Anthropological Institute*, 5(3): 399-421.

Smith, A. D. 1991. *National Identity*. Harmondsworth: Penguin.

Trevor-Roper, Hugh. 1983. The invention of tradition: The highland tradition of Scotland. In Eric Hobsbawm and Terence Ranger, eds., *The Invention of Tradition*, pp. 15-41. Cambridge: Cambridge University Press.

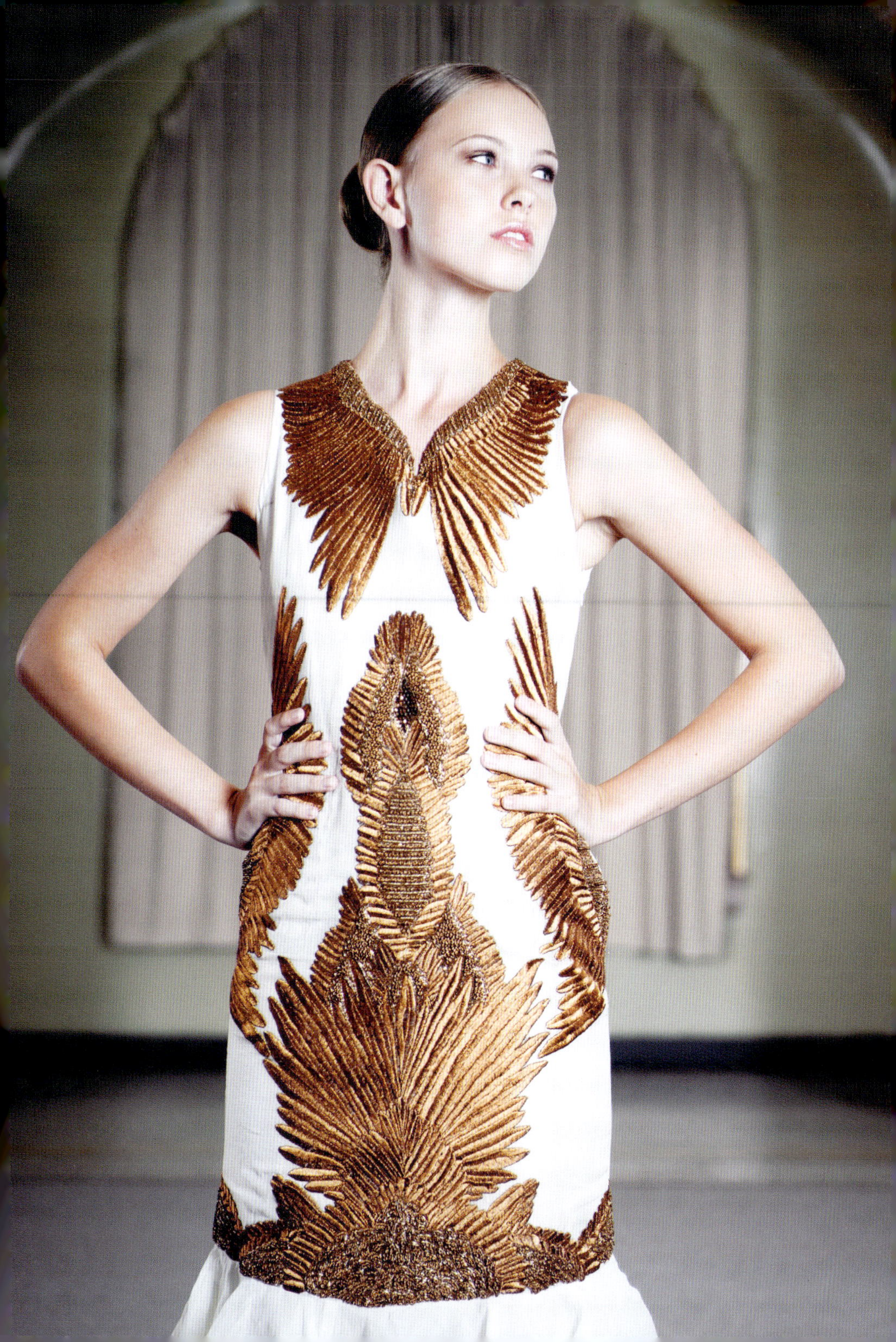

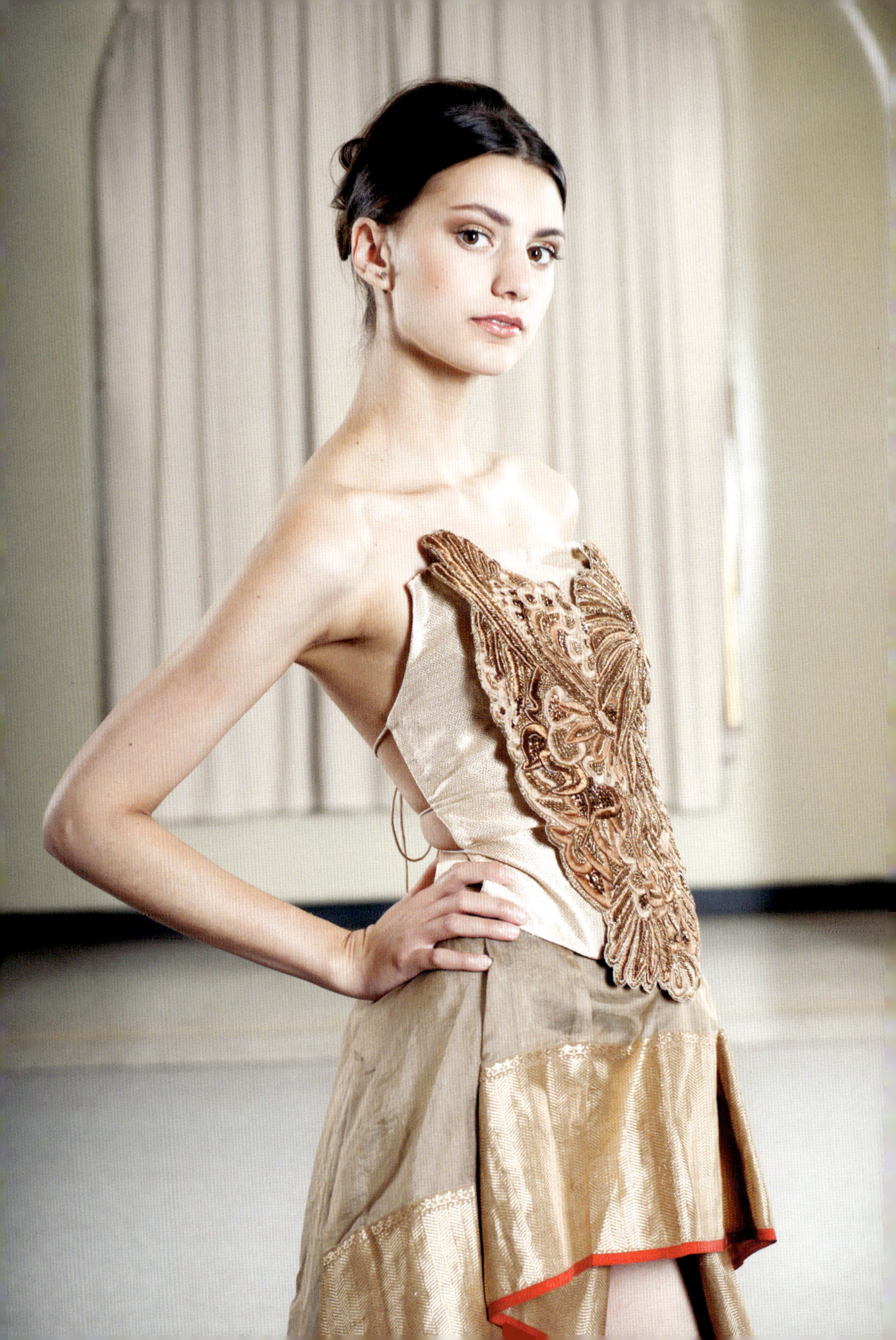

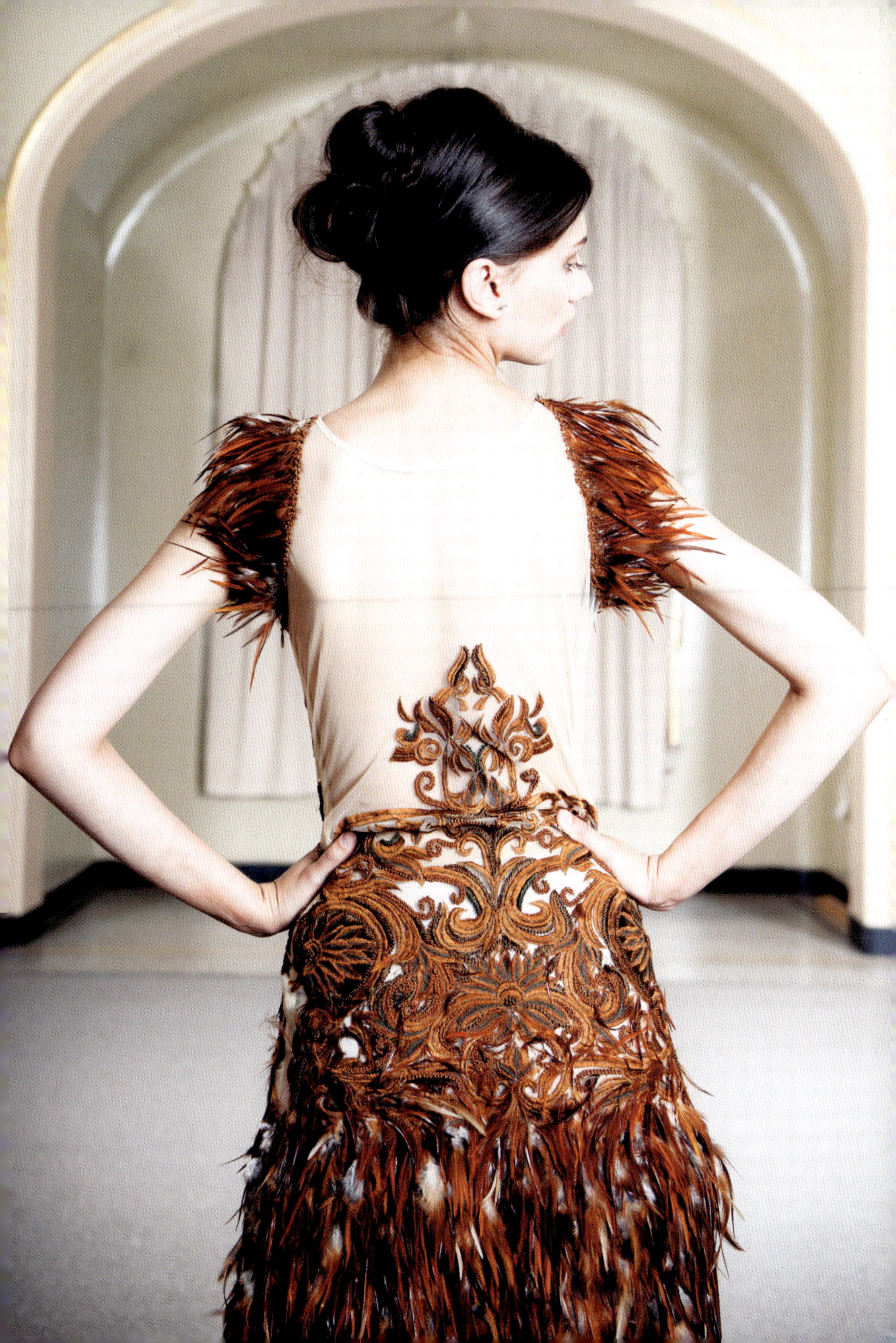

# Author Biographies

**Tereza Kuldova** is a research fellow and curator at the Department of Ethnography, Museum of Cultural History, University of Oslo. She finished her PhD in anthropology in 2013 with a thesis entitled *Designing Elites: Fashion and Prestige in Urban North India*. Her main research interests are material culture, contemporary India, theory of value and fashion industry. Recent publications include an article entitled 'Fashionable Erotic Masquerades: Of brides, gods and vamps in India', published in *Critical Studies in Fashion & Beauty* 2012. For more details see http://www.terezakuldova.com.

**Nilanjana Mukherjee** teaches English Literature at Shaheed Bhagat Singh College, University of Delhi. She has finished her doctoral research from Jawaharlal Nehru University, New Delhi. Her Ph.D. dissertation titled 'Articulating Colonial Space: British Representations of India' dealt with the idea of spatial construction of India through varied cultural forms such as landscape paintings, travel writings and cartography. She is interested in areas of visual culture, culture studies, post-colonial studies and ideas of spatiality. She has published research articles in many scholarly journals such as Postcolonial Studies and Journal of the School of Languages, JNU.

**Paolo Favero** is an associate professor in Film Studies and Visual Culture at the University of Antwerp and works in the area of visual and digital culture. With a PhD from Stockholm University Paolo has devoted the core of his career to the study of India and Italy. He has also created various visual projects aiming at translating anthropological questions in languages available to wider audiences. He is the author of *India Dreams: Cultural Identity among Young Middle Class Men in New Delhi* and director of the film *Flyoverdelhi* (screened by Swedish and Italian national broadcasters).

**Marion Wettstein** is a postdoctoral researcher in anthropology at the University of Vienna, with a current project on dance in Nepal. She has been doing research on material culture in Nagaland from 2003 to 2010. Her interests include material culture and arts, performance, ritual and mythology, and identity processes.

**Meher Varma** is a currently a fourth year student in the graduate anthropology program at UCLA. She is conducting research on the Indian fashion industry and will be completing fieldwork next year in New Delhi and Mumbai. Her academic interests include costume studies, material culture, and cinema studies: particularly in South Asia.

**Janne Meier** is an anthropologist from Copenhagen, with a research background in the fashion business, textiles and sustainability. Together with Tushar Bhartiya, a fashion designer from the National Institute of Fashion Technology, New Delhi, she has now opened a fashion and lifestyle label *Doo*.

**Caroline Osella** is reader in South Asian Anthropology at the *School of Oriental and African Studies*, London. Current projects include research with Zayed University, Abu Dhabi, on Arab-Gulf encounters. Among recent publications is a book entitled *Islamic Reform in South Asia* (2013), published by Cambridge University Press in New Delhi.

**Constantine V. Nakassis** (PhD University of Pennsylvania, 2010) is an Assistant Professor of anthropology and of the social sciences at the University of Chicago. Constantine is a linguistic and cultural anthropologist with interests in semiotics; mass media and film theory; trademark, brands, and counterfeiting; youth culture; codeswitching and codemixing. His regional focus is Tamil Nadu, India.

**Catherine Willems** is a doctoral researcher at the School of Arts, KASK, University College Ghent, where she also coordinates the shoe design studio of the fashion department of the school of arts. She is working on a larger interdisciplinary research on footwear, studying the creation process and the use of three types of footwear with input from design sciences, biomechanics and anthropology. Her project 'Future Footwear' is a six-year PhD project in the arts funded by the University College Ghent, School of Arts, KASK in collaboration with Ghent University and University of Antwerp.

**Kristiaan D'Août** is a biologist and biomechanist at the University of Antwerp and also the Centre for Research and Conservation, Belgium. He has a strong interest in the evolution of upright walking in early hominins, and in various aspects of gait (especially barefoot and shod-foot function) in different contemporary human populations.

**Némésis Srour** is a PhD student at *l'Ecole des Hautes Etudes en Sciences Sociales* (EHESS) in Paris. Affiliated to the Department of Anthropology and South Asian Studies, research in the fields of anthropology of the body and visual anthropology, specializing in indian and middle-eastern cinemas.

**Thomas Hylland Eriksen** is Professor of Anthropology at the University of Oslo and author of *Ethnicity and Nationalism* (1994; 2002) and *Small Places, Large Issues: An Introduction to Social and Cultural Anthropology* (1995; 2001).